CERTIFIED PUBLIC ACCOUNTING

A Sociological View of a Profession in Change

Publication of this book was made possible
by a grant from
ARTHUR ANDERSON & CO.

ACCOUNTING PUBLICATIONS OF SCHOLARS BOOK CO.

Sidney Alexander et al., *Five Monographs on Business Income*

Frank Sewell Bray, *The Accounting Mission*

Raymond J. Chambers, *Accounting, Evaluation and Economic Behavior*

John B. Geijsbeck, *Ancient Double-Entry Bookkeeping*

Henry Rand Hatfield, *Accounting: Its Principles and Problems*

Bishop Carlton Hunt, ed., *George Oliver May: Twenty-Five Years of Accounting Responsibility, 1911-1936*

Kenneth MacNeal, *Truth in Accounting*

George O. May, *Financial Accounting: A Distillation of Experience*

William A. Paton, *Accounting Theory*

W. Z. Ripley, *Main Street and Wall Street*

DR Scott, *The Cultural Significance of Accounts*

C. E. Sprague, *The Philosophy of Accounts*

George Staubus, *A Theory of Accounting to Investors*

Robert R. Sterling, ed., *Asset Valuation and Income Determination*

Robert R. Sterling, ed., *Institutional Issues in Public Accounting*

Robert R. Sterling, ed., *Research Methodology in Accounting*

CERTIFIED PUBLIC ACCOUNTING

A Sociological View of a Profession in Change

Paul D. Montagna

Scholars Book Co.
4431 Mt. Vernon
Houston, Texas 77006

To Doris

Ni dans son élan ni dans ses constructions, la science ne peut aller aux limits d'elle-même sans se colorer de mystique et se charger de foi.

—Tielhard de Chardin

Contents

Part One
The Professional Life of the Large-Firm Accountant

Part Two
Analysis of a Profession in Change

List of Tables

Preface

This study is the product of two years of interviewing and general discussion with members of the certified public accounting profession, made possible by a New York University Predoctoral Fellowship and a National Science Foundation Grant (GS-804). Primary emphasis is placed on the analysis of those who work in professional firms, because these firms, especially the large ones, determine the direction in which the profession will develop. The initial idea for examining them originated in discussions with John M. Black, formerly associated with one of the large firms. Expansion was made feasible by the late Dr. Erwin O. Smigel, through his study *The Wall Street Lawyer,* published in 1964 by the Free Press. Professor Smigel gave me the opportunity to examine early drafts of his work, and he served as my advisor for the Ph.D. dissertation, an earlier analysis of accounting firms.

One of my earliest contacts with the firms under study was with Richard Gifford of Price Waterhouse & Co., who provided the major contacts with the "Big Eight" firms. These were the important bases for bringing the study into its preliminary phases of obtaining permission to examine the firms and of making pilot tests and pretests.

Several of the firms continued to participate fully in the study: Ernst & Ernst; Haskins & Sells; Lybrand, Ross Bros. & Montgomery; Price Waterhouse & Co.; Touche Ross & Co.; and Arthur Young & Co. Several smaller firms also agreed to participate: Anchin, Block & Anchin; Eisner & Lubin; George S. Olive & Co.; and Smith & Harder. Conversations with a large number of the partners and employees of these firms are interspersed throughout the text. In some instances these have been paraphrased from the original discussion in the interests of conciseness and readability. The interpretations of these data should not be associated with a specific firm or one of its members except where explicitly noted. Interviews were conducted and questionnaires distributed at the Firms in the latter part of 1965.

To the members and employees of these firms, who necessarily must remain anonymous, I extend my thanks for their interest and for the time given from their busy schedules. The research staff of the major association of certified public accountants, the American Institute of Certified Public Accountants, supplied valuable information on the profession; and the library staff of the institute was helpful in locating innumerable sources of data.

Portions of chapter 5 are based on my article "Professionalization and Bureaucratization in Large Professional Organizations," in the *American Journal of Sociology,* volume 74, number 2, (September 1968).

The book has two parts. Part One serves primarily as an introduction for the nonaccountant, the prospective CPA, and those who are interested in the sociology of work and the professions and want to learn about the work history and life-style of the typical CPA in a large firm. The practicing CPA may want to lightly scan this material and move on to the critical analysis of the Big Eight and the profession itself, which is the focus of Part Two.

While I was writing the later versions of this work, I was fortunate to have two CPAs criticize the entire manuscript—Professor Maurice Moonitz of the University of California at Berkeley and Dr. Douglas R. Carmichael, Director of Technical Research at the American Institute of Certified Public Accountants. Many of their comments initiated significant changes. However, changes were made only where I saw fit, so that I accept the sole responsibility for the contents of the book. The final draft was completed in 1969.

I dedicate this book to my wife, whose critical readings of the innumerable drafts and continued moral support from the beginning have contributed so much to what style and depth it has.

P.D.M.

Introduction

Large international firms that offer a professional service are unique to the public accounting profession. Paul Montagna's study of those large firms has added significantly to the body of knowledge on the public accounting profession. The study considers the impact of the large firm both on the professional life of the accountant in the large firm and on the entire profession.

Accountants have written a good deal about the "professional" nature of their work, but they have only to a limited extent tapped the vast amount of research findings and theory developed by behavioral scientists. Behavioral scientists have studied professions as a unit of social organization, compiling a body of knowledge that holds fresh insights for the independent public accounting profession.

Accountants' discussions of their own profession sometimes appear to be exercises in self-aggrandizement. On the other hand, the perspective found in the branch of behavioral science commonly called "the sociology of professions" is a source of objective knowledge. Behavioral scientists realized long ago the emptiness of the question of whether a particular discipline was really a profession; therefore, they have directed their attention to questions such as: How does the process of professionalization take place in an occupation? What role do professional associations and codes of ethics play in the process? How does professionalization relate to other social processes, such as bureaucratization? Professor Montagna deals with the general aspects of the professionalization of public accounting and the interaction of the large firm in that process.

The relevance of the knowledge accumulated by the behavioral sciences is apparent when the public accounting firm is studied as an organization with problems similar to other organizations—the problem, for example, of maintaining the firm as a viable entity. In an organization of any size, bureaucratization —that is, rationalized efficiency—is necessary for organizational survival. Professor Montagna shows us how professional organizations as large as some public accounting firms cope with the problems of bureaucratization. For example, he observes that a direct correlation seems to exist between the degree of professionalization of an organization and the size of its administrative component. The smaller the administrative component, the more professional the organization. The formal decision-making structure of large firms is highly centralized; this allows the time spent on administration of the firm to be held to 12 percent of the total professional work time.

Professor Montagna does not, however, confine his study to problems of operating the firms. He deals with problems faced by the entire profession—for example, the charge that professional judgment is being abandoned in favor of more numerous, more specific, and more authoritarian professional pronouncements. But behavioral scientists view increased standardization and enforcement of external rules by a professional association as a normal part of the professionalization process. They also note that rationalization of one body of knowledge may lead simultaneously to the development of another. Thus, decreasing uncertainty in auditing practice could lead to expansion of the function of management services.

This book should appeal to a wide audience. Young college students who are considering a career in public accounting will find a wealth of information not otherwise available on what a career in a large firm would hold in store for them. Behavioral scientists who are interested in the role of professions in our society will be introduced to a field laboratory for observing professional change. Finally, accountants interested in taking an introspective look at their own profession will have a rare opportunity to view public accounting through the eyes of an objective observer.

D. R. Carmichael
Director, Technical Research
American Institute of CPAs

Abbreviations

AAA	American Accounting Association
AIA	American Institute of Accountants (incorporated in 1957 into the AICPA)
AICPA	American Institute of Certified Public Accountants
ARS	Accounting Research Study
CPA	Certified Public Accountant
EDP	electronic data processing
FTC	Federal Trade Commission
GAAP	generally accepted accounting principles
GAAS	generally accepted auditing standards
SEC	Securities and Exchange Commission

PART ONE

The Professional Life of the Large-Firm Accountant

Because the work of the large-firm public accountant is virtually unknown outside the profession, a detailed description of its main features is given. In the first chapter there is a brief history of the profession, a discussion of the reasons for conducting a study of the Big Eight, and an introduction to the major thesis of the book. In chapter 2 the size and formal organization of the firms is presented, followed by the breakdown of the accountant's work in this organization within the framework of the technical body of knowledge and rules of accounting. Specialization in the major sections of accounting (auditing, taxes, and management services) for the total information system is examined. Incorporated within the internal hierarchical system, specialization becomes the focus for an examination of the career pattern of a typical large-firm accountant. Here, the main components of the informal organization are exposed, and the peculiar promotional device—the up-or-out policy—and its effect on the formal organization are analyzed. Finally, how accountants feel and think about themselves is explored in chapter 4.

Public Accounting and the Big Eight

The profession of public accounting is perhaps the least known of the major professions in America today. Yet in numbers alone it is one of the largest. What is even more important is that in a business-oriented economy the most influential technical advisor to the great majority of large companies is the public accounting firm—specifically, the eight largest firms.* So little is known about these firms—what they do, who they serve, and the greatly increased scope of their services—that even the professional organization watchers (that small band of sociologists, administrative scientists, and economists who inquire into the mysteries of the large-scale group) have not carried out an extensive analysis of them. The task of this book is to begin such an inquiry.

The Big Eight, as they are called in the financial world, are among the first and the largest of a new type of organization that is now developing. This type is characterized by the combining of persons from several related professions in order to operate in a group practice in which temporary teams are constructed on the basis of the problem to be solved. Some of the questions raised by a preliminary examination of these firms were: How can the firms operate with such an unusually small amount of bureaucratic overhead? Can CPAs (certified public accountants) maintain a high professional stance in an increasingly rationalized area of services? What is the relation between these two questions? What does this form of organization indicate for the future of professions and for human organizations and institutions in general?

To attempt to answer these questions and other more specific ones, a theoretical perspective was established (see the section of chapter 1 entitled "Theoretical Overview"), and two major sources of data were tapped (see interviews of a cross section of people in the firms; these were supported by questionnaires that were more comprehensive in coverage. In many instances throughout the book I have quoted directly the comments of respondents because they expressed a point of view so well. The second source was a survey of the available literature in accounting and related areas that deals with the topic. This aided in verification of comments of those interviewed and it supplied a historical account of developments in the profession.

*The eight firms, in alphabetical order, are: Arthur Andersen & Co.; Coopers & Lybrand; Ernst & Ernst; Haskins & Sells; Peat, Marwick, Mitchell & Co.; Price Waterhouse & Co.; Touche Ross & Co.; Arthur Young & Company.

ACCOUNTING: A HISTORICAL PERSPECTIVE

Examining the wealth of individuals and organizations by evaluating their worth (accounting) and verifying their records for third parties (auditing) has constituted the lifework of a small minority of men since the beginnings of civilization. Those who owned or directly controlled large amounts of wealth employed persons to record and periodically audit their holdings in order to determine depreciation or appreciation of value. The accounting and auditing of goods and services have been done not only to satisfy the tax agents of a government but also to determine the efficiency of use of these goods and services, or, in more formal economic terms, their "utility," in the social environment. As far back as ancient Egypt, financial records were kept and audited by order of the Pharaohs. At the time that the Parthenon was built in Greece, auditors estimated that it cost $500,000. And the emperors of Rome, to keep track of their far-flung lands, required quaestors to examine personally the accounts and inventories of the provinces. Their reports were "heard" in Rome —thus the word "auditor" was coined. In thirteenth-century England the "customals" were the accounting records of rents and services owed to a lord by his tenants.[1]

As a system of rational notation that accurately records events of an economic nature, accounting has been considered by some social theorists as the key to the development of modern industrial society. The logic of double-entry bookkeeping—for every input there is an output, for every debit a credit—was set forth by an Italian, Fra Lucia Pacioli, in his *Summa Arithmetica* in the late 1400s. His method was highly praised by men of such diverse backgrounds and temperaments as Leonardo da Vinci and Goethe. Double-entry bookkeeping began to play an increasingly important role in organizations as the need developed for a method of accounting for larger and more numerous transactions that cover long periods of time. Both Max Weber and Werner Sombart list this method of accounting as one of the few basic reasons for the growth and development of modern capitalism.[2]

1. These and other points are found in Willard E. Stone, "Antecedents of the Accounting Profession," *Accounting Review* 44:284-291 (April 1969). The description of England is given by George C. Homans, *English Villagers of the Thirteenth Century* (Cambridge, Mass.: Harvard University Press, 1941), p. 8. Also, A. C. Littleton and Basil S. Yamey, eds., *Studies in the History of Accounting* (Homewood, Ill.: Richard D. Irwin, 1956), and Richard H. Homburger, "Accounting in Historical Perspective," *Southwestern Social Science Quarterly* 43:215-222 (December 1962).

2. Max Weber, *The Protestant Ethic and the Spirit of Capitalism,* trans. Talcott Parsons (New York: Scribner's, 1958), pp. 21-22; Max Weber, *General Economic History,* trans. Frank H. Knight (London: George Allen & Unwin, 1927), chap. 22; Werner Sombart, *Der moderne Kapitalismus: Historisch-systematische Darstellung des gesampteuropäischen Wirtschaftslebens von seinen Anfängen bis zur Gegenwart,* 3 vols. (Munich and Leipzig: Duncker & Humblot, 1917-1927), vol. 2, chap. 10, "Die Bedeutung der systematischen

With the advent of the "revolutions" of the twentieth century—mass production, communications, automation, and, now, information—techniques of accounting have changed along with the changes in the types and amounts of information they measure. As the pieces of information become more complex and numerous, so too do the methods and concepts for measurement of this information. A distinct body of accounting knowledge developed and expanded, and when the corporate form of ownership became dominant, the role of the accountant as a policeman for interested third parties took on increased importance. He was the outsider, able to obtain a fresh view of the organization and able to utilize the experience that he had accumulated from accounting and auditing other similar organizations. The popularization of the joint-stock company, which has led to widely held public ownership of private corporations, has increased the desire for an independent examination of the "state of health" of the business enterprise. Whereas the accountant formerly was engaged mostly in detailed accounting of a company's finances for that company's own information, he now examines the completed financial statements of the company. He also expresses an overall opinion to interested parties (stockholders, the public, the government, the company itself) of what these statements purport to represent. He is a *public* accountant. In addition, he engages himself as an expert in such areas as tax services; the design and installation of accounting systems; production control; mergers, consolidations, reorganizations, and acquisitions; and advice in systems and procedures related to finance and accounting. He offers these services to public and private corporations; partnerships; federal, state, and local governmental units; voluntary organizations; nonprofit organizations; banks; railroads; utilities; and individuals.

In short, the public accountant has extended his work into nearly every type of organized economic entity. Most of this has been accomplished during the past fifty years, mainly through two types of organization: professional associations and partnership firms. Also, an important event, the economic depression in the United States in the early 1930s, instigated a series of federal acts that greatly increased the significance of the accountant's reporting; it became law that all corporations registered with stock exchanges be audited by a certified public accountant. Presently, this means that CPAs are required for the auditing of the approximately 2,500 publicly traded corporations, whose stock has a total market value of more than $500 billion.[3]

With this expanded importance of their societal role, public accountants are found more and more often in key positions in private and governmental organizations. Public accountants have served as president or chairman of the

Buchaltung für die Entwicklung des Kapitalismus," pp. 118-124. At this writing, a new volume has been issued dealing with the history of accounting: John L. Carey, *The Rise of the Accounting Profession* (New York: AICPA, 1969).

3. Herman W. Bevis, *Corporate Financial Reporting in a Competitive Economy* (New York: Macmillan, 1965), p. 2.

board of such corporations as General Motors, General Electric, Western Electric, Chrysler Corporation, Ford Motors, TWA, Western Union, Sun Oil Co., I.T.&T., and IBM. They have also filled the posts of Director of the Bureau of the Budget, Secretary of Defense, and Secretary of Commerce.

THE PUBLIC ACCOUNTING PROFESSION

Certification in public accounting is acquired by passing a formal written test on the technical knowledge of the profession. Although there are public accountants who are not certified, the emphasis that educators, professional associations, and state and federal bodies have placed on certification has resulted in the great majority of public accountants being certified. Certification was first instituted individually by states in the late 1800s, and by 1900 there were 243 CPAs. With the steadily increasing demand for them, their number expanded to 5,000 in 1920, 20,000 in 1940, 70,000 in 1960, 87,000 in 1965, and it is estimated that by 1980 there will be 200,000.[4] Presently, CPAs constitute less than 10 percent of the more than one million accountants, auditors, and bookkeepers in the United States.[5]

Approximately 60 percent (55,000) of all CPAs are members of the largest professional association of accountants—the American Institute of Certified Public Accountants, or AICPA. The major requirement for membership in it is certification; therefore, it is made up primarily of practitioners of accounting. The second largest association of accountants, the American Accounting Association (AAA), which has about one-fifth the membership of the AICPA, is composed largely of accounting educators, many of whom are CPAs. For the AAA, there are practically no restrictions on membership. The AICPA is the spokesman and the rule-making and rule-enforcing body for the certified public accounting profession, generally. The AAA serves more as a sounding board for theoretical and conceptual formulations and opinions of such, and it often criticizes the AICPA.

The partnership firm is the most common unit of practice in certified public accounting, more than 50 percent of all CPA units being partnerships.[6] The largest firms dominate the profession in terms of their own size, the number and size of their clients, and their influence in the business community. Based on data available and percentages taken from the study sample (see table A-1, appendix A), we can estimate that approximately 15 percent of the 90,000

4. From an article in *The Philadelphia Enquirer*, November 1, 1963, pt. 20. The estimate is given by John L. Carey, *The CPA Plans for the Future* (New York: AICPA, 1965), pp. 342-343.

5. The figure of one million is given by John L. Carey, ed., *The Accounting Profession: Where Is It Headed?* (New York: AICPA, 1962), p. 29.

6. Carey, *The CPA Plans*, pp. 422-425.

CPAs in the United States today work in one of the approximately 35 firms that employ more than 50 CPAs each.

WHY STUDY THE BIG EIGHT?

The Big Eight employ about 12,000 CPAs, an even greater number of accountants who are aspiring to the certificate, and several thousand non-CPA technical specialists. Together they perform approximately 90 percent of auditing and its related services for big business in this country. Each of these eight largest firms maintains scores of offices in major cities of the United States, and each maintains and/or is affiliated with accounting firms in all parts of the free world. This facilitates services to the large, decentralized clients. They are the world's largest professional organizations.* Yet, their work and the extent of their influence in our society are little known, generally. This gap in knowledge was the initial impetus for choosing the topic for this study. Secondly, being the largest of their kind, these firms would supply valuable information for the growing body of knowledge on large professional groups and large-scale organizations. Finally, these firms are important for understanding the profession, because they dominate it in their scope of operations and in prestige.

The eight firms are the elite of the accounting profession, if by "elite" we mean those superordinate positions in a social system that claim and are granted highest prestige. The independence, competition, and licensing attached to public accounting give it a greater amount of prestige than private accounting, and the dominance of the large public accounting firms in the amount and types of practice and the opportunities resulting therefrom (such as greater independence, wider experience, more comprehensive training) give them more prestige than the individual practitioners and smaller firms.

The Big Eight have as clients the majority of the largest economic organizations in the world—the industrial corporations, commercial banks, insurance companies, merchandising firms, transportation companies, and utilities.[7] The work of the Big Eight consists primarily of auditing (forming an independent opinion based on examination of financial records and transactions) these organizations. Tax services and management counseling services are increasing in importance, together taking up more than one-third of the professional time of the firm (see table 5). The accounting of these economic organizations

*A group of practitioners organized as a firm to offer services for a fee is a professional *organization*. A group organized to initiate and promote general objectives of a profession or a segment thereof is a professional *association*.

7. The U.S. has more than twice as many billion-dollar (in net sales) industrial corporations than the rest of the world combined. See *The Fortune Directory* (New York: Time, Inc., 1968).

—recording of transactions and constructing of financial statements—is done by the accounting departments in these organizations.

The influence of the Big Eight within the United States is even greater. Tables B-1 through B-4 (see appendix B), which are based on figures in *The Fortune Directory* (1965), are clear evidence. In every major organizational group (the 500 largest industrial, 50 largest merchandising, 50 largest utilities, 50 largest transportation) the Big Eight are the choice of the largest clients, with very few exceptions. For example, in 1964 only 2 of the 55 billion-dollar industrial corporations in the U.S. were not clients of one of the Big Eight. The tables also indicate that there is little difference in the size of the firms. A firm that is "heavy" in one area, such as Touche Ross & Co. in merchandising, will be light in another, such as industrials; this tends to equalize the firms in size and scope of operations. As the question of size is a sensitive point among the Big Eight, it will be dealt with separately in the next chapter. However, for purposes of this study we can say that the firms are approximately equal in size.

Collectively, the Big Eight audit over $300 billion in net sales of the industrials and merchandising corporations. These corporations constitute less than one-half of 1 percent of the total number of corporations of their kind in the United States, but they account for about 30 percent of the total national sales volume for all corporations in their group.[8] And the revenues and assets of the largest transportation and utility companies ($13 billion and $78 billion, respectively) account for as large a percentage of their respective industries, for even though the smaller organizations in these industries are larger than the small business companies, they are fewer in number. The Big Eight audit 80 percent of those companies that are listed with the Securities and Exchange Commission and about the same percentage of those listed on the New York Stock Exchange.[9] But their clients include a large number of the unlisted and smaller organizations and of the wealthiest individuals, too. For example, Peat Marwick audits the oil holdings of the billionaire H. L. Hunt. They also audit more than 1,000 banks, about 700 savings-and-loan associations, 700 insurance companies, and more than 1,200 nonprofit institutions, including universities, hospitals, and local, state, and federal governmental bodies.[10] An average Big Eight firm handles more than 10,000 clients.

Some smaller accounting firms are considered to be excellent in their judgmental abilities and their command of accounting technique—in certain situations equal to or even better than those of the Big Eight. But they lack all the advantages of size: geographical comprehensiveness, accompanied by flexibility

8. Based on figures in *Dun & Bradstreet Million Dollar Directory, 1966* (New York: Dunn & Bradstreet, Inc., 1965), p. iv, and the *Statistical Abstract of the United States: 1965* (Washington, D.C.: U.S. Government Printing Office, 1965), pp. 487-496.

9. T. A. Wise, "The Auditors Have Arrived" (Part I), *Fortune* 62:151 (November 1960).

10. T. A. Wise, "The Very Private World of Peat, Marwick, Mitchell," *Fortune* 74:91 (July 1, 1966).

of operation; specialization within a wide range of services; elaborate formal training programs; and because of these advantages, the ability to attract personnel of highest quality. The large clients need these advantages, so they go to the big firm. The big firm knows how to handle the large clients, how to handle their tax planning, how to save them money, how to advise them on expansion, and so forth. Aside from the question of whether they *are* the most ethical group in the profession (which has long been debated in the profession), the Big Eight are *considered* to be very ethical and extremely competent by the financially aware public. So, when a company goes "public—that is offers its stock on the market—it considers the prestige that would accrue from the name of a Big Eight firm, for such a firm is *accepted* as "best"—it has prestige.11 With the big firm's name on the financial statements, third parties are supplied with a basis for confidence in making their financial decisions. A recent study noted that during the period 1955-1963, 83 companies among the 500 largest industrials switched from one accounting firm to another. Only 5 left the Big Eight; 8 moved from one small auditor to another; 31 switched from a small firm to a Big Eight firm; and the remaining 39 switched from one Big Eight firm to another.12

Therefore, to study the personnel of the largest accounting firms is to study a considerable part of the profession of public accounting. Certainly they form the most significant group of workers in the profession in terms of professional influence and control.

There is some disenchantment with the Big Eight on the part of other CPAs, but it is not prevalent enough to endanger their position as the elite with regard to prestige within the profession. There has been, for example, some effort by smaller firms to organize and offer coordinated services on a regional or national basis in an attempt to compete with the Big Eight. However, though there is this division between large and small firms (and individual practitioners, as described in chapter 9), no minority group consistently and intentionally applies power over others in the profession—that is, a power elite does not exist.

11. Wise, "The Auditors Have Arrived."

12. John C. Burton and William Roberts, "A Study of Auditor Changes," *Journal of Accountancy* 123:31-36 (April 1967). There were a total of 137 changes, but 54 were due to mergers and thus were not considered as real changes but rather as additions.

In its broadest perspective, the purpose of this book is to examine the nature and types of social structure and organization of these eight largest public accounting firms in the United States, utilizing concepts from organizational analysis and the sociology of the professions to develop and test a theory of organizational change. It is what sociologists call a functional analysis of a profession in that it "sees a profession largely as a relatively homogeneous community whose members share identity, values, definitions of role, and interests."[13] But it is also functional in that interdependent groups and sub-groups imply relative autonomy and reaction against one another (coercion, conflict), as well as equilibrium, in an integrated social system.[14] Both the equilibrating and disruptive effects in the public accounting profession and in the Big Eight in particular will be given as empirical evidence for the theory.

As large-scale organizations, the Big Eight accounting firms operate under established procedures that organize and control social processes. These procedures were first emphasized by the German sociologist Max Weber in his discussion of ideal bureaucratic types;[15] they have since been utilized by many students of organizational theory. Several authors have emphasized the rational efficiency of bureaucracy in their examinations of organizations, but at the same time they have pointed to its routine and oppressive nature.[16]

13. "The sociology of professions has largely been focused upon the mechanics of cohesiveness and upon detailing the social structure of given professions"—a critique of the theory and research in the sociology of professions by Rue Bucher and Anselm Strauss, "Professions in Process," *American Journal of Sociology* 66:325 (January 1961).

14. Cf. Alvin W. Gouldner, "Reciprocity and Autonomy in Functional Theory," in *Symposium on Sociological Theory* ed. Llewellyn Gross (Evanston, Ill.: Row, Peterson & Co., 1959), pp. 241-270; and Pierre L. van den Berghe, "Dialectic and Functionalism: Toward a Theoretical Synthesis," *American Sociological Review* 28:702 (October 1963); a commentary of Bert N. Adams, "Coercion and Consensus Theories: Some Unresolved Issues," in the *American Journal of Sociology* 71:714-717 (May 1966); Gerhard E. Lenski, *Power and Privilege*, (New York: McGraw-Hill, Inc., 1966), pp. 17-22.

15. H. H. Gerth and C. Wright Mills, eds. and trans., *From Max Weber: Essays in Sociology* (New York: Oxford University Press, 1946), pp. 196 ff.

16. Robert K. Merton, *Social Theory and Social Structures* (2d ed.; New York: The Free Press, 1957), pt. 2; Philip Selznick, *TVA and the Grass Roots* (Berkeley: University of California Press, 1949); Alvin W. Goulder, *Patterns of Industrial Bureaucracy* (New York: The Free Press, 1954); Peter M. Blau, *The Dynamics of Bureaucracy* (Chicago: University of Chicago Press, 1955); Harry Cohen, *The Demonics of Bureaucracy* (Ames, Iowa: Iowa State University Press, 1965).

Concurrently, many researchers have analyzed the increasing professionalization of modern industrial society.[17] Some have shown that as the number and types of professionals in the work organization have increased, their conflict with the bureaucratic process has generally intensified.[18] Others have gone further in order to show that a "reconciliation" can be achieved between the forces of bureaucracy and professionalism,[19] that in fact the two are necessarily interdependent.[20] Most recently it has been argued that bureaucracy is not an important factor in determining the structure and goals of the "professional collectivity" in the larger organizations in which they work. Rather, there is a loose coalition of constantly warring factions that operate under an elaborate set of political rules.[21]

17. Nelson N. Foote, "The Professionalization of Labor in Detroit," *American Journal of Sociology* 58:371-380 (January 1953); Howard M. Vollmer and Donald L. Mills, "Nuclear Technology and the Professionalization of Labor," *American Journal of Sociology* 67:690-696 (May 1962); Harold L. Wilensky, "The Professionalization of Everyone?" *American Journal of Sociology* 70:137-158 (September 1964); William A. Faunce and Donald A. Clelland, "Professionalization and Stratification Patterns in an Industrial Community," *American Journal of Sociology* 72:341-350 (January 1967).

18. Among the earlier examinations of this development are: Logan Wilson, *The Academic Man* (New York: Oxford University Press, 1942); Blau, *The Dynamics of Bureaucracy;* Roy G. Francis and Robert C. Stone. *Service and Procedure in Bureaucracy* (Minneapolis: University of Minnesota Press, 1956); Harold L. Wilensky, *Intellectuals in Labor Unions: Organizational Pressures on Professional Roles* (New York: Free Press, 1956); Alvin W. Goulder, "Cosmopolitans and Locals: Toward an Analysis of Latent Social Roles—Parts I and II," *Administrative Science Quarterly* 2:281-306, 444-480 (December 1957, March 1958).

19. For example, Mary E. W. Goss, "Influence and Authority among Physicians in an Outpatient Clinic," *American Sociological Review* 26:39-50 (February 1961); Ronald G. Corwin, "The Professional Employee: A Study of Conflict in Nursing Roles," *American Journal of Sociology* 66:604-615 (May 1961); George Strauss, "Professionalism and Occupational Associations," *Industrial Relations,* 2:9 (May 1963); Howard M. Vollmer, "Professional Adaptation to Organizations," in *Professionalization,* ed. Howard M. Vollmer and Donald L. Mills (Englewood Cliffs, N.J.: Prentice-Hall, Inc., 1966), pp. 275-282; Richard H. Hall, "Some Organizational Considerations in the Professional-Organizational Relationship," *Administrative Science Quarterly* 12:461-478 (December 1967); Gloria V. Engel, "The Effect of Bureaucracy on the Professional Autonomy of the Physician," *Journal of Health and Social Behavior* 10:30-41 (March 1969).

20. William Kornhauser, *Scientists in Industry: Conflict and Accommodation* (Berkeley: University of California Press, 1962), p. 197; Peter M. Blau, *The Dynamics of Bureaucracy* (rev. ed.; Chicago: University of Chicago Press, 1963), p. 9, describes an interdependence maintained in an environment of continual change; Richard H. Hall, "Professionalization and Bureaucratization," *American Sociological Review* 33:104 (February 1968).

21. Rue Bucher and Joan Stelling, "Characteristics of Professional Organizations," *Journal of Health and Social Behavior* 10:3-15 (March 1969).

As large *professional* organizations, the Big Eight epitomize the situation of interdependence. They are constituted almost entirely of professional people, and they are large enough to encounter all the factors of bureaucratization—the division of labor, a hierarchy of authority, a system of abstract rules, and so forth. Yet they never have become overbureaucratized, that is, dysfunctional through excessive routine, rigidity, and red tape, as many corporate and governmental organizations have.* Why haven't they? I hypothesize first that the system of rules, perhaps *the* most important characteristic of bureaucracy,[22] is largely *external* to the accounting firms. Therefore, the firms do not have to concentrate so heavily on these bureaucratic tasks; they can devote more time to professional work. For example, in his study of the twenty largest law firms in the country, Smigel found the profession's associations handling most of the rule-making and rule-enforcing.[23] Second, I hypothesize that the development of new knowledge in such areas as management advisory services requires the firms to adjust structurally, and, most important, it provides the practitioners with new areas of unrationalized knowledge. These areas of uncertainty, of judgment potential, provide the dynamics for organizational change. For with new knowledge each firm must individually take it upon itself to develop appropriate codes and rules for governing that knowledge. This presents the firms with bureaucratic problems of routine. However, at the same time, practitioners are freed from the constraints of the highly rationalized body of old knowledge. They can explore new areas, and they can innovate, until that new area becomes circumscribed by the rule-making parent (the external rules of the professional association). This rule-making in turn rationalizes the field of knowledge, but at the same time it reduces the firm's internal bureaucracy (hypothesis number 1). Internal bureaucrats, with their vested interests, cannot

*There are two types of bureaucracy: the first is the objective, ideal type bureaucracy of rationalization and efficiency; the second is the bureaucracy of routine (with its attendant dysfunctions). This distinction is made by Michel Crozier in his book *The Bureaucratic Phenomenon* (Chicago: University of Chicago Press, 1964).

22. Empirical studies have shown that the degree of development of a system of rules covering rights and duties of positions of incumbents in an organization in large part determines the degree of efficiency in that organization. The rules criterion of bureaucracy was the single measure of bureaucracy in an industrial organization, according to a work by Alvin W. Gouldner *(Patterns of Industrial Bureaucracy,* especially pp. 19-24, 158). Other studies conducted in civil-service organizations underline the importance of rules in the bureaucratic milieu. Francis and Stone *(Service and Procedure in Bureaucracy)* analyze, in several contexts, the professional's conflict between procedural rules and service to the client; and Blau *(The Dynamics of Bureaucracy)* points out the functions of statistical records as bases for rules. Schutz, in a factor analysis of social control, shows the important relationships between cluster items of rules and authority, rules and efficiency, and rules and the group (W. C. Schutz, *FIRO: A Three-Dimensional Theory of Interpersonal Behavior* [New York: Holt, Rinehart & Winston, 1958]).

23. Erwin O. Smigel, *The Wall Street Lawyer: Professional Organization Man?* (New York: The Free Press, 1964), pp. 275, 278.

fully develop in this constantly changing environment. The "vicious circle" of bureaucracy is thereby circumvented. However, bureaucracy is never eliminated. Rather, a *professional bureaucracy* is maintained: professional because external rules are developed to protect autonomy and because new knowledge increases judgment potential; a bureaucracy because external rules increase rationality and because new knowledge initially requires individual organizations to construct, administer, and police a body of rules in order to control that knowledge. The "external rules" pattern has been tested by Smigel in his examinations of the largest law firms. The "new knowledge" concept has been analyzed by another sociologist, Litwak.[24] Both these authors use the term "professional bureaucracy" to describe their ideas. In chapter 4 I shall use the same term to designate a theory that utilizes the ideas of both in order to depict a process of organizational change.

This theory puts the study of a profession into a historical perspective. Advances in knowledge are traced over time to see how they have affected the large firms and the profession as a whole. By doing this, the analysis not only becomes historical but also political. New knowledge is not usually found to be the preserve of a single profession or discipline. Therefore, many of the relationships between professions are power relationships, and public accounting is no exception. Led primarily by the Big Eight, public accounting is moving rapidly into management consulting (weakly disguised as "management advisory services"). Today, management services departments of the Big Eight could be found among the twenty largest management consulting groups in the United States.[25] Following our theory, the traditional area of the audit has been rationalized, reduced largely to a series of predigested and predirected checks of data. With this rationalizing of technique there is a loss of power, because power lies in the control over areas of uncertainty.[26] An alert profession will move rapidly to attain control over one or more of these areas. Auguste Comte said it thus: "Savoir pour prévoir, prévoir pour pouvoir."

To a great extent, then, the study of an occupation or profession is a study of power relations, and this study will be pursued here.

24. Smigel, *Wall Street Lawyer*. Eugene Litwak, "Models of Bureaucracy Which Permit Conflict," *American Journal of Sociology* 67:182 (September 1961).

25. Felix Kaufman, "Professional Consulting by CPAs," *Accounting Review* 42:713-720 (October 1967).

26. The relationship between power, rationalization, and uncertainty is examined by Michel Crozier, *The Bureaucratic Pheonomenon* (Chicago: The University of Chicago Press, 1964).

For purposes of comparison, medium-sized firms are included as part of the study. Medium-sized firms are not the firms next in size to the Big Eight. There are about eight large-sized firms that list more than fifty partners, with a total of two or three times as many CPAs as partners. These are no more than one-tenth the size of a Big Eight firm. Then there are the thirty or forty medium-sized firms that have between ten and fifty partners, with two to three times as many CPAs.[27]

The very rough generalization can be made that the medium-sized firm is a small-scale model of the largest firms. These firms too are large; their total personnel numbers in the hundreds and is located in several offices around the country and, in a few cases, in other countries. They also have the same internal formal organization in terms of hierarchy of positions and areas of specialty. Their salary levels are equal to or near those of the Big Eight, and their personnel is of the highest quality, many of its members becoming leaders in the profession. There are, however, some major differences between these and the largest firms, such as in job integration and in the proportion of professional time spent in administrative work. These and other similarities and differences are analyzed in following chapters.

27. These are the only figures available on size of firms, compiled by the AICPA in 1965.

2

The Public Accountant's World of Work

In order to be able to form an idea of the work environment of the public accountant, one must empathize with his background, with his career, and with the nature of his work and its basic technical aspects. The Big Eight have gone through several changes in organizational style and complexity. These changes can be traced through growth patterns in terms of size and type of services performed.

THE HISTORY AND GROWTH OF THE FIRMS

The Big Eight show a remarkable similarity in their histories and in their patterns of growth. There are differences, to be sure, some of them major, but generally they resemble one another closely enough for a picture of a typical firm to be sketched. Four of them (Haskins & Sells; Lybrand; Peat Marwick; and Arthur Young) were founded in the 1890s and were home-based on the Eastern Seaboard. One firm resulted from the establishment of a New York City office in 1901 by the British firm of Price, Waterhouse & Co., itself established in 1865. Two others were founded in the Midwest in the early 1900s: Ernst & Ernst at Cleveland (1903), and Arthur Andersen at Chicago (1913). Touche Ross, the youngest firm, is the result of the merger in 1959 of three firms of long and close association, themselves among the earliest firms in America.

These professional organizations experienced considerable growth during their early years. In 1903, Haskins & Sells reported that it had 40 accountants, 60 assistant accountants, and 40 clerks; fifteen years later, it reported that it had 10 partners and 268 employees in 14 offices, one of which was in London.[1] Ernst & Ernst expanded to 16 cities in the decade from 1910 to 1919, and its annual volume of billings passed $3 million.[2] In the 1930s, new federal regulations were passed that did much to increase the amounts and types of work done by public accounting firms. The most important regulations were the Securities Act of 1933, which regulates new securities that are issued to the public or are

1. "Introducing the Department of Professional Training," *Haskins & Sells Bulletin* 1:1-4 (March 15, 1918).
2. *Ernst & Ernst: A History of the Firm* (Cleveland: Ernst & Ernst, 1960), pp. 28-29. Similar historical facts can be found in *Arthur Young and the Business He Founded* (Boston: privately printed by The Merrymount Press, 1948).

involved in interstate trade, and the Securities Exchange Act of 1934, which regulates stocks on all securities exchanges to the extent that all companies listed on them must submit periodic financial reports to be audited by independent public accountants.[3] However, the curtailment of business activity during these years was great enough that the accounting firms felt the squeeze too. It was not until the beginning of World War II that services expanded significantly. The increase in size and complexity of business and government in the postwar years led to still more expansion. In Ernst & Ernst the number of partners admitted to the firm more than doubled from the decade of the thirties to the decade of the forties—from 20 to 47.[4] In the 1930s there was only 1 office added to this firm, as compared to 39 in the 1920s. During the 1940s only 6 offices were added, but the number of partners had increased from 30 to 65.[5] In a 1964 recruitment brochure, Peat Marwick shows that it had 30-odd partners in the 1940s.

However, the last fifteen years have seen the greatest increase in growth. With the post-Korean War expansion and the decentralization of U.S. industries in the 1950s, the Big Eight located new offices near the branches of these industries. In some cases, local firms were "bought out," that is, their names were changed to that of the purchasing firm for a price. In other cases, new branches were started by sending one or more members of the firm to the new location to build up a practice in that area.

The professional services that the Big Eight render to the largest businesses in this country have always required their presence in several foreign countries, but it has been only within the last fifteen years that international expansion has occurred in the majority of firms. This phenomenon of the international firm is unique to this profession. An international firm is an association of firms established as a single "firm," the firms being linked in some cases by one or more "international partners" in each associated firm. In other cases a firm will establish a contract association with foreign accounting firms, thereby expanding its international base through these firms by carrying its name in the title of the associated firm. One example of how an international firm could be used would be to examine the accounts of an overseas plant of a U.S. manufacturer who is audited by a Big Eight firm. In this way, auditing methods that approach uniformity produce more accurate reports. Another example would be to examine the accounts of a joint organization that has been set up by two or more countries and operates in these several countries.

3. Public Act No. 22 (1933) and Public Act No. 291 (1934), Seventy-third Congress, *United States Statutes at Large*, vol. 48, pt. 1, pp. 74-95 and 881-909. Regulation S-X of the SEC covers the specific requirements for audit.

4. *Ernst & Ernst*, pp. 53-67.

5. Ibid., pp. 52, 69.

Based on the figures in table 1, the *typical* Big Eight firm has 200 U.S. partners, a little more than half being located in its New York City offices and the remainder being spread through 50 other U.S. offices. Internationally, there is an average of 80 offices in 40 foreign countries. Less than 40 percent of these offices are correspondents or affiliates. By stating these figures, no inference is made as to the size of any specific firm. Nor should a linear trend for any firm be assumed, for the changes have been dramatic in some firms and minimal in others. Also, gauging a firm's size by the number of its partners would only lead to gross inaccuracies, because in some firms the responsibilities of a partner are of a much greater scope than in others. The list of offices, although it is not

TABLE 1

Number of Partners and Offices of the Eight Largest
Public Accounting Firms

Firm	Number of Partners		No. of U.S. Offices[c]	No. of No. of Foreign Foreign Offices[c] Countries[c]
	1960[a]	1962[b]		
Arthur Andersen	171	176	33	30 in 21 (1966)
Ernst & Ernst	132	82*	107	74 in 37 (1965)
Haskins & Sells	176	67*	58	97 in 42 (1964)
Lybrand	126	156	43	− in 27 (1965)
Peat Marwick	190	238	87	161 in 55 (1966)
Price Waterhouse	101	130	46	− in 48 (1962)
Touche Ross	71	−	31	106 in 34 (n.d.)
Arthur Young	104	92	40	109 in 51 (n.d.)

[a]These estimates are taken from T. A. Wise, "The Auditors Have Arrived" (Part I), *Fortune* 62:152 (November 1960). The author notes that these are "estimates," unconfirmed by the firms themselves. Many firms consider these figures to be completely unreliable.

[b]These figures are taken from "Registered Certified Public Accountants and Copartnerships of Certified Public Accountants Registered between 1962-64," *University of the State of New York Bulletin,* September 1963. Some firms appear to have listed only those partners licensed *only* in New York State, or those licensed in New York State plus those licensed reciprocally to practice in New York State. Where this is the obvious case, the average rate of increase has been inserted and indicated by an asterisk.

[c]The figures on number of offices and countries are taken from the house organs, publicity brochures, and pamphlets of various firms. The year is the date that the figures were printed, where the date was given.

subject to changes as rapid as the changes in lists of partners, must be interpreted with even greater caution. An office, in certain instances, may be no more than a room with a desk, unoccupied except for visits by the firm's representative to that area. In the case of an international firm's offices, the total number of offices might include offices that are not directly affiliated. These are "correspondents" or "representatives," with whom the firm cooperates in referral of business or in coordinating international work. Again, like the U.S. offices, some of the international offices may be very small. However, all of the Big Eight firms maintain large offices in the major foreign centers of commerce and industry.

These discrepancies in measurement indicate the difficulty in determining the size of a specific firm by using these figures alone—"playing the numbers game," as some respondents tagged it. As a result of analysis based on these figures and on figures reported in news media, the financially educated public would probably name Peat, Marwick, Mitchell & Co. as the largest public accounting firm.[6] But in reality, these firms are similar in so many respects, and the figures used to determine their size are so difficult to interpret in many cases, that the phrase "I'm the largest" would appear to be almost meaningless as a general statement representing an entire firm. Almost every firm is "largest" in one or several areas: Price Waterhouse in industrials; Peat Marwick in banking and finance; Arthur Andersen in utilities; Touche Ross in merchandising; and so forth. Some firms are "very strong" in several areas (tables C-1 through C-4 attest to those statements). In earlier decades, several firms grew by concentrating in certain areas. But the tendency has been towards diversification, which one firm includes as part of its formal policy.

In this study *it will be assumed that all eight firms are equal in size.* It is not significant for our examination whether one firm has one hundred more partners than another, or fifty more offices than another, because these firms are all large enough that they engage in the same type of work, with the same international scope and with the same quality of personnel. They are similar enough that any random switches of clients between firms in most cases could be handled by any one of these eight firms.

Another figure that is frequently used for comparative purposes is the total billings to clients. This is perhaps a better indicator of physical size, as billings give a rough indication of the number of man-hours that a firm has expended during a given year. But it does not indicate how these man-hours were spent, that is, in what type of work the personnel were involved—such as technical, routine, or high-level advising. Nor does it indicate how the work was *organized, directed, and influenced,* that is, the formal and informal organization of the firms, the amount of personal and office autonomy within the firm, and the

6. A great many inaccuracies exist in these figures. Compare, for example, an article in the *Wall Street Journal* of May 24, 1965, with figures given by Peat Marwick as of January 1966 in its recruitment brochure—the latter being more conservative.

influence of the firm on groups external to it, and vice versa. What the work is and how it is organized is the focus of this chapter. Authority and power relations within firms and with outside organizations is taken up later in the book.

Size, then, is not only determined by the number of positions or offices, but, more importantly, by what underlies these numbers—social organization and influence. So, the question of size is not asked in order to determine which firm is largest. Rather, it is asked in order to analyze the process of professionalization in public accounting (through analyzing these firms, because they are so important to the profession) and to analyze the relationship of this process to bureaucracy in the firms.

THE FORMAL ORGANIZATION OF THE FIRMS

The wide variety of services and the world-wide scope of the Big Eight necessitate a formal organization that is very complex for a professional organization. Basically, the organization can be broken down into two major components, technical and administrative, which correspond to some extent to the line and staff (respectively) designations used on the organizational charts in industry. The technical component is made up of three major sections: auditing, taxes, and management services. The administrative component includes: (1) the senior partner (similar to the position of president or chairman of the board in a private corporation) and the managing or executive committee, including the managing partner; (2) the specialized departments, such as personnel, communications, client relations, and the like; and (3) the office manager. Neither of the two components is purely line or purely staff. In many firms those who are considered administrators also are engaged to a limited extent in client work. On the other hand, an individual from any one of the three areas of the technical component may serve on occasion in an advisory capacity to almost any department of the firm. It should also be mentioned that all areas of the two components would not be found formally listed as such in each firm. But in every firm each area has a counterpart, unnamed or with a different name, that performs the same function.

Excluding the international offices, the total number of personnel for each firm runs into the thousands. Two firms contain about 5,500 people each; one has about 5,000; two more have about 3,500; one has about 3,000; and two have about 2,000 each.* About 40 percent of these people are based in the New York City offices. The firm's professional hierarchy is separated into several levels. The top level is that of partner. State law (with a few states excepted) allows only *certified* public accountants to join in a partnership. Only partners

*These figures are based on interviews and on the recruitment brochures of two firms.

19

are "members" of a firm. All others are "employees." The partners collectively hold final responsibility for all decisions made by the firm.

The next highest level consists of managers; in some firms they are called "principals." The manager works closely with the partners and with the men in the field (those in the lower levels work at the clients' offices). He acts much of the time as the liaison between the firm and the client. The third level, that of "supervisor," is used only at two firms. The next level of positions is given the name "senior." The beginner is called a "junior" or a "staff assistant."

These are the four or five formal levels of professional positions in the firms. There is also a special set of corresponding positions fitted to the nonaccountant specialists employed by the firm. To list them here would only confuse the picture. They will be enumerated in the chapter on career patterns. Approximately 35 percent of the professional staff, mostly juniors and some seniors, are non-CPAs. This is a relatively constant figure that is determined by the promotional system of the firms.

The levels of a typical New York City office, by the size of level, are as shown in table 2.

TABLE 2

Estimated Number and Percentage of Personnel, by Position,
of a Typical Big Eight Office in New York City [a]

Position	Number	Percentage
Partner	100	10
Manager	100	10
Supervisor/Senior	300	30
Junior	500	50
Total	1,000	100
Professional Accounting Staff	1,000	67
Other Professional Specialists	200	13
Nonprofessional Staff	300	20
Grand Total	1,500	100

[a]Figures were compiled from statements made during interviews and, in a few cases, from firm recruitment brochures.

20

TABLE 3

Organization Chart of a Typical Big Eight Firm

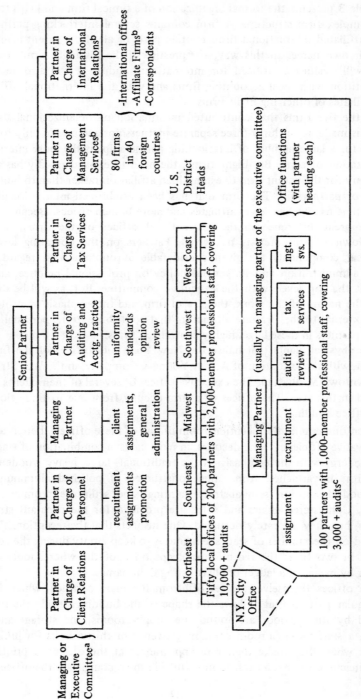

aPart of U. S. partnership.

bStaff may be or may not contain a separate partnership.

cThe proportionately smaller number of audits performed by the New York City office is due to the larger size of the clients handled.

Table 3 presents the formal organization of a typical firm and helps to clarify the complex firm structure. A firm contains several interlocking partnerships. Most affiliated international firms contain parts or all of the parent firm's name in their own name. In this way, the prestige of the Big Eight firm's name (its "goodwill" value) is utilized for international audits. It can also be used in competition with local accounting firms and with the international offices and the affiliates of other Big Eight firms.

Of the five firms that contributed information on organizational structure, one was made up of thirty-three separate partnerships and one of only four. One reason for a large number of interlocking partnerships is the loose international organization of some Big Eight firms; the need to expand rapidly has made it necessary for the parent firm to establish an affiliation rather than to build up an office or partnership. The firm that has been established internationally for a longer time usually has fewer affiliates and more branch offices. Because there is such a great difference in the international offices of the firms, a further breakdown of this area is not given. Partners on the operating levels (the technical component) are given considerable autonomy. With regard to the firm's administration and its general policy on professional practice, authority rests at the top level, with the executive committee. But, as will be discussed later, the nature of the work, the size of firm, and the emphasis on professional rules external to the firm are all factors that contribute to the personal autonomy of partners in these large, highly centralized firms.

The physical plants that house the New York City offices of the firms are located, with the exception of Arthur Young & Company, in the Wall Street area of downtown Manhattan. The executive offices of several of their clients are also located in this area. The offices of a firm occupy from one to three floors of a large office building.

When one enters the reception room of one of these offices, there is an air of conservative efficiency. The decor is, in most cases, a combination of traditional and modern, with the emphasis on the traditional—large, heavy wooden doors, but with the attached firm name constructed of polished aluminum; large hardwood desks, but semi-abstract paintings and sculpture prominently displayed. Upholstered chairs and sofas are provided for the constant stream of visitors, but they are rarely occupied. One suspects that the receptionist's salary is based on the number of seats she manages to keep empty during the course of a day. In two firms the receptionist keeps track of the whereabouts of each partner by means of a ledger or chart listing their names.

The offices themselves are set off from the main corridor, which forms a rectangular pattern that follows the shape of the building. Inside the rectangle formed by the corridor are found the supply rooms, the storage and filing rooms, a staff room (a room containing twenty or thirty desks for juniors and seniors when they make their rare appearances at the office), a printing and office-machine room, and rest rooms. Outside the rectangle are the offices of the partners and managers. The partners have the offices with the best views. At some firms they are situated so that they command a magnificient view of New York harbor, but the telescope associated with the Wall Street banker is usually not seen. Other noticeable features are the large-sized desks; the wall-to-wall carpeting; the long work table behind the desk; extra chairs for interviews and conferences; a few paintings, reflecting the tastes of the occupant; and on the desk, a photograph of his wife and children. The senior partner is the "president" of the firm. To him come the major problems with regard to the firm's policy and administration. He works closely with a managing or executive committee of partners on these matters. The offices of these few partners are the largest, and in some cases their secretaries also command private offices. The senior partner's office is equipped to hold small conferences. As might be expected, the managers and supervisors are located in less desirable areas; they have smaller offices and sometimes smaller desks, fewer chairs, and less carpeting.

The symbols of status are, upon close inspection, quite evident in these firms. The amount of pressure put on the professional in these firms by the unusual career pattern (generally, you can remain in the firm only if continually promoted) and the demands of the job produce quite an elaborate informal organization. Those in the lower levels of the hierarchy are given indications of their progress by informal designations of status. "Semi-senior" indicates progress toward promotion to a senior. "Heavy senior" evidences nearness to the position of supervisor or manager. "Acting manager" signifies that you are practically there. And so forth.

Other indicants are more subtle, such as a person's being allowed a bit more responsibility than is normal for his position, or being assigned to the less boring jobs. Thus, the unusual pressures put on the individual in these firms are relieved somewhat by the informal organization, which lets a man have a better indication of where he stands in the system.

THE NATURE AND SCOPE OF THE PUBLIC ACCOUNTANT'S WORK

The average public accountant spends the major part of his career as an auditor. Why, then, is he called a public *accountant* instead of a public *auditor*? And why is he called a *public* accountant? To answer these questions, it is necessary to describe the fundamentals of accounting and the specialized work areas of the public accountant. Because these work areas are more esoteric, the descriptions of them are more extensive than would be necessary if a better known profession, such as medicine or law, were being studied.

In 1940 the AICPA Committee on Terminology issued its first Bulletin, in which accounting was defined as "the art of recording, classifying and summarizing in a significant manner and in terms of money, transactions and events

23

which are, in part at least, of a financial character, and the results thereof." In 1958, this definition was greatly expanded to include the observing, measuring, interpreting, reporting, and inspecting of these events or data.[7] The data were termed "economic" data, that is, data concerned with the management of funds (financial events) in the total process of production, distribution, and consumption of goods and services.[8] However, several years later, in 1966, the AICPA limited somewhat this broad definition in an official statement of policy by emphasizing financial data instead of economic data, though the actual wording "financial and other information" is still rather ambiguous.[9]

Through a series of research studies, the AICPA has attempted to define and describe the more important aspects of public accounting. The first such study, written by the accounting theoretician Maurice Moonitz, covered the basic postulates, that is, the assumptions, or "givens," of accounting. In a prefatory remark he states that: "In their economic aspects, all organized societies of which we have knowledge are concerned with the production and distribution of wealth; all use entities of one kind or another to accomplish this result. Accordingly, accounting is and always will be closely identified with *wealth* and with *entities.*"[10] Several accounting texts in the past have listed one or more of these assumptions as premises of the discipline, but this is the first major work devoted solely to their construction. Although these postulates have been hotly debated, the generality and scope of them are important enough that they should be listed and briefly defined, as many parts of the discussion will touch upon them.

> A-1. *Quantification.* Quantitative data are helpful in making *rational economic decisions,* i.e., in making choices among alternatives so that actions are correctly related to consequences [italics supplied].

7. "Reports of Committee on Terminology," Accounting Research Bulletin No. 7 (November 1940), issued by The Committee on Accounting Procedure of the American Institute of Accountants, p. 58; Herman W. Bevis, "The Accounting Function in Economic Progress," *Journal of Accountancy* 106:27-34 (August 1958).

8. Ibid. John L. Carey, ed., *The Accounting Profession: Where Is It Headed?* (New York: AICPA, 1962), p. 11, comments: "Accounting can and does measure and communicate data not only in terms of money symbols, but also in nonmonetary units, such as material, labor, and time. Accounting, therefore, embraces that part of the control function of management which utilizes measurement and exhaustion of material and human resources, and the efficiency of their utilization."

9. "A Description of the Professional Practice of Certified Public Accountants," *Journal of Accountancy* 122:61 (December 1966). See also the discussion on this statement by John L. Carey, "What Is the Professional Practice of Accounting?" *Accounting Review* 43:1-9 (January 1968). A year before the statement was released the author of an Accounting Research Study had defined accounting in its more limited meaning: Paul Grady, *Inventory of Generally Accepted Accounting Principles for Business Enterprises,* Accounting Research Study No. 7 (New York: AICPA, 1965), p. 4.

10. Maurice Moonitz, *The Basic Postulates of Accounting,* Accounting Research Study No. 1 (New York: AICPA, 1961), p. 51.

A-2. *Exchange.* Most of the goods and services that are produced are distributed through exchange, and are not directly consumed by the producers.

A-3. *Entities* (including identification of the entity). Economic activity is carried on through specific units or entities. Any report on the activity must identify clearly the particular unit or entity involved.

A-4. *Time period* (including specification of the time period). Economic activity is carried on during specifiable periods of time. Any report on that activity must identify clearly the period of time involved.

A-5. *Unit of measure* (including identification of the monetary unit). Money is the common denominator in terms of which goods and services, including labor, natural resources, and capital are measured. Any report must clearly indicate which money (e.g., dollars, francs, pounds) is being used.

B-1. *Financial statements.* (Related to A-1.) The results of the accounting process are expressed in a set of fundamentally related financial statements which articulate with each other and rest upon the same underlying data.

B-2. *Market prices.* (Related to A-2.) Accounting data are based on prices generated by past, present or future exchanges which have actually taken place or are expected to.

B-3. *Entities.* (Related to A-3.) The results of the accounting process are expressed in terms of specific units or entities.

B-4. *Tentativeness.* (Related to A-4.) The results of operations for relatively short periods of time are tentative whenever allocations between past, present, and future periods are required.

C-1. *Continuity* (including the correlative concept of limited life). In the absence of evidence to the contrary, the entity should be viewed as remaining in operation indefinitely. In the presence of evidence that the entity has a limited life, it should not be viewed as remaining in operation indefinitely.

C-2. *Objectivity.* Changes in assets and liabilities, and the related effects (if any) on revenues, expenses, retained earnings, and the like, should not be given formal recognition in the accounts earlier than the point of time at which they can be measured in objective terms.

C-3. *Consistency.* The procedures used in accounting for a given entity should be appropriate for the measurement of its position and its activities and should be followed consistently from period to period.

C-4. *Stable unit.* Accounting reports should be based on a stable measuring unit.

C-5. *Disclosure.* Accounting reports should disclose that which is necessary to make them not misleading.[11]

The factors that distinguish a public accountant from other types of accountants are, first, that he serves the public rather than a single employer and, second, that he is an attestor to certain financial statements of the clients he serves.[12] In order to attest to these statements, the public accountant must perform an audit, an examination of the records of the client organization. This examination covers the flow of information, the system of internal control over transactions, the counting of amounts of raw material, material being processed, and finished goods (technically known as inventory), and so forth. Auditing is the inspecting of economic data in its manifestations in an organized group.

The purpose of the audit is to give an independent judgement of the financial condition of a business enterprise for presentation to the client and/or to one or more interested third parties (stockholders, the general public, the government, and so forth). The physical form that this judgment takes is the statement of the auditors that is attached to the financial reports of the client. It is commonly known as the "opinion." The form it takes on the report to stockholders of publicly traded corporations (corporations in which stock is sold on an exchange) is:

We have examined the balance sheet of X Company as of June 30, 19— and the related statement(s) of income and retained earnings for the year then ended. Our examination was made in accordance with generally accepted auditing standards, and accordingly included such tests of the accounting records and such other auditing procedures as we considered necessary in the circumstances.

In our opinion, the accompanying balance sheet and statement(s) of income and retained earnings present fairly the financial position of X Company at June 30, 19—, and the results of its operations for the year then ended, in conformity with generally accepted accounting principles applied on a basis consistent with that of the preceding year.[13]

This opinion lends credibility to and reliance on the financial reports by implying "that the data presented are appropriate for the purpose of the representation, that there is objective evidence underlying the data, and that the judgments exercised in interpreting the data are such as to justify the opinion."[14] These judgments are concerned with the substance of a business entity

11. Ibid., pp. 52-53.

12. Bevis, "The Accounting Function," p. 32.

13. This example is given in *Auditing Standards and Procedures: Statements on Auditing Procedures No. 33,* Committee on Auditing Procedure of the AICPA (New York: AICPA, 1963), p. 57.

14. Herman W. Bevis, "The CPA's Attest Function in Modern Society," *Journal of Accountancy* 113:28 (February 1962).

rather than with its form, as the partner of one firm put it; with realistic rather than legalistic action, as the member of another put it.

The CPA may be engaged in the construction of the financial statements, auditing of them, and other related activities (all part of the broad definition of accounting), or he may be involved only in the auditing. Whatever, he must be familiar with all the information systems that are used throughout the organization to deal with economic data.[15] In his audit function, the CPA accounts for the accuracy of information and control systems. "Other experts deal with similar data but usually for more specialized purposes; sometimes broader, as in the case of economists in reports or studies on the gross national product; sometimes narrower, as in the case of a statistician concerned with only one specific problem."[16]

Accuracy in measuring these data is achieved by adherence to "generally accepted accounting principles" (GAAP) and "generally accepted auditing standards and procedures" (GAAS). Basic principles were first formulated by the AICPA in the early 1930s in conjunction with the New York Stock Exchange, and new principles have gradually been added over the years. Accounting principles have been discussed in writing, but they were never codified until quite recently, and this has been done from two very different points of view. One view presents them as they stand today; the other as they ought to be, following from the basic postulates.[17]

Auditing standards and procedures are used for the inspection of accounting records. For example, the first standard of reporting requires that the accounts of the client be in line with the GAAP. Auditing standards are measurement requirements applied to the accounting that the actual performance of the auditing procedures must fulfill. Both "auditing procedures" and "accounting procedures" are the more detailed processes subsumed under the GAAP and GAAS.

Take an example of how the entire set of standards and concepts are utilized: Imagine that the management of a corporation decides to rate its current assets on its balance sheet by $50,000 more than its auditors feel is appropriate. The question can immediately involve several basic postulates or concepts: the amount may be large enough to "materially" affect the financial statements; the auditor has the obligation to give a conservative estimate of the situation;

15. Robert M. Trueblood, "The Management Services Function in Public Accounting," *Journal of Accountancy* 112:37-44 (July 1961), as quoted in Carey, *The Accounting Profession*.

16. John L. Carey, "The Integrated Accounting Service," *Journal of Accountancy* 120:63 (November 1965).

17. Grady, *Inventory*, presents the current principles; Moonitz, *Basic Postulates*, presents them as they ought to be. Grady, *Inventory*, p. 43, notes this distinction. He also prefers not to call them postulates (because this depicts them as the definitive givens), but rather concepts, i.e., "ideas" (this appears to be the intention of the change in name—PDM).

objectivity must be maintained by the auditor in determining the extent of the business cycle, which thus affects the amount of money involved. The principle that pertains to the situation is "Items classified as current assets should be carried at not more than is reasonably expected to be realized within one year or within the normal operating cycle of the particular business."[18] The specific auditing standards to be followed include (1) that "sufficient competent evidential matter" shall be obtained and (2) that the auditor, when he prepares the report, shall state whether the financial statements are in accordance with GAAP.[19] Certain accepted auditing procedures for confirming the current assets are used, just as one of several accepted accounting procedures was used by the client's private accountants to obtain the original higher estimate. The accounting procedure itself may not be in question, only the estimate derived from it.

All this tells us what the public accountant does in very general terms. However, what he does depends to a large degree on the size of the firm in which he works. In the largest firms he is engaged mostly in specialized areas of auditing and management services. The accountant in a medium-sized or small firm performs more accounting and integrated management services in proportion to auditing services than does the accountant in a large firm. One important reason for this is that the largest firms are engaged by the largest clients; and all of these clients have their own staffs of private accountants who prepare most of the information for audit. It is not economically feasible for the smaller clients to have such staffs, so they ask their auditing firm to perform these services for them. On the other hand, it would be economically infeasible for the large clients to engage high-priced public accountants for the mountain of routine accounting groundwork that is required in preparing data for an audit or for other internal control purposes when less expensive accounting help is available.

The work of the large-firm public accountant falls within all three major areas of the technical component: auditing, taxes, and management services. All three contain some aspects of accounting work, and each (with some exceptions in taxes and management services) owes its basis for existence to the accounting function.

Auditing

The largest area is the audit area. The accountants who answered the questionnaire indicated that 52% of their time was devoted to auditing. The audit of a client company involves many steps and sometimes several months of work before the partner-in-charge will sign the name of the firm to the resulting

18. Grady, *Inventory*, p. 222.

19. For a summary listing of GAAS (General Standards; Standards of Fieldwork; Standards of Reporting) see *Auditing Standards and Procedures, No. 33*, pp. 15-16.

opinion. These steps may include a physical count and observation of inventories, a random check of the accounts receivable (checking to see whether the list of creditors and amounts due are valid), a similar check of the accounts payable, counting of cash or securities, and checking to see whether consistency has been maintained in accounting methods employed by the client during the course of the year. Or, in more complex business and governmental organizations that have the latest technological devices, these steps may include constructing and running a test deck to audit the computer's information program and constructing dynamic accounting-system models to test against the client's computer program for accounting.

The requirements of the law have played a very important part in shaping the growth and type of work of the public accounting profession. The Securities and Exchange Commission, the arm of the federal government that administers the Securities Act and the Securities Exchange Act, requires independent audits of all corporations issuing securities to the public, all corporations listed on stock exchanges, and registered brokers, dealers, and investment companies. The Rural Electrification Administration, a federal lending agency, requires independent audits of electric and telephone companies that borrow from them. The Small Business Administration, another federal agency, requires independent audits of small business investment companies to which it has granted licenses.[20] However, many organizations, such as banks, insurance companies, and railroads, are not included in this list.

Auditing has been mentioned in connection with the phrase "measurement and control data." The dependability of any audit has to do with the objective measurement of both the accounting and the administrative system of internal control of an organization.[21] The auditor examines the internal control system for efficiency of operation and for correct accounting procedures, as a check against collusion. He will examine the system of authorization that deals with all levels of exchange in the organization. He will also examine the systems of administrative controls for their operational efficiency. This includes controls only indirectly related to financial records, such as statistical analyses, time and motion studies, performance reports, employee training programs, and quality controls.[22] "The internal information system is the nerve center of every organization . . . [It] includes the recording, accumulation, classification, analysis and transmission of economic data."[23] The relation of the audit to internal

20. These legal requirements of federal bodies are taken as listed by Carey, *The CPA Plans for the Future* (New York: AICPA, 1965), p. 157.

21. Grady, *Inventory*, p. 37, feels that dependability of data through internal control underlies objectivity.

22. *Auditing Standards and Procedures, No. 33*, p. 28.

23. David F. Linowes, "Professional Organization and Growth," *Journal of Accountancy* 120:27 (July 1965).

control is such that the audit is the only full-scale internal control system in small businesses.

A final major consideration of auditing is the auditor's responsibility for presentations to interested parties. The auditor's responsibility is a "secondary" one.[24] He is responsible only for his opinion as to whether the financial statements have been fairly presented according to generally accepted accounting principles, as the opinion statement expresses. The accounts of a company are the responsibility of its management.[25] The most important external purpose of accounting is to supply the information that is required in order for management to fulfill its fiduciary responsibilities to interested parties.[26] Legal precedence for this matter was established in 1939 by *In the Matter of Interstate Hosiery Mills, Inc.*, 4 SEC 721:

> The fundamental and primary responsibility for the accuracy of information filed with the Commission and disseminated among investors rests upon management. Management does not discharge its obligations in this respect by the employment of independent public accountants, however reputable. Accountants' certificates are required not as a substitute for management's accounting of its stewardship, but as a check upon that accounting.

In other words, if the auditor is competent and has made a reasonable effort to detect irregularities, he cannot be held responsible for not uncovering fradulent practices of his client. The question of responsibility for audit statements had already been tested in courts in *Touche* v. *Ultramares*, 225 N.Y. 88, 174 N.E. 441 (1931). The judgment rendered in this case was, in essence, that the defendant (the audit firm) is considered liable for fraud not only if he has knowledge of the fraud and intends to deceive the plaintiff, but also if he pretends to have knowledge when in reality there is none.[27]

The current, generally accepted accounting principles of the public accounting profession are standards set primarily for meeting responsibilities to investors and to interested parties other than management. The accounting procedures used in preparing reports for management (for example, examination of a system of employee benefits) are the basis for a management service that is separate from the reporting to external parties.[28]

24. Grady, *Inventory*, p. 5.

25. *Restatement and Revision of Accounting Research Bulletins*, Accounting Research Bulletin No. 43, Committee on Accounting Procedure (New York: AICPA, 1953), p. 10.

26. Grady, *Inventory*, pp. 56-57. See also, *Auditing Standards and Procedures, No. 33*, p. 9. A critique which refutes the fiduciary nature of the relationship is given by R. J. Chambers, "A Matter of Principle," *Accounting Review* 41:450-451 (July 1966).

27. Robert H. Montgomery, *Fifty Years of Accountancy* (New York: privately printed by Ronald Press, 1939), p. 289, gives a concise summary of this case.

28. Grady, *Inventory*, p. 5.

Taxes

Tax services, or "taxes," constitute the second major area commanding the time of public accountants in the Big Eight. The questionnaire sample indicated that 18 percent of their time was spent in this area. About one-third of this time is spent in preparation of tax returns for businesses and individuals. The remainder is spread over a diverse area that includes advising clients on tax implications of organizational changes (mergers, reorganizations, liquidations, and so forth), representing clients before the Internal Revenue Service, estate planning, and special tax surveys.

Much of the work in this area involves the public accountant as an advocate for his client, in contrast to his role as an independent observer when he is auditing. At Arthur Andersen & Co., 25 percent of the tax accountants have law degrees.[29] In this area of the accountant's work there is a constant need to represent the best interests of the client, because tax laws encourage the minimizing of payments by offering alternative forms of computing tax payments. This "forensic accounting" is also carried on in areas other than taxes. For example, the CPA often argues before the staff of the SEC in support of audit positions he has approved in the financial statements that his clients file with the commission.[30] On the question of responsibility in tax work, the CPA is again only responsible for decisions or advice that results from the information made available to him. Of course, it is understood that he should only pass judgment when such information is adequate for the circumstances.

Management Services

Concurrent with the rapid advances in methods of electronic data processing and with new experiments in organizational efficiency, accounting firms have developed a set of management services for clients. This third major area of the large-firm accountant, occupying 20 percent of his time, according to the questionaire sample, has been known by many similar names within the Big Eight. Three firms have called the area "management services"; two, "management consulting services"; one, "management advisory services"; one, "management controls";[31] and one, "administrative services." With the issuance in 1969 of two sets of "management advisory services" by the AICPA, this term may soon be universally accepted in the profession. I shall stick with the most common usage at present—"management services." There are other reasons that

29. As stated in the recruitment brochure of Arthur Andersen & Co. (1966).
30. Carey, *The CPA Plans*, p. 170.
31. One firm, Peat, Marwick, Mitchell & Co., publishes its house journal under the title *Management Controls*.

31

persuade me to use the shorter, more popular version; they will be examined in a later chapter.

Each firm employs between two hundred and five hundred people in this area, nearly all of them specialists. There are mechanical, chemical, and civil engineers; mathematicians, psychologists, and economists with Ph.D.s; and CPAs with a background in one or more of these specialized areas. As with the previous two areas, specialists in management services further specialize within their department. However, the department of management services is not as integral to the formal structure of the organization as are the other two departments. It has its own promotional hierarchy, and it has yet to be centrally related to the primary task of the firm—the audit.

A non-CPA cannot become a partner in a public accounting firm. Therefore, the non-CPA personnel in management services who attain high rank in the firm are given positions that bear the title "principal," or some similar designation, which signifies that the position is equal to that of a partner. The entire department thus has its own names for positions; they correspond to those of the audit and tax departments. Sometimes a CPA will head up the department of management services, and so will be designated a partner. About 10 percent of this department is composed of persons originally trained in public accounting.

The breakdown of specializations in this department in Arthur Young looks like this:[32]

General Management
    Over-all surveys of operating
      and financial policies
    Acquisitions and mergers
    Long-range planning
    General counseling
Accounting Costs and Budgeting
    Accounting applications
    Product costs planning
    Special costs analyses
    Government contract costs
    FTC cost justifications
    Profit planning and budgeting
Operations Research
Industrial Engineering
    Product and inventory control
    Maintenance control
    Quality control
    Work measurement

Organization and Personnel
    Organization planning
    Incentive compensation
    Job evaluation
    Training programs
    Executive recruitment
Data Processing
    Machine applications
    Punched-card applications
    EDP applications
    Office methods and layout
Marketing
    Market research
    Product planning
    Distribution patterns
    Sales organizations and methods
    Sales incentives
    Sales forecasts

32. Recruitment brochure, Arthur Young & Company (n.d.).

Although several of these areas did not exist twenty years ago, the implication that management services are essentially new appears to be inaccurate. Many accounting authors have stated that "management services" is to a large extent a new name for work that the CPA has been doing for a long time. One indication of this is found in a 1929 listing of the functions of the public accountant, which includes the investigation service for the purchase and sale of businesses; reorganizations and consolidations; issuance of new and old securities; and consulting services.[33] A more concrete example is McKinsey & Company, Inc., a management consulting firm that was born more than sixty years ago as the outgrowth of the consulting services department of an accounting firm.[34] However, there has been a new period of growth for such services since the mid 1950s. Today management services are expanding at an annual rate of about 15 percent in the Big Eight, and the total of fees derived from them has increased to one-third or more of a firm's gross earnings.

Much of the work of management services is based on, or stems directly from, accounting.[35] Examination of the system of internal control could constitute a good part of the work of management services, depending on how broadly the system is defined. In fact, when the CPA firm is separated into three areas for purposes of description, the picture tends to become distorted by implying a wider gulf between the three than actually exists.[36] This distortion exists in the mind of many Big Eight practitioners, especially on the lower levels, where the accountant sees only a small part of the firm's total services.

The public accountant believes that the conditions of responsibility for his management services are essentially the same as for his auditing services. In management services, he is presenting the alternatives available for the making of a decision. His client makes the decision and assumes the responsibility for it.[37] As in the case of auditing, the responsibility of the consultant is a secondary one. He is responsible only to management or to other interested parties who have engaged his services to prepare a presentation based on information that is available and sufficient for him to complete the services.

33. Monard V. Hayes, *Accounting for Executive Control* (New York: Harper & Bros., 1929), p. 25.

34. As reported by Caroline Bird, "Young Man, Be an Accountant," *Esquire* 56:137-138 (September 1961).

35. One example: H. T. McAnly, "Current Cost Accounting Problems Give Impetus to Management Services," *E&E* 1:14-16 (Winter 1961-1962).

36. Paul Grady, "The Independent Auditing and Reporting Function of the CPA," *Journal of Accountancy* 120:70 (November 1965), feels that John Carey's book *The CPA Plans for the Future* does just this. Carey's comments on the relations between the three areas are located on pp. 123 and 260 of his work.

37. Trueblood, "The Management Services Function," p. 42. See also, Carey, *The Accounting Profession*, p. 88. This point is made emphatically in the Statements on Management Advisory Services, Nos. 1 and 2, in the March and April 1969 issues of the *Journal of Accountancy*.

Because of the nature of their work, accountants are very conscious of the importance of effective administration in an organization. As might be expected, this habit extends to their own firms. In the large accounting firms, four major administrative functions are performed; and in most cases, each of these requires the efforts of more than one person. In the Big Eight, one function is consigned to the personnel department. Consisting of about five people, it is engaged almost entirely in recruitment and in running the firm's training program. Another group, the managing or executive committee, makes the major policy decisions for the firm. This includes taking action on promotions to partnership and other positions. The personnel department supplies this committee with records of the individuals being considered, such as yearly written evaluations of the employee, which cover his technical competence and social behavior. The managing committee ranges in size anywhere from eight to twenty persons.

A third group performs assignment services. This is usually a small group of two or three persons whose major task is to assign employees of lesser rank to each partner in the firm. They match the technical qualifications of these people to the particular job (client) of the partner; they also match personalities—for example, they place a manager who is economically (in regard to accounting technique) and socially conservative with a like-minded partner and client. The managing partner of one of the large U.S. offices might perform this duty or parts of it; but as a member of the managing committee, he is more concerned with the assignment of clients to partners and with major decisions regarding administration of the firm. In some firms the assignment work is formally a function of the personnel department.

The fourth major administrative function is actually several related functions that can be grouped under the title "communications." This area involves the time of several people engaged in client relations, public relations (on a limited "information services" basis), and coordination of certain outside activities for the firm, such as scheduling a partner to speak at a civic or professional convention meeting.

About 8 percent of a firm's total professional time is assigned to these four administrative groups. Another 4 percent is spread throughout the entire firm's professional personnel. This 4 percent is made up of personnel reports on subordinates, the making out of time sheets on time chargeable to clients, and correspondence related to administration.

34

RELATIONS WITH ORGANIZATIONS
EXTERNAL TO THE FIRM

Clients

The public accounting profession has long been called the profession of business advice;[38] its primary recipients are its clients. Although the large accounting firm is an authority on accounting systems and on other information systems related to them, this has yet to be recognized by some clients.[39] However, it is becoming evident to most that accounting is the "language of modern business," that good accounting may mean the difference between profit and loss, or even between solvency and bankruptcy.[40] For this the client is willing to give a part of his yearly profits to the accounting firms. In 1962 a reported "standard charge" per hour for Big Eight firms (ethics forbid competitive bidding) was $7 for juniors, $10 for seniors, and $35 for partners.[41] This appears to be an average, because firms generally charge clients according to the salary of the partner assigned to the engagement. Two times a man's salary is given as a rough estimate. For a specialist, it is 2.25 to 2.75 times his salary, because not as much of his time can be charged directly to clients. Taking into consideration a $50,000 salary and the 30 percent of a partner's time given to administrative and other affairs (see table 5) that must be deducted from an average 37-hour week, the charge per hour would have been around $40 in 1966. But the hourly charges actually ranged from $30 to more than $100.

A 1964 study of what smaller companies think of their auditors indicated that the auditors had a good image and that the range of services is wide but that improvements could be made in both areas.[42] Meanwhile, these smaller companies are willing to pay accounting fees that run into tens of thousands of dollars, which is certainly above the minimum costs necessary to fulfill the legal requirements of audit. Yet, there still are problems today with large as well as

38. Robert H. Montgomery, *Auditing Theory and Practice* (New York: Ronald Press, 1912), p. 7.

39. An excellent example of losses that a company sustained due to lack of attention to the auditor's advice is given by Lewis D. and John J. Gilbert in their *Twenty-fifth Annual Report of Stockholder Activities at Corporation Meetings during 1964* (New York: L. D. and J. J. Gilbert, 1965), pp. 241-242.

40. An empirical study of ten successful and ten bankrupt companies by the Bureau of Business Research at the University of Pittsburgh disclosed that "business success is directly related to the full use of adequate records." As reported in Robert E. Witschey, "The Accounting Function for Small Business," *Journal of Accountancy* 106:34 (December 1958).

41. Jack J. Friedman, "Auditors: A Wasted Asset?" *Dun's Review* 80:51 (November 1962).

42. Elmo Roper, "As Others See You," *Journal of Accountancy* 117:32-36 (January 1964).

35

small clients. So many companies have been bringing suits against Big Eight firms that, as one partner reports:

> Currently, there are, I would say, about fifty suits against CPA firms in this country. There's one for each of the Big Eight at any one time you choose to pick. The Wise article [T. A. Wise, "The Auditors Have Arrived," *Fortune*, November and December 1960, which estimated size and total billings of each of the Big Eight] may have had more effect than we thought. Enough lawyers may have read it to create an increase of suits, consequently raising suit coverage. Suit coverage is almost prohibitive in expense to a firm, but we have to have it. It has risen because of the number of suits, and whether they're justified or not, the insurance company many times settles out of court because it's less expensive than bringing it through. Nor do the firms like it. The costs in partners' time and legal fees is tremendous.

Sometimes a firm does decide to test a case in court. A recent case involved Peat Marwick, which was sued by four banks, two of them the largest and second largest banks in the U.S. (Bank of America and Chase Manhattan Bank). Peat Marwick was sued for $6 million in damages, because they allegedly had not been explicit enough in their financial reports of a San Francisco coffee-importing firm. This may bring into focus the problem of what degree of explicitness is required in CPA reports to stockholders and to other parties who are legitimately interested in the finances of a company, a much debated problem in the profession today.

Professional Associations

The largest accounting association, and the one that is most important for large-firm accountants, is the American Institute of Certified Public Accountants. Large-firm CPAs are also members of several accounting associations or associations related to accounting, namely, the American Accounting Association, the National Association of Accountants, the Federal Government Accounting Association, the Financial Executives Institute, the Institute of Internal Auditors, the American Management Association, state accounting societies, regional associations, and others. But it is through the AICPA that the large-firm practitioner operates to voice his opinions to the profession and the public.

Members of the large accounting firms are well represented on the committees and boards of the Institute, and they have a great deal of influence—many times their numerical influence—on the entire membership. One good example of this was in the factional dispute between the Big Eight and small firms at the 1960 national meetings of the AICPA, which concerned rulings with regard to professional independence.[43] Their committee influence has been commented on by the senior partner of a small but influential New York firm: "The position of the Big Eight on the APB [the 21-member Accounting Principles Board of the AICPA] is quite a bit like that of the five permanent members of the U.N. Security Council—others come and go but the Big Eight will always be there."[44]

The Securities and Exchange Commission

In the 1930s the federal government, through the SEC, utilized the accounting profession to limit the unevenness in the financial reporting of business enterprises. The Securities Act and the Securities Exchange Act and their attendant regulations were powerful instruments. All companies registered with the SEC were required to submit financial statements that had been audited by a CPA. The SEC has the authority to determine the details of the contents of the financial statements and the methods to be used in obtaining these details. With some exceptions, the accounting profession has been allowed to steer its own course in making these determinations of accounting and auditing practice, and this has kept direct government interference in business reporting to a minimum. The large firms deal frequently and closely as intermediaries between their clients and the SEC. Corporation registration reports and annual financial statements are presented by the firms to representatives of the SEC. The complexities of dealing with the SEC requirements are important enough to require that the firms have special committees to keep abreast of current regulations and new developments in the area.

Relations between Firms

Although there is a very high degree of competition between Big Eight firms in practically every area, there is also considerable cooperation. Much technical information is shared by communications maintained through AICPA committee work, and there are occasional meetings of Big Eight technical or administrative specialists to discuss their mutual problems. The competition does provide an undercurrent of distrust regarding certain practices of another firm or firms compared to those of one's own firm, but this occurs mostly on the levels below partnership. Much of this distrust was denied by partners, indicating that the beliefs of these accountants were largely unfounded.

43. The story is given by T. A. Wise, "The Auditors Have Arrived" (Part II), *Fortune* 62:146-148 (December 1960).

44. Quoted in "A Matter of Principle Splits CPAs," *Business Week*, January 26, 1963, p. 57.

Occasionally, cooperation is found in an area of major importance. In its international expansion, Ernst & Ernst was aided considerably by Haskins & Sells and by Price Waterhouse.[45] This was a rather unusual gesture, considering that increased competition was, in certain instances, likely to result. An executive partner of one firm remarked:

> There is a relatively high level of cooperation among seven of the Big Eight—there's one progressive firm which doesn't go along with much of what we do together. For example, the managing partner of another firm made himself available in court for a case [we contested] with a client. And we would do the same for them [the managing partner's firm].

Other Professions

The most frequent contact that large accounting firms have with other professions is through their services to their associations and through group practices. In its recruitment brochure, Peat Marwick lists the American Medical Association, the American Library Association, and the American Bankers Association as clients in the "Associations" category. Price Waterhouse maintains an unusual contact with the legal profession. It acts as private auditor and consultant on areas of accounting and internal administration to large law firms—professional organizations that are nearly identical in formal organization to large accounting firms.[46] In a brief discussion, a member of Price Waterhouse commented on their operation:

> In our work for law firms we do some audits for a report to [the law firm's] partners only, of course. We do quite a bit of management advisory services. We install EDP equipment, and we are engaged in cost projects and other analysis projects.
>
> We also conduct an annual survey of financial operations of law firms. One hundred firms participate by completing a questionnaire on financial operations of their firms. We accept the questionnaires as they are, run them through a computer, and come up with a nine-page report. The law firms can then see how they have done competitively. Without this they

45. *Ernst & Ernst: A History of the Firm*, p. 76. Another unrelated and minor but rather unusual example is the publication of an article by the senior partner of Arthur Young & Company in the official journal of another firm. See Thomas G. Higgins, "Comments on Generally Accepted Accounting Principles," *Arthur Andersen Chronicle* 24:7-12 (April 1964).

46. Two Price Waterhouse specialists have written on their observations at the request of an American Bar Association committee: Clark Sloat and Richard D. Fitzgerald, *Administrative and Financial Management in a Law Firm*, Economics of Law Practice Series, Pamphlet 10 (New York: The Standing Committee on Economics of Law Practice of the American Bar Association, 1965).

would not be able to see their position with respect to the other firms. This is a significant relationship, and is further examined in Part Two, in the discussion on power, decision-making, and "generalists."

The Public

Most people can give the names of one or two of the Big Eight firms, and a good number of stockholders could list three or four. But hardly anyone is aware of the size and range of activities of these firms. This lack of knowledge is due chiefly to restrictions on advertising imposed by the CPAs themselves in their code of ethics and by the nonpersonal nature and the confidentiality of most of their work. These points are elaborated on in the next chapter. At this point it should be noted that relations with the general public are very limited, and only recently have the profession's associations attempted to remedy this situation.

The Government

In 1965 twenty-six federal agencies utilized outside accountants in more than 40,000 cases—double the number of 1959.[47] It can reasonably be inferred that a fair proportion of these cases involved the Big Eight. In addition to conducting its engagements with private companies, every Big Eight firm maintains an office in the nation's capital in order to serve these federal agencies. A recent example of this close association is the appointment of a managing associate of the Washington, D.C., office of Arthur Young as project director of a federal government study to review the management of automatic data-processing activities in the executive branch.[48] A landmark was reached in 1967, when for the first time the federal government, through the office of the president, formally recommended the use of outside auditors for a government activity—in this case pension funds. Services of this sort are becoming more common as the expertise of the large-firm accountant is increasingly sought by the organization with the world's largest budget.

Local, state, and federal governments have shown great interest in a new accounting method for planning poverty and rehabilitation programs. Called social accounting, it attempts to measure quantitatively the needs of the population and the resources available to meet these needs, to assess alternative plans to

47. Reported by Lyman Bryan, in *Journal of Accountancy* 121:22 (April 1966). See also Carey, *The CPA Plans*, p. 157.

48. As reported in *Management Services* 1:8 (February 1964).

allocate resources, to simulate the alternatives, and to measure social indicators (statistics on literacy, crime, unemployment, welfare, hospital care, and so forth) in order to obtain feedback that will serve as a basis for anticipating future changes. This technique was tested by the city of Detroit, which hired Touche Ross as professional consultants.[49]

49. Robert Beyer, "The Modern Management Approach to a Program of Social Improvement," *Journal of Accountancy* 127:37-46 (March 1969); Jean-Paul A. Ruff, "Poverty Programs—A Business Management Approach," *Quarterly/Touche, Ross, Baily & Smart* 12:24-32 (June 1966); David F. Linowes, "Socio-Economic Accounting," *Journal of Accountancy* 126:37-42 (November 1968).

3

The Career Pattern of a Large-Firm Accountant

PRE-FIRM PATTERNS

Unlike the professions of medicine or law, the accounting profession does not arouse conscious interests in the individual at an early age. Young children do not list accounting as an occupation to be considered for their future—most of them have no knowledge at all of accounting. Along with many other occupations, it has no place in the youngster's world of fantasy. Youths of high school age are almost equally in the dark. One contact with accounting is the book-keeping courses in the "commercial" section of their school,[1] but college-bound persons recognize that bookkeeping training leads to positions that are among the lowest in prestige for white-collar workers. Or, they might know the local CPA, an individual practitioner who does the auditing and accounting of small businesses and handles personal income tax returns.

For nearly all college entrants, including those in business schools, this is the extent of information about accounting. Candidates for the Bachelor of Science degree in a college of business administration are exposed to theory and methods of accounting in the required courses during their first two years. It is based on these two years of exposure that the majority of public accountants presumably decide to make a career of accounting. During the second year the choice must be made formally to enroll for the advanced training in accounting, which comes in the final two years of college. Because the majority of accounting graduates do not enter public accounting, courses specifically designed for CPAs are not usually given much emphasis in the advanced accounting curriculum. Thus, it is ordinarily not until the final year of his college training or later that the individual decides on public accounting as a career. This usually occurs just before or during the recruiting season. Each of the Big Eight has a year-round program in which recruiting takes place at more than one hundred selected colleges and universities in all parts of the country. They are looking for the top graduates in each class. The national recruiting director of one firm commented

1. Evidence of early influences of this nature are documented in the replies of 775 undergraduate and graduate male students who were members of chapters of accounting honor societies across the nation. The report is given by Ray M. Powell, "Career Choices Among Beta Alpha Psi Members," *Accounting Review* 41:525–534 (July 1966). The AICPA has engaged the Bureau of Applied Social Research at Columbia University to expand this study.

on the competition involved in this system of recruiting: "We want the top 10 percent of this year's crop. There are approximately 10,000 graduates. All the firms are after these 1,000 people, and, of course, we [his firm] don't get only the top ones."

Once the initial weeding-out has been accomplished by the campus recruiters, the selected persons are invited, at the firm's expense, to visit their home office or one of their major branch offices to meet and talk with representatives of the staff. This is where the candidate looks over the firm and where the firm looks him over. The firm knows through the individual's college grades that his technical abilities meet at least their minimum standards. They are primarily interested in the less tangible factors: How does he handle himself with others in new situations? Is he nervous? Does he talk too much? Is he very opinionated and antagonistic in nontechnical matters? This process may take only an hour, or it may cover an entire day, in which case wining and dining are in order. A candidate may be alone, or several may visit in a group.

The firm also wants to interest the candidate in the attractive and unique features it offers. A day-long interview would probably include a tour of the office, a private chat with a "junior" and a "senior" and perhaps with one of the firm's specialists whose area the candidate is considering.

If the candidate is one of the sought-after 10 percent and he visits several firms, he may notice that each firm has a distinctive "personality." Sometimes the differences are not great, but they are still evident. For example, two firms are almost identical in the mood they project onto the visitor. There exists the same conservatism, the same casualness, the same mannerisms, the same style of clothing and manner of wearing them. That is, the same *Betriebsklima* or atmosphere is apparent—with one exception. In the first firm, the people are open, friendly, gregarious, while in the second they are quiet, reserved, and restrained. In addition to this, administrative and technical procedures and rules of the firms vary greatly.

The popular candidate is also in the position to bargain for his beginning salary. The salary for beginning positions is standard among the large firms, due to the intense competition for new people. The same situation exists for large law firms, where the base salary is known as the "going rate."[2] The going rate for new recruits in the large accounting firms in 1968 was $8,600 to $11,000, depending upon qualifications. "Qualifications" would include a very high grade-point average, in which case bidding would be erratic and the extent of bidding would depend a lot on the candidate's ability to "play the field," to see who would match and go beyond another's offer. Another qualification is the amount and type of higher education. In 1968 new M.B.A.'s in accounting

<hr />

2. For a discussion of the going rate of large-firm lawyers, see Erwin O. Smigel, *The Wall Street Lawyer: Professional Organization Man?* (New York: The Free Press, 1964), pp. 57-58.

received about $10,800 for their first year, whereas an M.B.A. with a bachelor's degree in engineering or physical science started at around $11,000.[3] Consideration is also made for other specialties. A growing number of large-firm accountants have law degrees (mainly for tax specialization), and for the management services department a few are hired with master's or doctorates in mathematics, engineering, economics, and related fields. Qualification in these specialties results in higher initial salaries.

For those candidates who receive more than one offer, the importance of firm "climate" becomes central. This, in fact, was the most important consideration for two candidates with whom I talked while I was observing recruitment interviews. One applicant had visited three firms, all of whom had made approximately the same offer in terms of position, salary, benefits, and promotional opportunities.

THE FIRST YEARS IN THE FIRM

The majority of entrants into the Big Eight are graduates of business schools, and most of them have majored in accounting.[4] Examination of the questionnaire sample reveals that 88 percent hold a degree in business administration (see table 4). Nearly all new men entering one of the firms begin in the audit area. Some exceptions are made for experienced specialists in taxes and management services, but these are unusual cases. Ordinarily, management-services and tax personnel obtain one or two years of audit experience so that they can learn the basic procedures in order to be able to relate their work to that of the auditors. This practice of "auditing first" is borne out by the percentages of time that beginning accountants spent in the four major work areas (see table 5), as compared to the percentages that personnel in higher positions spent.

Not only is the neophyte started with immediate on-the-job training, he is also enrolled automatically in an elaborate formal training program that spans several years of his career. The program comprises four or five major phases or schools, each phase or school being conducted every year in order to accommodate the yearly inflow of recruits. The initial indoctrination course is scheduled during the first year of the new person's employment, and it lasts from one to four weeks. Intensive training is given in the firm's procedures in accounting and auditing.

During his first years of work, the junior is exposed to a fairly wide range of clients in order to gain maximum breadth of experience. Much of the work he does, however, is dull and uninspiring; it is known to accountants as "detail

3. Figures are reported in the March 1969 issue of *Journal of Accountancy*, p. 19.

4. Arthur Andersen & Co. reports this to be the case in its recruitment brochure, dated 1966.

TABLE 4

Educational Background of Big Eight Accountants (N=111)

Major Area[a]	Number
Business Administration	53
Liberal Arts + Business Administration	26
Business Administration + Business Administration	12
Business Administration + Law	4
Liberal Arts + Business Administration + Law	2
Liberal Arts	7
Other (includes engineering, and doctorates in liberal arts, business, and law)	7
Total	111

[a]All fields listed after a "+" indicate degrees received at the master's level.

TABLE 5

Apportionment of the Time of Big Eight Accountants, by Area of Work and by Position in Firm (N=111)

Position in Firm	Partner (N=12)	Manager (N=8)	Super-visor (N=26)	Senior (N=39)	Junior (N=26)	Total all Positions (N=111)
Area:						
Auditing	31%	34%	34%	48%	95%	52%
Taxes	19	27	25	24	2	18
Management Services	21	31	31	21	1	20
Administration	23	10	10	6	1	8
Other	6	1	2	2	1	2
Total time	100%	103%[a]	102%[a]	101%[a]	100%	100%

[a]Due to rounding.

44

work." Some examples are: "vouching," the verifying of entries on statements by examining the original documents on which they are based; recomputing arithmetical calculations; physical examination and counting of inventories; formally confirming financial transactions with external parties; scanning ledger accounts; and counting securities.5 During the busy season of the profession, from mid-December to mid-April, the junior may be assigned to one or more large clients. As a result, he may spend weeks just counting securities or confirming accounts receivable. On the other hand, he may be more fortunate, in which case he may work with smaller clients and travel to several locations to accomplish his work. It is more interesting to examine the entire accounting system of a small firm than to be assigned to a small, repetitive part of the system in a large firm. But it also requires fortitude to spend Saturday mornings alone in cold factories, inspecting bales of paper pulp or recomputing long lists of inventory values on adding machines. It is true that some of this work has been speeded up or eliminated by computerization, and it is expected that more will be transferred to the computer in the future, so that much of this present monotonous routine may soon be spared the junior.

The progress of the junior is documented in his personnel record by means of evaluations by his immediate superiors and by the partners for whom he has worked during the year. Generally, an evaluation includes progress in work, aptitude for responsibility, ability to get along with clients, relations with colleagues, interest in work, and progress on the CPA examination. Sometime during his first year the junior usually sits for the first two parts of the four-part CPA examination. Most firms conduct formal courses at their offices in order to prepare their staffs for this examination.

After the first year, or sometimes two, the junior will be promoted within his level. In two firms the junior level is formally separated into the beginning position and a higher junior position. In the higher one the work becomes more technical, and the junior may be directly responsible for the work of two or more men on a large audit or may be given responsibility for several areas of an audit of a smaller client. At this point he has the opportunity to show some creativeness; he is allowed to handle the problems of an audit situation.6 In all firms, experienced juniors are given this opportunity.

The junior is rarely seen at the firm's office. Nearly all the audit and accounting information is at the offices of the clients. There he is a member of

5. R. K. Mautz, "Duties of the Junior Accountant," in the Supplement to the *CPA Handbook,* ed. Robert L. Kane, Jr. (New York: AICPA, 1953), pp. 52-53. See also the analysis by William L. Campfield in the June 1968 issue of *Journal of Accountancy,* pp. 81-83.

6. Of the limited literature on these points, see Stuart F. Kaufman, "Opportunities for the Junior with a Large Public Accounting Firm," *The Price Waterhouse Review* 1:29-35 (December 1956); and Charles G. Walker, "Responsibility of the Junior Accountant for His Professional Development," *Arthur Young Journal* 5:12-16 (January 1958).

an audit team, ranging from two accountants for a small client to as many as several hundred for the largest. The majority of teams range from three to eight accountants, four being the most common size. They are put together by the managing partner or by the assignment manager, and they are placed in operation upon the acceptance of the partner-in-charge.

Because he is a visitor to the offices of the client and because he must go to where the records are stored, the junior will find himself in a different situation on each assignment. At one client's office the audit team may be ensconced in one room set aside specifically for their use, and all records will either be available there or will be brought to them. At another client's office the junior may be working alone in an unoccupied storage room for records, or he may be in a very busy, large room of clerks and managers, where he will be asking questions, tracking down papers, or telephoning his immediate senior, who is working in another office ten floors below.

The average number of years that a person spends at the junior level is four. During all this time he continues to receive formal training in technical areas. In the second year there may be several weeks devoted to tax courses. The third year may be taken up with advanced auditing procedures and with courses in management services.

At the end of his third year of experience in audit work, the accountant is allowed to sit for the last two parts of the CPA examination.* That it is not easy to pass these parts, even with the training that the firms offer, is evident from inspection of tables 6 and 7. Most seniors are over twenty-six years of age (table 6), yet only half of them are CPAs (table 7).

Promotion from junior to senior is based on many factors, among the most important of which are the individual's personnel record, the verbal evaluations of superiors, and his progress on the CPA examination, although not too much weight is given to the last if the reports on the candidate's technical abilities and development are good and several superiors on the manager or partner level put in a good word for him. If at any time during these first years the firm feels that the junior is not acceptable, he is notified and is offered assistance in locating a new job in private accounting or finance. Many who are considered undesirable or are uninterested are weeded out during these first three or four years. At the end of four years, about half of those who started remain. When the time for promotion arrives, there are very few who are passed up for promotion to senior. If they are, the message is clear that their chances of progressing are slim. By age thirty-four, no juniors are left in a large public accounting firm.

*This is the New York law. The laws vary from state to state.

TABLE 6

Age of Respondents, by Position in Firm (N=140)

Position	Age							Total	Per-centage
	20-26	27-33	34-40	41-47	48-54	55-61	62+		
Partner			6	11	3	1	1	22	16
Manager		8	10	3				21	15
Supervisor		15	7		1			23	16
Senior	9	32	4	1				46	33
Junior	24	4						28	20
Totals	33	59	27	15	4	1	1	140	100
Percentage	24	42	19	11	3	1	1		100

TABLE 7

CPAs and Non-CPAs, by Position in Firm (N=140)

Position	CPA	Non-CPA	Total
Partner	20	2[a]	22
Manager	18	3	21
Supervisor	18	5	23
Senior	24	22	46
Junior	–	28	28
Total	80	60	140
Percentage	57	43	100

[a]Nonpartner specialists are given ranking equal to partnership.

Promotion to senior brings with it promotion in almost all aspects of the public accountant's work life. His work becomes more interesting, his salary is increased, and new formal training programs are instituted for him and his colleagues at this level. In effect, the firm is saying, "We like you. You are qualified for more important tasks, and you are in line for further promotion if your progress is maintained."

The new senior is twenty-seven years old (give or take three years) and has his CPA certificate or is fairly confident that he will obtain it soon. He has some experience in directing the work of a small group of men, he has been exposed to accounting and auditing work in a wide range of formal organizations, and he has received follow-up training in the firm's formal program.

A senior is a man who is in charge of accounting and audit operations on the job. He assigns the juniors to the various accounting duties to be performed, and he sets up the specific audit procedures and programs that are to be used for obtaining the audit information. He checks on the client's consistency in upholding accounting principles. He also evaluates the work of the juniors under him.[7] If the individual begins to specialize at this level, he is known informally as a tax senior or, in management services, as an associate consultant. Whenever a problem arises on which a major decision must be made, the senior contacts the manager of the job or the partner who is in charge of the audit. If there is a question of changing the audit procedure or if irregularities in the accounts of the client are discovered or if differences of opinion arise with the client,[8] the senior immediately contacts his supervisor for instructions. The senior receives about $12,000 yearly, which includes about 10 percent for overtime pay.

Table 8 points out the trend toward specialization at the senior level. Whereas there is no specialty at the junior level other than auditing, more than one-third of the seniors are equally divided between specialization in taxes and in management services. The senior's advice is increasingly sought after as his background broadens and as his judgment is tested and found sound

By age twenty-nine, the large-firm public accountant has passed the CPA examination and is certified by state law to practice as a public accountant. With this achievement he has proven himself a valuable senior and so is ready for the

7. Description of the work of the senior can be found in John C. Martin, "Duties of the Senior Accountant," in the Supplement to the *CPA Handbook,* ed. Robert L. Kane, Jr., pp. 77-118; Nicholas A. Bogoluboff, "Responsibilities of Staff Seniors," *Arthur Young Journal* 4:14-20 (July 1956); James A. Barnes and Derrick M. Brown, "Additional Thoughts on Senior Accountants' Responsibilities," *Arthur Young Journal* 4:29-33 (October 1956); David K. Miller, "What the Staff Assistant Expects of the Senior," *Arthur Young Journal* 10:28-33 (January 1963).

8. Martin, "Duties of the Senior Accountant," p. 106.

TABLE 8

Primary Area of Work, by Position in Firm (N=140)

Area	Position in Firm					Totals	%
	Partner	Manager	Super-visor	Senior	Junior		
Auditing	7	11	9	25	28	80	58
Taxes	2	6	4	9	–	21	15
Management Services	6	3	8	8	–	25	17
Administration	3	1	1	1	–	6	4
Combination of Two Areas	4	–	1	3	–	8	6
Totals	22	21	23	46	28	140	100

next step in promotion. In most firms this step is informal—the person is known as a "heavy senior" or as an "acting manager." Two of the Big Eight firms have formalized the level, giving it the title of supervisor. In one firm the position is so informal that the respondent to the questionnaire was unable to give himself a designation other than "veteran senior."*

At this point in a public accountant's career, the moving from senior to supervisor or its equivalent, another weeding-out process takes place. All non-CPAs except nonaccountant specialists in management services are automatically eliminated from the competition. Those who are not interested enough to remain in public accounting—industry offers much more lucrative positions to public accountants at this level—leave for the corporations they once audited. A few take academic positions. Those who managed to get by the previous less severe screenings are now discreetly told if their chances to attain partnership are very slim. (In several firms this occurs at the manager level.) The reason may be their lack of high-caliber technical ability, but just as likely it may be due to personal habits or eccentricities that disturb the smooth flow of work and relations with the client. This process of elimination, which continues all the way to the partner level, has been called the "up-or-out" policy. It is also used as a promotion mechanism by the largest law firms in the United States,[9] and by

*Thus, supervisors are slightly underrepresented in the sample. A few seniors were definitely called heavy seniors, and therefore were placed in the supervisor category.

9. Smigel, *The Wall Street Lawyer*, chap. 4.

the academic departments of major colleges and universities.[10] Unlike members of the academic profession, however, large-firm lawyers and large-firm accountants cannot aid the progress of their careers by techniques of bargaining and by transferring to another employer. In these firms, playing the field is not accepted at the higher levels.

The work of the supervisor or heavy senior is an extension of the work and responsibility of the senior. The supervisor will usually direct more than one client engagement at a time, and he will supervise and review the work of seniors and juniors at these engagements. He may be called in for advice on major decisions involving the clients with whom he is familiar. At this level he will still be attending the firm's formal training programs, which cover the highly technical aspects of all areas of the firm's work. Topics that are covered range from corporate organizational structure and financial planning to methods of electronic data processing and techniques of personnel supervision. Utilizing this knowledge, the supervisor might even be permitted to handle a small client on his own, his work being checked carefully by the manager and the partner-in-charge. Increased specialization occurs at the supervisor level in the three major departments. There is also a marked increase in administrative tasks (see table 5).

The next level, that of manager or principal, as it is known in a few firms, ultimately has room for most supervisors, because most of the attrition has taken place by this time. The less interested, the less talented, and those who are less amenable to the ways of the firm have already left. For those who leave, the opportunities in industry are very attractive. Positions there are usually for the asking, as the diversified background of the large-firm CPA in the handling and interpretation of financial and internal control data are in great demand. The firms have a continuing policy of helping staff members to relocate. This eliminates some of the fears of the staff member regarding his prospects for the future. This policy is also used as an inducement to the college graduate to come to work at the firm. A senior at one firm commented on this system:

> Like the legal world, we have a fraternity. There's an effort to place people. People sort of weed themselves out, and there's some weeding out by the firm. You can stay here for two years while looking for a job, and they [the firm] arrange your schedule accordingly to make it easy for you to go looking. You must tell the firm first, or they'll let you go immediately without helping if they find out you're looking without first informing them.

A distinct advantage of this system to the firm is that its "alumni" strengthen relations with the client, and in some instances they bring a new client to the

10. Theodore Caplow and Reece J. McGee, *The Academic Marketplace* (New York: Basic Books, 1958), chap. 3.

firm. So, the firm does not try to keep the knowledge of good jobs quiet.11

It is very unusual for someone to transfer from one firm to another at the higher levels or to come in from outside public accounting. This is due to each firm's long and highly specialized training program and the special knowledge and techniques associated with each client that have been accumulated over the years. This becomes a close and irreplaceable relationship between a partner and a client, which, if it is passed on at all, can be done only by the manager's concurrent long association with the client. In this respect, it is interesting that less than 1 percent of the five hundred largest industrial corporations change auditors in any given year.12 The pressure in the accounting firms of going either up or out is manifested in their reaction against nepotism. Four firms emphasize the point in writing that persons who are related to any professional in the firm will not be hired by the firm. In a nonprofessional organization the risk of going "out" is lessened, because even though one may not go "up," he at least can remain in his position; he has his union or his seniority. Only the very aggressive companies maintain a semblance of the up-or-out policy of these large professional organizations, but there is much more high-level interchange between companies. And then, the executive who finds himself "out" can much more easily obtain a position equal in prestige elsewhere. Whereas, for the independent CPA there is no position comparable in prestige to partnership in a large or medium-sized firm.

The policy of emphasizing the placing of alumni has its weaknesses. One of the most critical is the degree of turnover. All firms recognize that it is very high, and few see a remedy for the situation. The partner of a medium-sized firm commented: "We have all the disadvantages of the big firms. We have a high turnover. Everyone is restless. The younger people see public accounting as a stepping stone. As soon as they get an offer from some company, they're gone." The average turnover in a Big Eight firm is about 20 percent of the nonpartner professionals per year. The mode is at 20 percent, with the range extending from 15 to about 45 percent. For the medium-sized firms, turnover averaged about 15 percent in the three that were questioned on this point.

The second highest level of the firm, the level of manager, is reached by the successful aspirant at age thirty-two, give or take five years. In the typical firm, ten years elapse from the time that a person begins to work at a firm until he is promoted to manager. The period of time will be a few years shorter or a few years longer, depending on the firm's policy and the historical forces affecting the firm from within. The responsibilities of the manager include all matters

11. A point emphasized by Jack J. Friedman, "Auditors: A Wasted Asset?" *Dun's Review* 80:146 (November 1962).

12. Based on figures for the ten-year period 1955-1964. Results for the first nine years are taken from John C. Burton and William Roberts, "A Study of Auditor Changes," *Journal of Accountancy* 123:31-36 (April 1967). I compiled the results for the last year.

leading up to the final decisions on the audit. For example, he will order additional accounting procedures if he feels that further information is justified in certain areas of the client's organization.[13] He is the liaison between the members of the firm (the partners) and their staff of supporting professionals, an especially important task in the case of large audit teams. Also, where smaller clients are handled entirely by the manager, the partner relies heavily on the manager's judgment when conducting his final review of the client's statements.

The manager will take on anywhere from fifteen to forty-five engagements during the course of a year, the average being thirty-five. He usually has four or five in process at any one time. He has to maintain close contact with the staff on the job in order not to lose track of the progress and direction that the work is taking from week to week. At a luncheon engagement with several partners of one firm, it was mentioned to me that perhaps the "toughest" job in the firm is that of the manager. The others agreed on this point and added that the manager works with as many clients as the partner, sometimes more, and, as liason, the manager is kept very busy. This was evident during the interviews. The manager was the man who was most rushed. In almost all cases his interviews were the shortest; sometimes they reached the point of curtness.

The manager is assigned to an audit team by the managing partner of his office. The managing partner of one firm stated that he bases his decisions on (1) the manager's availability at the time, (2) his technical ability for the specific job, (3) whether the job will help in his professional development, and (4) whether he fits in with the partner-in-charge—personnel are never assigned against the desires of a partner. For his work the new manager receives a salary of about $13,500, which increases at a rate based on his ability, to a maximum of $25,000 to $30,000. A veteran manager may also participate with the partners in the earnings of the firm.

During his time as manager, the individual devotes part of his time to continuing his education in the firm's formal training program. He concentrates on his specialization and closely related fields. The tax manager may attend two or three week-long sessions on the tax implications of corporate mergers, consolidations, and acquisitions; corporate gift taxes; and tax planning. The audit manager might attend a series of lectures on management administration, attend a one-week course on auditing computer-programmed accounting systems; or he might spend a week dealing with procedures and problems in business consulting. The equivalent to the manager in the management services area—who is known as as associate, a managing associate, a manager, or by some other name—will be attending advanced courses in operations services (scientific techniques applied to management decision-making), EDP, work measurement, and related areas. The manager begins to serve on informal committees of

13. John M. Waterman, "Managers' Responsibilities as to Auditing Procedures," *Arthur Young Journal* 3:1-8 (April 1956).

specialists in various fields of auditing, taxes, or management services. He can be found in at least one of more than thirty specialties, for example, committees on banking, transportation, investment trusts, hotels, educational institutions, associations, cooperatives, voluntary organizations, steel manufacturing, auto manufacturing, electronics, mining, and so forth.

The manager remains in his job for approximately five years, when, at an annual meeting of partners, he is selected to become a member of the firm. Selection is based on the question "Will the man make a good partner, or is there someone better we have on tap?" A "good" partner will be able to get along with all types of people, is liked by all, will do much to carry the firm's image to outside contacts, and will enhance that image by his bearing. Those inadequate in accounting techniques will have been weeded out by this level. Therefore, this is not one of the bases for selection, unless the candidate has shown signs of becoming an outstanding contributor to his specialization even though he is admittedly weak in other technical areas.[14]

Some managers who are passed over for partnership are placed in very high managerial positions in industry, many times on the top executive level as controller or financial manager. In some firms there is room for the know-how and experience of the veteran manager (or supervisor) who wishes to stay with the firm but who knows that there is little probability of his being promoted. The very important jobs of assisting in the training of personnel at all levels below partnership,[15] of working in an unusual specialty, and sometimes of handling the less glamorous tasks is the work of a "permanent manager," as this position is informally known in some firms.[16] Although he is outside the firm's promotional hierarchy and does not command the status of the up-and-coming prospective partner, the benefits of his position are considerable. As one senior noted: "It's a position of high regard and high salary, sometimes $25,000 and more. And he has the prestige of working for a top firm."

When they realize that they have little chance of becoming a partner, those managers who leave the firm do so primarily because they will not attain the prestige of being a partner. It is hardly ever a question of money at this point, as it is with lower levels, although this cannot be eliminated as a contributing factor. One Big Eight managing partner, discussing the job of permanent manager, emphasized that this position is one of a topflight technician or administrator, or both, but that it possesses fewer of the characteristics of the partnership

---

14. The conditions for becoming a partner in a large law firm are discussed thoroughly by Smigel, *The Wall Street Lawyer,* pp. 97-110.

15. The responsibilities of partners and higher-level people in personnel development are discussed by Ralph F. Lewis, "Managing with and for Distinction," *Journal of Accountancy* 125:34-38 (March 1968).

16. The largest law firms have a similar but somewhat less attractive position called the "permanent associate." Smigel, *The Wall Street Lawyer,* p. 85.

level than do the jobs of those with whom he is competing.

> For most of these men, we hope they will stay on with us forever. It's those who aren't carrying their weight who are a problem. If they become the majority of permanent managers, you suddenly have a whole new stratum and a serious problem for the firm, because then those below don't get the training, and there are fewer openings for promotion to this level.

For those who have passed the final mustering, the rewards of partnership are theirs to be shared.

PARTNERSHIP AND LEADERSHIP IN THE PROFESSION

The average age at which a person is admitted to partnership in the Big Eight is thirty-six, a total of about fourteen years having elapsed since he entered the firm. However, this total is quite variable, even within the Big Eight. In one firm the range is from eight to twenty years.[17] The pressures of keen competition during these years are tremendous, and manifestations of these pressures were obvious during the interviews: schedules purposely overloaded by a man in order to push himself to his limits, carefully worded conversation so as not to in any way endanger his position, and deference to superiors in nontechnical and, in some cases, in technical discussions.

But the rewards for attaining partnership are great. The salary of the new partner may increase only slightly from his previous year's salary, the minimum for a partner being $30,000. But within five to ten years this can increase up to $100,00 and higher. Highest earnings range up to a quarter of a million dollars yearly. The way to reach these heights is explained by one managing partner:

> This isn't the order of importance, but the ways a partner's salary is determined are, first, technical competence; second, initiative and creativity in dealing with and using this competence; third, personal characteristics, for example, his judgment, his willingness to make sacrifices when needed, his civic contributions. It's a collective judgment, where the senior partner finds the general consensus from the [managing] committee. It's not based on the number of clients he handles, necessarily. Nor is it based on the clients that the partner may be able to attract to the firm.

A few rough estimates, received in interviews, placed partner earnings being shared at around 50 percent of the total billings (total fees from clients) of the

---

17. In the large law firms, the average length of service upon admission to partnership is ten years (Smigel, *The Wall Street Lawyer,* p. 92), but the age of admission is probably the same as that for CPAs, due to the lawyers' later entry into the firm, which is caused by the longer *average* length of time spent by the lawyer on higher education (seven years) as compared to that of the large-firm accountant (five years).

firm. About 10 percent more is used for the firm's training program, and the remainder is used for staff salaries and overhead. Calculations based on this information would put an average firm's annual total billings at about $40 million, although the range among the Big Eight stretches widely from that mean. Peat Marwick's U.S. earnings were reported to have been more than $100 million in 1964.[18] The partner level is the level at which the years of hard work and heavy pressures in public accountancy pay off financially. Accountants in private industry earn up to $30,000 a year for top positions,[19] whereas, as mentioned before, partners in large accounting firms begin at this amount.

What does a partner do to earn this money? First, he assumes the final responsibility for the opinion that he signs in the name of the firm. For the publicly traded corporation, the financial statements that this opinion represents take three different forms: one form is for the management of the corporation, a second is for the SEC, and a third simplified form is presented to the stockholder in the annual report of the corporation. The partner is responsible to all three groups for representations made on the basis of the information supplied to him by his client.

A partner's average number of clients is thirty-five, but again there are large differences from one partner to the next. One partner answered the question concerning the number of clients by stating:

> It depends on the size of the client, mostly. But it also depends on the partner. One of our partners is acquisition-minded, so he spends a lot of time with each client on this matter, consequently he only has seven or eight clients. Another partner, who works rapidly and specializes in small businesses, handles over seventy. One of our personnel men handles thirty clients on the side.

The responsibility for the representations is not spread amorphously throughout the partnership but is placed squarely on the shoulders of the partner who signs them. Although review committees check the work of each partner, the final comprehensive review occurs after the opinion has been issued. Each client is covered by a specified partner. If something goes wrong, the firm accepts the charges against it, but everybody in the firm knows who slipped up if a mistake is made. An executive partner commented on this:

> The audit partner calls the signals on the job. He can consult on his problems with any specialist in the firm. One partner reviews all opinions, but this comes after the fact, after the opinion is issued. The partner is responsible to the partnership for his work, but he has complete autonomy within the firm.

18. From an article in the *Wall Street Journal,* May 24, 1965.
19. *Occupational Outlook Handbook,* Bulletin No. 1450 (1966-1967 ed.; Washington, D.C.: U.S. Government Printing Office), p. 30.

The firms maintain a check on the reports of partners by conducting "prelimi-nary" or "concurring" reviews before the report goes to the client. The extent and depth of the review depends on the nature of the specific engagement (a thorough review would be conducted of a new large client) and the experience of the partner.

The work of the partners is more diverse than that of any other level in the firm (see tables 5 and 8). Partners spend less time in actual audit work than do the personnel at any other level (table 5). This is also true for personnel in the areas of taxes and management services, except for those at the bottom levels. Administrative tasks become heavier for the partner, and for some this becomes the main form of activity. Those who want to have a hand in managing the firm or who have a flair for administration become involved in the work of organizing and maintaining the flow of work and information in the firm. This ultimately covers all functions of the firm.

The people who handle this work are the "executive" partners, "administra-tive" partners, and "managing" partners. A few firms carry one of these titles; most carry two. These people are a part of the home office or the international executive office. They are more concerned with problems of firm-wide admin-istration, of client relations, of setting up new offices, and of changes in personnel at the national or international level. The largest branch offices also have a managing partner. He controls the recruitment and promotion function for the office and passes judgment on deadlocked technical or client problems,[20] or, if a problem is serious enough, he brings it to the national managing (or executive) committee for resolution. The senior partner is the head of this committee and is elected by it. He is the head of the entire firm, the court of last resort. Final solutions, if not found elsewhere, are solved here. But, as one audit partner put it, "It remains that for the client, Brown, Smith, & Company is the partner in charge of the engagement, the manager, and the supporting staff of seniors and juniors, and no one else."

Partners are in most cases specialists in one of the three major areas of work. They also specialize in one or two fields within an area. They serve as chairmen and key members of the informal committees in these fields, organizing the vast amounts of accounting experience and knowledge acquired through the years by the firm's staff. Much of the synthesis of this material he presents at professional meetings, in talks at gatherings of business and financial organizations, and in journals or books.

These committees and other informal groups of the large firms may share their information by working on committees sponsored by the AICPA. Important summaries of several fields have developed from the combined efforts of AICPA members. The experience and manpower that the large firms command enable

20. Richard C. Rea, "What is a Good Managing Partner?" *Journal of Accountancy* 126:78-80 (July 1968), details some of the administrative tasks of the managing partner.

their partners to take the lead in these fields, and there is an expectation by the profession and by industry and finance that they will fulfill this role. For this reason, and for more important reasons discussed in chapter 6, a large proportion of large-firm partners participate and lead in the growth and development of the profession. They are found as leaders on AICPA committees, as contributors to professional journals, as members of civic foundations and associations, and as advisors to state and federal agencies.

A partner is at the top of his firm, and the large-firm partner is at the top of his profession. He is freed from the competition and pressures of the up-or-out policy and from the unusual work load produced by it. But his habit of hard work, the expectations of the firm that he will spread its name in the highly competitive public accounting market, and his leadership role in the profession make his work life a full one. As the center point and final arbiter for all accounting and auditing matters with his 35-plus clients, he must remain accessible to his staff and to his clients, and so he is found in his office a good part of the time. This was of little aid in the interviewing, however, because a partner has the fullest and most carefully planned schedule of all. If he is not "in conference" with other partners, he is on the phone with one of his staff or with a disgruntled or mystified client. The major amount of his communication with clients is probably indirect via the telephone. About half the interviews that I had with partners were conducted during their only "free" time of the day —lunch. This gave me the opportunity to see part of the world of the Big Eight partner—the environment of the less formal gatherings with staff and with clients. Partners of the New York offices lunch in the best downtown restaurants and private clubs. Some firms spread their partners out in order to maintain sufficient representation in all the more important clubs. The business lunch can be an important part of the day for accomplishing the firm's business. That day usually begins at 9:30 A.M. and concludes at 5:30 P.M., the latter stretching into the evening during the busy season.

THE LATER YEARS: STATESMANSHIP AND RETIREMENT

Those partners who have excelled in their fields build a reputation for their expertise, and in later years they become statesmen of the profession. They are virtually unknown outside their profession, with the exception of a select circle in industry and in government, but they are admired and respected by all who know them. They are usually (but not necessarily) prolific writers, are very active in professional and civic affairs, and are engaged in the dialogue at the frontiers of knowledge in accounting. Their firms now comfortably established, today's statesmen give even more time to the development of the profession than the legendary founders and builders, many whose names are inscribed in the title of the firm.

57

Retirement from active work in the large firm is early, age sixty or sixty-two being the most common time. In some firms, after retirement the partner is permitted to carry on part-time services for the firm and to maintain an office at the firm's quarters. But there are rules that make it not worthwhile to continue practice for several years beyond the retirement age. A few retired partners remain close to the firm, offering valuable counsel to the staff and joining in on events of the firm. Most retired partners, however, are seldom seen at the offices.

In summary, the career pattern in these large professional organizations is an unusual one. During the first half of his career, the large-firm accountant must either be promoted or leave the large-firm scene. If he lasts, he becomes a member in the firm, and for the last half of his career he has tenure as a partner. There are no reported recent cases of partners being relieved of their membership in the firm—the system of promotion, relentless in its process of elimination, disposes of the erratics, the technically unqualified, the uninterested.

4

Professionalization and Ideology

TOWARDS A THEORY OF OCCUPATIONS

Much has been written by CPAs in the last decade about the state of their profession. They are very much aware of their status, and primarily through the AICPA, they have begun to closely scrutinize areas that they feel can improve their position among the competing professions. A large body of social-science literature has centered on the "attributes" of a profession—the factors that determine the standing of a profession.[1] A summary of this literature, some of which has been utilized by CPAs, indicates at least ten important attributes:

A set of values. There is an idea of a career, a "calling" in the service of the public, which through authority in its sphere of knowledge, monopoly in all matters related to its service, and objectivity in its theory and technique will advance social progress.

A body of knowledge that is formulated in a systematic theory or set of theories; a developed intellectual technique.

An established and formalized *educational process,* which imparts a body of knowledge that the professional group decides is necessary.

A standardized *formal testing* on a body of knowledge in order to be admitted to the professional group.

Formal recognition of the status of the profession by the society through

---

1. Among the more important sources are: Alexander Carr-Saunders and P. A. Wilson, *The Professions* (London: Oxford University Press, 1933), pp. 284-287; Roy Lewis and Angus Maude, *Professional People in England* (Cambridge, Mass.: Harvard University Press, 1953), pp. 55-56; Ernest Greenwood, "Attributes of a Profession," *Social Work* 2:45-55 (July 1957); Richard M. Lynch, "Professional Standards for Management Consulting in the United States" (Ph.D. diss., Graduate School of Business Administration, Harvard University, 1959), pp. 30-31, 138-139, with permission of the author; William J. Goode, "Encroachment, Charlatanism, and the Emerging Profession: Psychology, Sociology, and Medicine," *American Sociological Review* 25:902 (December 1960); William Kornhauser, *Scientists in Industry: Conflict and Accommodation* (Berkeley: University of California Press, 1962), p. 11; Bernard Barber, "Some Problems in the Sociology of the Professions," *Daedalus* 92:672 (Fall 1963). See *Standards of Education and Experience for Certified Public Accountants* (Ann Arbor: Bureau of Business Research of the University of Michigan, 1956) for a list of seven attributes, which is descended from the work of Abraham Flexner.

means of state and federal licensing, thus limiting entrance into the professional group.

A *code of ethics* governing relations with colleagues, clients, and other external organizations; included are such areas as client confidence, service motive (professional independence) over personal gain, fees, and advertising.

Symbols. Such meaning-laden items as insignias, emblems, history, folklore, argot, the heroes and the villains, and the stereotypes of the client, the layman, and the fellow professionals.

A *professional association* to facilitate relations and communications among colleagues and to act in concert in aiding the development, maintaining, or changing of the above seven attributes.

Personal qualities beyond the technical competence, such as commitment to the profession through work in its associations and good judgment and poise in social relations both at work and in civic activities.

Unwritten rules of behavior in social situations. Over and above the written rules and codes, these are the accepted, appropriate, and proper ways of doing things, all the way from the "correct" way of seeking employment to securing promotion, to grooming a protégé, or to challenging outmoded theory.

Each of these attributes can be considered an ideal type, that is, an accentuation of reality. The ideal profession would be a "perfect" profession, one that had attained perfection in each of these attributes. This state is impossible to attain. The idea is merely a mental construct conceived in order to roughly compare realities (in this case, different professions) to one another. All we can do is say who has more or less of some attribute, holding constant the ideal—the "most"—which is itself almost always difficult to conceptualize. However, at the present rudimentary stage of development of the sociology of occupations, the inability to quantify is not necessarily a drawback; some would consider it a blessing in disguise.[2]

Rough measures of professions have existed for as long as the professions themselves. They are adjudged higher professions, emerging professions, paraprofessions, and so forth. Implicit in these titles is an estimate of the degree of attainment of one or more of the attributes of a profession. These measures can be further clarified by considering their position on a continuum of professions.

---

2. Don Martindale, "Sociological Theory and the Ideal Type," in *Symposium on Sociological Theory,* ed. Llewellyn Gross (Evanston, Ill.: Row, Peterson & Co., 1959), pp. 57-91.

para-professions	emerging professions	full professions	established professions	higher professions learned professions

direction of professionalization ➡

◀ direction of deprofessionalization

An increase in activity of any occupation on this continuum that results in movement of attributes toward their ideal types is "professionalization." Any activity that results in movement of attributes away from their ideal types is "deprofessionalization." Usually, movement will take place among several attributes simultaneously and in the same direction, for the profession's activity (or lack of it) is a social process.[3] As such, the attributes are interdependent.

It must be stressed that this is a continuum of professionalization and that, although all occupations may be placed on this continuum, since "there is no absolute difference between professional and other kinds of occupational behavior, but only relative differences with respect to certain attributes common to all occupational behavior,"[4] it is practical to place on it only those occupations that are intent on professionalizing, those that are deprofessionalizing, or those that are useful for comparative purposes. Physicists, philosophers, and mathematicians, for example, are far from being professionalized, with the exception that they have a body of knowledge and symbols, yet they consider themselves "professional" people. They are professionals in that they *profess,* that is, they declare or affirm a certain body of knowledge. Also, there are differences in the method of developing that body of knowledge: the scientific (primarily deductive logic) and the experiential ("artistic," primarily inductive reasoning). Compare economics and public accounting[5] or sociology and social work.[6]

Perhaps an ideal type should be constructed for those who are not interested in professionalizing, where such factors as a written code of ethics and licensing

3. Howard M. Vollmer and Donald L. Mills, "Some Comments on 'The Professionalization of Everyone?'" *American Journal of Sociology* 70:481 (January 1965). These authors also define a profession as "an *ideal type* (in the Weberian sense) . . . of occupational structure characterized by certain specified elements."

4. Barber, "Some Problems," p. 671. A similar view is held by Howard M. Vollmer and Donald L. Mills, eds., *Professionalization* (Englewood Cliffs, N.J.: Prentice-Hall, Inc., 1966), p. 2.

5. The dichotomy exists within accounting itself between the CPA-Ph.D. academic accounting researcher and the CPA practitioner. The conflicts between these two groups are discussed by Edward L. Summers and Robert M. Hermance, "Professors and Practitioners," *Journal of Accountancy* 128:85 (August 1969).

6. Talcott Parsons discusses the growth of "applied" behavioral sciences from their "pure" bases in his book *Social Structure and Personality* (New York: The Free Press, 1964), pp. 352-354. Also see his discussion of professions as being concerned with applying knowledge, and scientific disciplines as being concerned with the advancement of that knowledge, in his article "Some Problems Confronting Sociology as a Profession," *American Sociological Review* 24:547 (August 1959).

are less important goals than the purpose of developing knowledge. We might call this type a learned society. Comparisons of the empirical research on the two models might provide similarities and distinctions upon which a theory of occupations could be built.

How does public accounting fit into this picture? First, it is generally considered an established profession,[7] as compared to general accounting, which is an emerging profession.[8] Second, it is making a directed effort to become a higher profession, to dwell in that rarified atmosphere of the elite professions of medicine, law, dentistry, and university teaching. Most indications are that the public accountant will make it. And if he does, it will be due to the efforts expended by him during the crucial decade of the 1970s.

In what ways is public accounting attempting to reach this pinnacle? Perhaps the best way to begin an examination is by taking a look at the development of their professional attributes. As is the case with all social groups, the problem exists of distinguishing between reality and ideology, or between professionalization and professionalism. Although these terms are often used interchangeably, here the term "professionalism" will refer to ideology, to shared beliefs and values that legitimate the collective claims of the profession regarding its attributes. Professionalization will refer to what changes are actually taking place in the professional attributes.[9] Ideology may influence tremendously the growth or decline of a profession, through the influence of the ideology on members of the profession and on those outside the profession. If it is more than a simplified guide to understand and evaluate experience and action, or if it systematically and consciously distorts reality for private ends that may possibly be harmful to others, it can cause serious damage. The reaction to the intensified political action of the American Medical Association over the past few years is a case in point.

Our task is to compare professionalization and professionalism where possible when examining the attributes. One indication of their feelings about the relative importance of each attribute was given by the Big Eight accountants when they were asked the importance of each in distinguishing their profession from nonprofessions (see table 9). Their responses are analyzed as each attribute is considered.

7. Harold Wilensky, "The Professionalization of Everyone?" *American Journal of Sociology* 70:137-158 (September 1964).

8. Barber, "Some Problems," p. 676.

9. Vollmer and Mills, "Some Comments," p. 481. The definition of ideology is from Burkhart Holzner, *Reality Construction in Society* (Cambridge, Mass.: Schenkman Publishing Co., 1968). See especially chap. 10, "The Social Organization of Ideological Knowledge."

TABLE 9

Public Accountants' Choices of the Order of Importance
of Attributes of a Profession Distinguishing Public
Accounting from Nonprofessions (N=111) in Percentages

Attributes	Order of Importance of Attributes				
	Very Important	Important	Not Very Important	Unimportant	Other[a]
Set of Values	32	37	26	4	1
Body of Knowledge	42	50	5	1	2
Formalized Educational Process	32	52	11	1	4
Formal testing	45	44	7	2	2
Formal Recognition through Licensing	51	36	11	1	1
Code of Ethics	73	25	1	–	1
Symbols	1	3	20	75	1
Professional Association	32	55	11	–	2
Personal Qualities	41	43	14	–	2
Unwritten Rules	14	43	29	8	6
Other (in numbers)	5	2	–	–	1

[a]Contains "no answer," "can't tell," and "coder can't tell" responses.

THE ATTRIBUTES OF A PROFESSION ANALYZED FOR PUBLIC ACCOUNTING

The Set of Values

The service ideal of selflessness in serving "society," "the public," "the public good," "the public interest," and so forth, has been espoused as the most important basis of a profession by students of the professions[10] and by public

10. Such as Harold J. Laski, "The Decline of the Professions," *Harper's* 171:676-685 (November 1935); Greenwood, "Attributes of a Profession"; Lynch, "Professional Standards."

accountants.[11] However, the Big Eight do not see this altruism as being very important. They list it as the third least important of all the attributes for public accounting. Similar results were recorded in a closely related profession;[12] and although the author interpreted this as one of the primary factors for management consulting not becoming professionalized, it just may be that the attribute is not as important as some make it. The attempt to interpose an ideology of professions serving the "public good," such as a "great corporation under government control," to counteract the motive of personal gain through service to clients was an early model.[13] Or, more recently, in a speech before the 20th National Credit Conference of the American Bankers Association (January 30, 1968), the Executive Vice-President of the AICPA stated that "the profession is confident that, by holding fast to its aim of serving and protecting the public, it is helping to preserve the free enterprise system."[14] In reality, it is the practitioner's service to the *client* which stands as an extremely important attribute of a profession for public accounting and for other professions as well. This was established in the courts as early as 1933, in *State ex rel. Steiner v. Yelle*, 25 P. ds 91, 174 Wash. 402:

> A profession is not a money-getting business. It has no element of commercialism in it. True, the professional man seeks to live by what he earns, but his main purpose and desire is to be of *service to those who seek his aid* and to the community of which he is a necessary part. [Italics supplied.]

In the early 1930s, in a series of letters exchanged between the AICPA (at that time the AIA) and the New York Stock Exchange, a letter dated September 22, 1932, by a special committee of the AIA, supported the interests of third parties:

> The only practical way in which an investor can today give expression to his conclusions in regard to the management of a corporation in which he is interested is by retaining, increasing, or disposing of his investment, and accounts are mainly valuable to him insofar as they afford guidance in determining which of these courses he shall pursue.[15]

11. Examples: Paul Grady, *Inventory of Generally Accepted Accounting Principles for Business Enterprises,* Accounting Research Study No. 7 (New York: AICPA, 1965), p. 1; James Wesley Deskins, "On the Nature of the Public Interest," *Accounting Review* 40:76-81 (January 1965); John L. Carey, *The CPA Plans for the Future* (New York: AICPA, 1965), pp. 312-313; David F. Linowes, "Professional Organization and Growth," *Journal of Accountancy* 120:27 (July 1965).

12. Lynch, "Professional Standards," pp. 280, 298-306.

13. Laski, "The Decline of the Professions."

14. As reported in the March 1968 issue of *The Journal of Accountancy.*

15. The letters are collected in a pamphlet, *Audits of Corporate Accounts* (New York: AIA, 1934).

This emphasis on investors is emphasized by Herman W. Bevis, the senior partner of Price Waterhouse, in his book on corporate financial reporting. According to Bevis, it is the investors (the grantors of credit to corporations) and the potential investors whom the public accountant must consider in his financial reporting, along with the stockholders and management.[16]

There is altruistic service to a client (and, as a result of that, to society), because the professional benefits from it.[17] It is in his interest in the long run to be selfless in the short run.[18] Furthermore, because of this, it is in the interest of the professional to follow the *rules* of the profession, which makes the situation "in the first instance institutional and not motivational" by having to go beyond the individual to the social system for an analysis of that motivation.[19] Professionals do not have to *feel* altruistic but only to *act* altruistic because the professional community has institutionalized altruistic behavior.[20]

The Body of Knowledge

The body of knowledge of a profession gives the practitioner a special technical skill, a unique competence upon which rests his authority to profess.[21] It allows the profession to claim the right to control the training, the licensing, and the distribution of rewards and punishment of its members. Some believe that the body of knowledge is the single most important characteristic defining a professional. The practitioner's autonomy is derived from his respect for this

16. Herman W. Bevis, *Corporate Financial Reporting in a Competitive Economy* (New York: MacMillan, 1965), p. 19.

17. Morris L. Cogan, "Toward a Definition of Profession," *Harvard Educational Review* 23:49-50 (Winter 1953), and Wilensky, "The Professionalization of Everyone?" p. 140, stress the service ideal.

18. Robert M. MacIver, "The Social Significance of Professional Ethics," *Annals* 101:7 (1922), notes that the altruistic motive is not a strong one because of the essential acquisitive interests of the business manner in which professionals operate. C. Wright Mills commented that professions, as bureaucratic organizations, are like business organizations—there is no altruism but rather the "merging of skill and money." See his *White Collar* (New York: Oxford University Press, 1951), pp. 136-141.

19. Talcott Parsons, *The Social System* (New York: The Free Press, 1951), pp. 472-473.

20. Robert K. Merton, *Some Thoughts on the Professions in American Society*, Brown University Papers No. 37 (July 8, 1960), p. 13. Parsons has long stressed the altruistic and the acquisitive factors as institutional rather than motivational. This whole problem was the basis for the formation of his "pattern variables." Parsons, *Social Structure and Personality*, p. 328. See also his article "The Professions and Social Structure," *Social Forces* 17:457-467 (May 1939).

21. Goode, "Encroachment," p. 912, states that "a professional community would be denying its own unity, and questioning its character and its self-image, if it accepted any higher authority, to which it would submit proofs of its own competence."

superior knowledge—it distinguishes the truly professional.[22]

The body of knowledge of public accounting is mostly experiential, because auditing and its accounting base are constructed almost totally through inductive procedures. The technical skill developed from this body of knowledge is *intellectual.* It involves reflection and highly abstract reasoning. Abstract principles are applied to a concrete situation in order to obtain a judgment of reality.[23] The carpenter, the plumber, and the electrician also command a special technical skill and requisite authority to profess, but the skill is technical in the sense that it is *mechanical* and detailed, with little room for reasoning.

The intellectual technique of a body of knowledge can gradually become mechanical and detailed through a comprehensive and rigid definition and systematization of rules, which limits judgment. In some cases, this might lead the client to ask the professional not "what to do" (judgment), but "how to do it" (technique) as the body of knowledge becomes easier to interpret. The special skills of judgment are the "mystique" of the profession. They protect the professional from having the client interfere in his work, and at the same time they protect the client (through his ignorance) from the moral burden of such judgments.[24]

Public accountants attach much importance to their body of knowledge. In the early 1960s, the AICPA established a special committee to explore the state of the body of knowledge in accounting and to make recommendations for changes and improvements. The results are published in the book *Horizons for a Profession,*[25] which indicates the deep concern of the committee members for the future of the profession--that it must broaden the base of its knowledge, especially into mathematics and the social sciences, and that it must learn to adapt to social and technological change with respect to the development of accounting knowledge and the method for constructing that knowledge (namely, conceptual viewpoints, the use of deduction).[26] The Big Eight sample agreed that this attribute is important. Combining the "very important" and "important" categories of table 9, it is seen as the second most important. But how accounting knowledge is to be developed is still a major issue. Practitioners

22. Donald I. Warren, "Power, Visibility and Conformity in Formal Organizations," *American Sociological Review* 33:951-970 (December 1968).

23. William J. Goode, "The Librarian: From Occupation to Profession?" *Library Quarterly,* 31:308 (October 1961).

24. David Riesman, "Toward an Anthropological Science of Law and the Legal Profession," *American Journal of Sociology* 57:121-135 (September 1951), discusses the protection of the client through the "mystery" of the law.

25. Robert H. Roy and James H. MacNeill, *Horizons for a Profession* (New York: AICPA, 1967).

26. Doyle Z. Williams has summarized a series of seminars conducted by leading accounting educators and practitioners at which the conclusions of the book were discussed. In *Journal of Accountancy* 127:81-84 (June 1969).

generally favor the experimental method; academicians favor the deductive method.[27]

To meet the burgeoning requirements of the technological revolution, ever since the mid 1950s the CPAs' body of knowledge has been expanding rapidly. Advisory services on systems analysis for subunits and entire organizations has become a specialty. Electronic data processing, management accounting, operations auditing, and social accounting are all being developed, and they offer large challenges to the creative people in the profession.

The Formalized Educational Process

"No true profession in America has been built without a sound educational foundation with emphasis on collegiate training for that specific profession. The accounting profession is no exception." So stated the participants of a University of Texas conference on accounting education in 1962, during a discussion of the common body of knowledge for accountants.[28] How far the profession has to go is illustrated by the fact that as of 1967 only thirty of the fifty-three accounting jurisdictions (the states and territories of the U.S.) require a bachelor's degree to qualify for the CPA certificate. However, this represents more than a three-fold increase since 1961.[29]

Large-firm accountants certainly do not lag behind other established professions in terms of formal education. Nearly all Big Eight accountants have a college degree, and almost half the sample held advanced degrees, 5 percent of which were doctorates. Although nearly half the sample held the bachelor's degree in business administration, almost all the rest held one of their degrees in an outside field. Their education continues in elaborate formal training programs constructed by the firms, and it extends over a period of several years (see chapter 3). This has long been a policy at several firms. Haskins & Sells, for example, established a Department of Professional Training in 1918, with a university professor as its head.

The formal educational process of public accounting barely manages to begin the adult socialization experience of the "student professional" in accounting. It is a further-reaching socialization than for the learner in the nonprofessional occupations,[30] but it is less comprehensive than that in the higher professions. The choice to become a public accountant is usually not made until towards the end of the accountant's formal academic training, so the student does not know

27. Summers and Hermance, "Professors and Practitioners."

28. *Accounting Education*, The Committee on Relations with Universities of the AICPA (New York: AICPA, 1963), p. 51.

29. As reported in *Journal of Accountancy* 126:24 (December 1968).

30. As cited by Goode, "Encroachment," p. 902.

enough about the field to consider it before then. Some socialization naturally takes place when rules governing the methods and procedures of accounting and auditing are discussed in textbooks and in class, also when fair presentation in reporting to clients and other interested parties is emphasized. In interviews, five respondents commented that they realized the full importance of the public accounting code of ethics during their college training, although, the remaining twenty-one answered that this realization came to them only after they had spent some time on the job.

Unlike medicine and law, public accounting does not now have a system of graduate schools developed to train its students. It is felt by most CPAs that experience is more valuable than continued formal education at this point in the public accountant's career.[31] In 1962 the AICPA Council (a board of more than ninety representatives of the AICPA membership) voted down a proposal to organize an Academy of Professional Accounting for graduate-level training in public accounting.

In terms of a formalized educational process in its major fields—accounting and auditing—public accountants fall behind the learned professions and a few of the less-established ones such as engineering and architecture. But the overall education of the average large-firm CPA is comprehensive, and in the case of a few percent, it includes more than one discipline. To an increasing number of his clients, the CPA is becoming known as a generalist, and his services are utilized on this basis. With the rapidly expanding body of knowledge, professional schools, because of their isolation, would harm accounting more than they would help it.[32]

The Formal Testing Procedure

The requirement to become a CPA is fulfilled by passing a nationwide examination that is given twice each year in various parts of the country by a coordinating AICPA committee. This formal testing procedure tends to eliminate many of the noncollege applicants from the CPA ranks—more than 90 percent of those who pass the examination are college graduates.[33] This is an important figure, considering that only half the jurisdictions require an applicant to have a college degree in order to qualify for the test. Two years' experience in

31. The dangers of this isolation are stressed by Julius Roller and Thomas H. Williams, "Professional Schools of Accounting," *Accounting Review* 42:349-355 (April 1967).

32. This attitude may be beginning to change. Raymond G. Ankers, "Should New York Require a Master's Degree for the CPA Certificate?" *New York Certified Public Accountant* 37:852–855 (November 1967), says yes, that accounting should require the degree if it is to follow the history of the established professions.

33. *Occupational Outlook Handbook*, Bulletin no. 1450, 1966-1967 ed. (Washington D.C.: U.S. Government Printing Office), p. 29.

auditing (reduced from three in 1968) is required to sit for the auditing part of the examination. It is suspected that this long waiting period deters many qualified young people from entering the profession, because they are afraid to take the chance of not being able to pass the final testing years after they have entered the profession. A commission of CPAs that studied this problem suggested a year-long postgraduate professional accounting program with about three months of the program consisting of on-the-job training, after which the CPA examination could be taken and the certificate issued. Other "transitional" programs were suggested for those jurisdictions now requiring only high-school diplomas.[34]

Large-firm accountants see the formal testing requirements as a very important attribute, distinguishing professional accounting from nonprofessions. The examination has been standardized and is rigorous; it has been an important part of the professionalization of public accounting during the last two decades. Law and medicine have more demanding educational requirements leading up to the testing, but they do not surpass public accounting in the degree of standardization of the formal testing of the body of knowledge.

Formal Recognition through Licensing

The CPA certificate allows one to legally render certain accounting and auditing services to the public. It certifies that the holder of the certificate has a certain minimum competence, and it protects him from errors that might be committed due to the unusual nature of his professing—the application of a great deal of judgment in his dealings with his client.[35] The uncertainty of the situation demands protection for mistakes, and a collective defense is built up against the lay world.[36] The method of attaining knowledge can affect whether licensing will take place in professionalization.[37] If the scientific method is applied to problems by an occupation, there is more concern with "academic traditions of proof" and less concern with "official certificates of competence."[38]

This qualification of the licensing attribute is only apparent and not real, if the picture of the learned society is brought into view again. The profession licenses its practitioners—the nonprofession (including learned societies) may or

34. See the commission's report, *Standards of Education and Experience* . . . , pp. 125-137.

35. Goode, "Encroachment," p. 913.

36. Everett C. Hughes, *Men and Their Work* (New York: The Free Press, 1958), p. 90, mentions this collective defense.

37. Goode, "Encroachment," p. 913.

38. *Ibid.* Also, p. 906.

may not license its practitioners. But all professions, scientific and nonscientific, attempt to attain formal recognition for their members through licensing. Learned societies and other nonprofessions do not have the same unvarying qualification.

Public accountants are attempting to further professionalize by standardizing the licensing of CPAs in all jurisdictions (states) and by strengthening penalties for infractions of rules by deviant members. Presently, nineteen jurisdictions are "permissive," that is, there are no restrictions on non-CPAs for practicing in any or all areas of accounting and auditing; whereas in the remaining thirty-four "regulatory" jurisdictions there are restrictions. Also, in eighteen jurisdictions, a CPA certificate may be issued to an applicant who has only a high-school education if he can pass the examination. At the same time, in order to protect their own CPAs, these states do not allow temporary interstate practice by out-of-state CPAs. Many permissive states allow the use of titles similar to "certified public accountant," such as "accounting practitioner" and "public accountant," which further confuses the issue.[39]

The AICPA also has its hands tied in policing public accountants. Unlike the associations of the legal and medical professions, the AICPA does not have the power to revoke or suspend the licenses of its members. All it can do is to expel or suspend a member from its association; but the individual may still continue to practice public accounting. It is the state regulatory bodies that have the power to revoke or suspend. But even if this occurs in one of seventeen "permissive" states, the CPA can still practice as a "public accountant." And in some states the CPA certificate has never been revoked.[40] There is clearly much room for improvement in this entire area of licensing in public accounting, even though Big Eight accountants judge it to be effective as an attribute.

The Code of Ethics

It is in the interests of the professional to follow the rules of the profession. This is accomplished by emphasizing service to the client through maintenance of a certain standard of professional relations. The formal rules of a profession that govern these relations are covered in its code of ethics. The large-firm accountants chose their code of ethics, by a wide margin, over other attributes as the most important attribute distinguishing public accounting from nonprofessions. The very first "article" of their code deals with relations with clients; and

39. John L. Carey, ed., *The Accounting Profession: Where Is It Headed?* (New York: AICPA, 1962), pp. 123-124. One of the results of this multiplicity of regulations is that in only about thirty of the more than six hundred companies with published annual reports is the name "certified public accounts" used. In 1949 the "accounting practitioner" was licensed in Indiana, according to a news report in *Journal of Accountancy*, May 1969, p. 12.

40. Carey, *The CPA Plans*, p. 337.

it was chosen by them as being more important than the combined remaining articles, by a two-to-one margin. The subarticle on independence was the most popular by far. The other four articles cover rules on technical standards, promotional practices, operating practices, and relations with fellow members.

The Code of Professional Ethics is the only national standard of ethics for public accountants. Forty-two state regulatory bodies have variations of this code. However, in only twenty-four of them is the code fully enforceable in that a violation may result in the loss of a license to practice public accounting.[41] The rule generally considered to be the most important by the profession is "independence," that rule against conflict-of-interest between the accountant's personal matters and those of his client. Adherence to this rule enhances objectivity on the part of the accountant. First formulated by the SEC and almost immediately modified by the AIA, Rule 2-01 of Regulation S-X stated that:

> an accountant will not be considered independent with respect to any person in whom he has any substantial interest, direct or indirect, or with whom he is, or was during the period of report, connected as a promoter, underwriter, voting trustee, director, or employee.

The word "substantial" was the modification made by the AIA.[42] In the latest revised code of ethics, Rule 1.01 clarifies several of the words and phrases of this passage and includes several additions. The rule is rigidly adhered to by the large firms, and several have enlarged the definition of what is a conflict of interest. Most large firms bar their professional people from owning stock in any company that the firm serves. A member or employee of Price Waterhouse, for instance, is barred by his firm from investing in approximately four hundred listed companies.[43]

However, complete independence in all areas cannot be maintained. In order to do so, the above rule would have to add that no fee could be accepted. As the public accountant sees it, you don't bite the hand that feeds you—unless the difference between what he (the client) wants and what you (the auditor) see becomes "material," that is, significant enough to make a statement false or misleading to the reader. There is, then, some leeway with which the CPA can play in favor of his client, that grey area of "nonmateriality," where a reasonable observer would not feel there was a conflict of interest.[44]

41. Carey, *The Accounting Profession*, p. 127.

42. Darwin J. Casler, "The Independence of the Public Accountant," *Ohio CPA* 23:151-167 (Autumn 1964), gives a comprehensive history of the independence function.

43. T. A. Wise, "The Auditors Have Arrived" (Part II), *Fortune* 62:147 (December 1960).

44. The AICPA Committee on Professional Ethics, in Opinion no. 12, "Independence" (New York: AICPA, 1965), p. 49, has defined the lack of independence as "relationships which in the eyes of a *reasonable* observer would suggest a conflict of interest."

The maintaining of this independence is often referred to as the "responsibility" of the CPA, a responsibility that manifests itself in the resulting audit opinion. The legal profession also issues opinions that are reasonably independent of their clients' demands.[45] For accountants and lawyers this independence extends to other interested parties. By attesting to financial statements, the CPA becomes responsible (legally, up to a certain point) to stockholders, grantors of credit, government agencies, and other parties who are directly interested. This is the unique professional service that public accounting offers, and it is properly recognized by its members. Again by a two-to-one margin, the interview sample of Big Eight accountants (N=33) listed the service to third parties as the unique function that distinguished public accounting from other professions. Many respondents noted that independence is maintained according to the type of economic organization served. One partner noted: "If it's a family corporation, it's to the shareholders. If it's AT&T, it's to the shareholders, plus he [the CPA] has a quasi-public responsibility. If it's the government, there are no shareholders, so it's directly to the public. If it's an industrial corporation where the shares are publicly traded, then it's to the shareholders, the management, and the directors." A manager of another firm emphasized that the public accountant's responsibility is "to all parties equally. This is like asking whether one is for God, Motherhood, or Country."

To introduce and maintain independence in management services is not as easy as it is in the case of auditing. Several of the total sample's respondents felt that independence was lacking for much of the management services work. Herman Bevis, the senior partner of Price Waterhouse, has been quoted as having said:

> We wouldn't, for instance, recommend to a client that he spend millions of dollars for a new plant . . . and then be in a position, as auditors, of having to evaluate that plant as an asset. Here we would obviously be losing our independence.
>
> The real test of the CPA's independence . . . stems from the professional environment in which he works. All phases of his . . . work . . . are, if challenged, subject to review, examination and criticism by his fellow practitioners.[46]

If, however, the practitioner in management services would be willing to undergo the scrutiny of his colleagues, then independence would not be put in jeopardy.[47]

45. Erwin O. Smigel, *The Wall Street Lawyer: Professional Organization Man?* (New York: The Free Press, 1964), pp. 343-344, points out the lawyers' ability to maintain independence from their clients.

46. As reported by Jack J. Friedman, "Auditors: A Wasted Asset?" *Dun's Review* 80:150 (November 1962).

47. *Ibid.*

A sizeable percentage of third parties sampled in a study of opinion on management services did not feel that there was a conflict of interest on the part of CPAs engaged in this area. Such groups as research and financial analysts of the brokerage firms, commercial loan and trust officers of banks, investment officers of insurance companies, and investment officers of domestic mutual funds were sampled, for a total of over 1,200 responses from small and large institutions.[48] Forty-three percent saw no danger to the independence of CPAs, 33 percent did, and 24 percent were "somewhat undecided." These results are not decisive and certainly cannot be interpreted as a strong case for independence in management services, as the author carefully notes.[49] Twelve percent of my total sample (N=140) felt that management services did not aid public accounting in its drive to further professionalize. One tax supervisor stated: "If anything, management services present a problem for the profession. The attest function could become more difficult in the face of greater business decision-making guidance by the management services CPA to his audit client."

The supervisor's statement focuses on an increasingly serious problem. On the one hand, the CPA naturally has advocacy sentiments for his clients. And rightly so, argues the director of management consulting services of Lybrand, and where reasonable, he should practice forensic accounting, because if he doesn't, he *prevents* independence. He would purposely narrow his vision so much as to fault the client in needed "perception, discrimination, or moral judgment."[50] On the other hand, there is the question of "perceived independence" by third parties and the public, as well as clients. Merely the appearance of the lack of independence may be almost as damaging as the reality.[51] Even the "potentiality" of loss of independence may, in certain instances, be enough to threaten

48. The study is reported by Arthur A. Schulte, Jr., "Compatibility of Management Consulting and Auditing," *Accounting Review* 40:587-593 (July 1965). The sample consisted of 504 persons of the 130 largest institutions, representing a 56 percent return; and a random sample of the total universe of institutions, for a total return of 756 persons, representing a 51 percent return. The total return from both samples was 53 percent from 76 percent of the institutions.

49. A study by Abraham J. Briloff, "Old Myths and New Realities in Accountancy," *Accounting Review* 41:492 (July 1966), further substantiates the divergence of opinions of the accounting profession and the financial community (excluding clients) on this point, from nearly universal agreement that independence is not threatened (15 of 17 Big Eight respondents) to incompatibility between the two (16 of 72 [22 percent] financial community respondents).

50. Felix Kaufman, "Professional Consulting by CPAs," *Accounting Review* 42:719 (October 1967).

51. John L. Carey and William P. Doherty, *Ethical Standards of the Accounting Profession* (New York: AICPA, 1966), p. 20. Perceived independence is discussed by D. R. Carmichael and R. K. Swieringa, "The Compatibility of Auditing Independence and Management Services—An Identification of Issues," *Accounting Review* 43:697-705 (October 1968): "The observer's opinion will be based on the meaning the auditor's actions have for the observer, not the meaning the auditor would like to convey."

professional standing.52 Until the courts and the profession have ironed out the major questions arising from new practices in *all* the specialty areas of public accounting, the firms will continue to anticipate the mood of clients and the public. The day that all questions are solved will be a long time in coming.

The code of ethics comprises the formal commandments protecting the service ideal. That they exist in such detailed form signifies the degree to which the altruistic motive must be helped along. In one sense they reflect attempted professionalization, a high-water mark of professional development. But all bodies of rules mask reality to some extent, and in order to see what actually takes place, the accountants themselves must be asked. Their "everyday world" must be examined. What is being done is reflected mostly in the stories and statements of the respondents. A tax supervisor asks: "Are we professionals [in the broad sense of independence], or are we more concerned about giving services to a client?" He answers: "There is a moral and ethical breaking point. The point may move, depending on the size of the client. You'd get many more disclaimers [the CPA opinion that refuses to certify the client's statements] if all firms were placed in a pool and each received a fair share of clients each year."

The CPA's opinion is an extremely powerful tool. There are four basic types of opinion that the CPA can give: a fully satisfactory, "unqualified" opinion of the financial statements of the client; a "qualified" opinion, in which the CPA takes exception to certain selected factors on the financial statements; an "adverse" opinion, which states that the financial statements are not in conformity with accounting principles, thus are not presented fairly; and a "disclaimer" of opinion, stating that there is not "sufficient competent evidential matter" to give an opinion on the financial statements of the client. Because of the rather wide range that CPAs give to nonmateriality (differences in judgments between client and auditor that are not considered to be significant in their effect on financial statements), the latter two types of opinion are exceptions that rarely occur, and the qualified opinion occurs only with moderate frequency. So, when they do occur, readers of the opinion know that something extremely divergent has caused the CPA to disagree with the management's presentation of the statements.

It follows that a prospective stockholder or investor is apt to be chary of supporting a company that has been given a poor opinion statement by its auditor. At the same time, however, the offended client is apt to dismiss the accounting firm from any further services. In some cases, this could mean the loss of several hundred thousand dollars in fees. The result, according to a senior partner of one medium-sized firm, is that "it's pretty hard even for a big firm to say no to a big client." A senior partner of another medium-sized firm noted an example of unethical practice bearing on materiality and consistency of reporting:

I had a run-in with a certain Big Eight firm, which I thought was unethical.

52. Carmichael and Swieringa, "Compatibility."

74

He did not agree with an inventory valuation I had made which was consistent with that of preceding years. He wanted to value it in favor of the client. Finally, after a very long argument, he agreed with my way, but only after I suggested that we mediate the argument before a panel of partners from both our firms. One of his final statements to me was, "We don't live in an 'Alice-in-Wonderland' world, you know." At another time, earlier, he said to me, "The client's pushing me; what should I do?" meaning that the client had to be satisfied, as far as he was concerned. I said, "Push him right back. You're the accountant, aren't you?"

This statement is not intended to generalize on large-firm versus small-firm ethics, but to point up the conflict between the reality of client service and the ideal of service in the "public interest." An incident that came to the attention of the general public a few years ago was the totally unexpected bankruptcy of the Yale Express Company. The collapse was due almost entirely to rapidly deteriorating systems of internal control and internal accounting. Service to the client in the form of strict adherence to their confidential relationship was the overriding element in the auditor's (in this case, Peat Marwick's) decision to maintain silence in the face of certain public and even stockholder discontent because of their doing so.[53]

Public accountants also feel that professionalization, regarding the independence factor, is seriously hampered by the federal government's intervention through the SEC. The paradox here is that the establishment of this body gave legal recognition to the importance of the independence of the public accountant, but at the same time the legal requirement for an annual audit overshadowed other functions of public accounting. A senior in a large firm felt that this was the main reason why public accounting was not being molded into one of the higher professions:

> Inherently, the profession, in the eyes of clients, does not serve the same kind of function [we feel we are accomplishing]. [To them,] we're a necessary evil. They don't have the concept of what we're doing to get to the little piece of paper [the CPA's opinion statement]. For example, I can see from talking with accountants from other countries that in those countries there is more reliance on the accountant. As long as they're [the clients] forced, they won't accept us.

In this situation the CPA has lost some of his responsibility for the construction of the rules that govern his independence with respect to his client. There is, again, a legal recognition of the public accountant's independence, but with a

---

53. Professionalization has here created a barrier to the distribution of the CPA's information about his performance, just as it does for a physician in clinical practice. See Eliot Freidson and Buford Rhea, "Knowledge and Judgment in Professional Evaluations," *Administrative Science Quarterly* 10:122-123 (June 1965).

corresponding loss of control over his establishing his own responsibilities regarding independence.[54]

Another element affecting the public accountant's independence stems from his unusual relation to third parties, in this case, to stockholders of the corporations that he audits. More and more, stockholders are having a say in deciding who is to be the auditor for the companies in which they hold an interest. In 1964, 908 corporations included in their proxy solicitations the request for stockholder ratification of the previous year's auditor. In 1965 this number increased to 949.[55] The average stockholder knows little about the workings of the public accountants' auditing of the companies in which he holds an investment, and he goes along with management's choice of auditor. But when an auditor has been accused of poor or improper work, the stockholder has questioned his integrity. If the case were important enough and received wide coverage in major news media, proven impropriety could seriously damage an accounting firm. Stockholder participation in the choice of auditor is becoming a strong impetus for the auditor to maintain "across-the-board" independence. This requires that a firm maintain a uniform rule of independence for all clients, no matter what the circumstance, so as not to endanger the entire firm by a single slip of one audit team.

This discussion of the independence concept in client relations is a central concern of much current accounting literature. Although the emphasis on the client is a basic weakness in maintaining strict independence, many improvements have been made, especially by individual firms, toward expanding and refining the definition of independence.[56] There is a definite trend of professionalization in the area of independence for CPAs, even though so much of it is covered with a film of professionalism. In a recent analysis of professions, independence was not considered to be a measure of professionalization. The conclusion was that norms covering client relations that require the professional to be impersonal, objective, and impartial do not clearly demarcate between professional and nonprofessional occupations.[57] True, the demarcation may not be clear; the sciences depict such norms. However, it still remains that the norm of independence, as part of the code of ethics, is a necessary and important attribute of a profession, and *along with other attributes* it measures the degree of professionalization of an occupation.

54. This point is discussed by C. W. DeMond, *Price Waterhouse & Co. in America: A History of a Public Accounting Firm* (New York: privately printed by The Comet Press, 1951), p. 220.

55. Lewis D. and John J. Gilbert, *Twenty-Fifth Annual Report of Stockholder Activities at Corporation Meetings During 1964,* and *Twenty-Sixth Annual Report of Stockholder Activities at Corporation Meetings During 1965* (New York: L. D. and J. J. Gilbert, 1965 and 1966), p. 246 and p. 251, respectively.

56. Comment in an editorial in *Journal of Accountancy,* December 1968, p. 31.

57. Wilensky, "The Professionalization of Everyone?" pp. 140-141.

In general, members of large firms feel that the AICPA and state codes of ethics are rigidly adhered to. One executive partner of a large firm commented that "there are very few complaints, but, of course, that's like in taxes—the only ones who are known as evaders are the ones who are caught." There are indications also that some jurisdictions hesitate to apply sanctions to violators. In some states a CPA certificate has never been revoked, and only approximately twelve certificates are revoked or suspended each year in the United States.[58] Yet the stigma of merely being listed for disciplinary action probably serves as a deterrent to disobeying a rule, though not as strong a deterrent as in some higher professions.[59]

The special role of the CPA also involves general ethical considerations. Sometimes the job situation will require a complete change of ethical rules. At the audit the CPA must be rigidly objective in his interpretations, whereas in handling the tax matters of the same client, he would be in the role of the pure advocate in his representation of the client in federal tax examinations.[60] A recurrent debate of whether there is a conflict of interest in the dual practice of the lawyer-accountant swirls around this issue. The argument in favor of dual practice is very strong: that the ethics of CPA and lawyer are practically the same. Therefore, the question of the CPA touting himself as a lawyer to his client will not come up, because he cannot advertise openly as a lawyer. In fact, as a lawyer, the CPA can give his client even better service; he knows the internal financial system, and he can make related legal decisions even more competently. Those opposed to this line of thought raise some problems: (1) That other outside opinions are needed. A single individual cannot possibly have the expertise of a specialist in each of these areas. It would best serve the client to have a lawyer *and* a CPA. (2) That confidential communications can be protected only through the attorney-client privilege. This would confuse the placing of responsibility and might endanger the position of the client in legal proceedings.[61]

Another odd circumstance is that the CPA often finds himself working to help the rich man become even richer, while by comparison he earns only

58. Figures given by Carey, *The CPA Plans,* p. 339.

59. For example, in law. See Smigel, *The Wall Street Lawyer,* p. 272.

60. Alexander W. Faber, "C.P.A. or C.P.S(chizophrenic)?" *New York Times,* April 12, 1959, sec. 6, p. 73. A more recent view is given by a CPA, William H. Westphal, "The Future of the CPA in Tax Practice," *Journal of Accountancy* 127:40–44 (June 1969).

61. Two comprehensive articles on this debate are: W. D. Sprague and Arthur J. Levy, "Accounting and the Law: Is Dual Practice in the Public Interest?" *Journal of Accountancy* 122:45-52 (December 1966), and Philip D. Brent, "Accounting and Law: Concurrent Practice Is in the 'Public Interest,'" *Journal of Accountancy* 123:38-46 (March 1967). The problem of confidential communications is covered by O. J. Anderson, "Accountant-Client Privileged Communication," *Nebraska CPA* 2:9-12 (Fall 1967) and 3:6-9 (Spring 1968). Further arguments on this debate can be found in these sources.

pittance for doing so. However, a client who has a large income means more business—there are possibilities here for setting up trusts, new commercial ventures, estate-planning, and extension of services to heirs and benefactors. In determining the price for professional services rendered, the client does not bargain, and the professional norm is that a fair price is *asked* by the practitioner. At the same time, in his work the practitioner must, in regard to his client, uphold the free enterprise precept to bargain with intent to exploit.[62] Another writer disagrees with the latter statement, saying that the accountant objectively measures and reports the progress of corporate management toward the profit goal.[63] This, of course, would result in increased independence at the expense of service to the client (for example, not bothering to emphasize the interests of the client in areas of nonmateriality), which is considered poor judgment and a very real danger to public accounting in some quarters.[64]

We might conclude by examining the comment heard so often during the interviews: "Time is what we offer." Time is only of value in terms of what services the CPA offers in that space of time. Even if the independent audit were not required by law, the client would still engage the public accountant for two very important reasons: (1) *independent* judgment, which is something that is not available to the company accountant; and (2) broad and well-founded judgment based on a wide familiarity with particular types of businesses, which again, is available only to the public accountant.

Symbols

The symbols of the profession of public accounting—its folklore, argot, stereotypes—were considered by far to be the least important attribute in distinguishing public accounting from nonprofessions. This is primarily because there are so few and because those that do exist are utilized so infrequently. One reason is that public accounting is still relatively young as a profession. It takes a while for myths and legends to build and spread, and normally it is not until several generations have passed by that the stories become strongly embedded in the professional subculture.[65] That time is just arriving for public accounting.

62. John J. Willingham, "The Accounting Entity: A Conceptual Model," *Accounting Review* 39:549 (July 1964).

63. Thomas R. Prince, "The Motivational Assumption for Accounting Theory," *Accounting Review* 39:554 (July 1964).

64. See, for example, Paul Grady, "The Independent Auditing and Reporting Function of the CPA," *Journal of Accountancy* 120:69 especially (November 1965).

65. The requirement of this generational lapse is mentioned in an editorial in *Journal of Accountancy* 120:28 (August 1965). See also the comments of Grady, "The Independent," p. 67.

Another reason is that the nature of the work of the public accountant does not lend itself readily to symbolism. A Touche Ross recruitment brochure notes: "We have no Nathan Hales, Patrick Henrys, or Walter Reeds to venerate in the history of our profession. No statue exists anywhere to commemorate the memory of a public accountant who laid down his life in the Battle of Profit Determination or the Siege of the Internal Revenue Service." Their memorials and legends are esoteric; they do not lend themselves to a public understanding of service and sacrifice, courage and excitement.[66]

A third reason, perhaps the most important, is that the development of symbols has not been actively pursued by the profession as a whole. Public accounting has a potential storehouse of tales that could be developed and perhaps directed to archivists, novelists, and the like, who describe the culture of our society. Stories of dedication and integrity on the part of the higher professions abound—Perry Mason defending the rights of the poor or the small-town MD braving the elements to save a life. Although rarely brought into the open, public accounting has a body of lore in its own history. There is the story of David B. Chase, who once pursued an Internal Revenue Service over-charge of $3.06 to a nurse through years of appeal, and finally won.[67] One accountant recalls the rough, exciting, and sometimes dangerous life of auditing Venezuelan, Colombian, and Carribean subsidiaries of oil companies. John Henry Barcena wrote of his experiences: "Life was a bit rough in the earlier years. Living in oil company compounds, particularly in the early stages of their development, was not unlike Army life in an outpost. Flying in these years across the Northern Coast, into the interior of Venezuela and up and down the Magdalena River was a thrill, but it was always good to feel terra firma."[68] Another accountant chronicles the abnormally long hours devoted to work by Charles James Marr, a partner of Price Waterhouse from 1902 to 1925.[69] These true-to-life examples are an indication of the dimensions that public accounting symbolism can take, but that still have to be developed.

66. The lack of understanding of the work of the chemist is another example of a poor image, which is pointed out by Anselm L. Strauss and Lee Rainwater, *The Professional Scientist: A Study of American Chemists* (Chicago: Aldine Publishing Co., 1962), p. 212.

67. As reported by Caroline Bird, "Young Man, Be an Accountant," *Esquire* 56:140 (September 1961).

68. As quoted in DeMond, *Price Waterhouse & Co. in America,* p. 241.

69. *Ibid.*, p. 51.

The profession of certified public accounting has existed as an organized and effective group for little more than half its eighty years of life.[70] The major association of CPAs during this organized existence has been the American Institute of Certified Public Accountants. As of February 1, 1966, the AICPA membership totaled 55,357, which was more than 50 percent of the entire number of CPAs in the United States. Each state contains a society of certified public accountants; the total membership of these state societies includes between 60 and 70 percent of all CPAs, just a bit more than the total membership of the single largest national association, the AICPA.

The purposes of the AICPA, adopted by its membership, are summarized as:

> The formalizing and codification of auditing standards and procedures, accounting principles, and a continuing refinement of the code of ethics. Organization of a technical training program, a consultation service for technical problems, and a practice review committee to encourage by persuasion rather than disciplinary action the compliance to GAAP and GAAS.[71]

This body has served as the spokesman for the profession in virtually all matters of practice through its multifarious committees. These groups have produced reports, opinions, proposals, rules of ethics, and research reports in many critical areas of technique and professionalization.

The AICPA has scores of committees to carry out its major functions. One such committee is the Committee on Long-Range Objectives, which makes certain broad proposals covering mostly areas that concern themselves with professionalization of public accounting. For example, one of its 1960 proposals dealt with the coordination between the AICPA and state societies with regard to voluntary agreements on a uniform code of ethics and enforcement procedures. It was adopted by the AICPA Council. A year later, it presented a set of proposals covering areas of professionalization in management services.

The AICPA protects its members from dissatisfied clients or third parties. One documented case of this protection is that in which a Big Eight firm fell back on the authority of the AICPA in a disagreement with its client U.S. Steel.[72] The AICPA also indirectly aids clients and interested parties who deal with its members. For instance, in 1965 an AICPA tax committee presented to Congress eighty-nine recommendations for amendments to the Internal Revenue

70. Carey, *The CPA Plans*, p. 348.

71. Grady, *Inventory of GAAP*, p. 11, lists these as six separate areas.

72. Richard Leo Smith, "A Case Analysis of External Accounting Influence over Managerial Decisions" (Ph.D. diss., Graduate School of Business Administration, Harvard University, 1955).

Code of 1954, in order to obtain more reasonable tax laws.[73] In 1959 the AICPA established a Washington, D.C., office, and it now acts as consultant to eighteen federal agencies through this office.[74]

One area that the AICPA has given much attention to is the CPA's public and client image. In 1962 an "objective" was presented by the Committee on Long-Range Objectives, which dealt with the attest function. It was accepted by the AICPA Council, and an "implementing resolution" was added in order to inform issuers and users of economic data and the interested public of "the purpose, nature, and value of the CPA's attest function."[75] The problem of the image of the accountant is such a serious one that the major accounting associations, which meet annually, brought up for consideration the matter of publicity for careers in accounting.[76]

The CPA has good reason to be concerned with his image. Although over the years his work has changed considerably, especially at the level of the large firm, where new and sophisticated techniques and areas of specialization have produced more challenging tasks and a more glamourized atmosphere, his image has not. Elbert Hubbard's description of the typical auditor, written decades ago, is still held in the minds of some today:

> ... a man past middle age, spare, wrinkled, intelligent, cold, passive, noncommittal, with eyes like a codfish, polite in contact, but at the same time unresponsive, calm and damnably composed as a concrete post or a plaster-of-Paris cast; a human petrification with a heart of feldspar and without charm of the friendly germ, minus bowels, passion or a sense of humor. Happily, they never reproduce and all of them finally go to Hell.[77]

Such a scathing obloquy does not fit the general image held today; it has been watered down. But still, the picture of the accurate calculator, faultless with figures and an admirer of anything pertaining to them, persists. A *Life* magazine

---

73. *NEWS: From American Institute of Certified Public Accountants* (release of June 15, 1965).

74. Lyman Bryan, the Director of the Washington office, lists them in the April 1966 issue of *Journal of Accountancy*, p. 22, as: Civil Aeronautics Board; Office of Economic Opportunity; Federal Home Loan Bank Board; Federal Power Commission; Federal Trade Commission; Interstate Commerce Commission; National Defense Department; Securities and Exchange Commission; Department of Agriculture; Department of Commerce; Federal Aviation Agency; Federal Budgeting and Accounting; Federal Maritime Commission; Department of Health, Education and Welfare; Department of Housing and Urban Development; International Development; Department of Labor; Small Business Administration.

75. Carey, *The Accounting Profession,* p. 169, discusses this and other activities of AICPA committees.

76. *The CPA,* a monthly newsletter published by the AICPA (February 1965), p. 9. The major associations at this annual meeting are AAA; AICPA; Financial Executives Institute; Institute of Internal Auditors; National Association of Accountants.

77. As quoted by Bird, "Young Man," p. 71.

story of April 2, 1965 (p. 94), asked: "Its [basketball's] symbol is not the hero at all but the scoreboard—and who but a certified public accountant could love a basketball scoreboard?" A radio advertisement for the producer of certain wines brags: "The brass always backs the winemaker;" but not the cost accountant, who wants to keep down the retail cost of the wines by not importing necessary rare herbs. Posters in New York City subway stations assert:

ACCOUNTANTS
listen to radio
W O R
It adds up!

Leonard Spacek, senior partner of Arthur Andersen & Co., reported that an Opinion Research Corporation survey in 1961 revealed that less than half the public stockholders were familiar with basic accounting and economic terminology and concepts, except for the meaning of profits.[78] To the public, numbers mean precision, and they expect CPA reports to reflect this. Consequently, judges and juries do not understand the wide areas of judgment that are involved in giving an opinion on financial statements. Therefore, the risks involved in being sued are out of proportion to the fees received by the accountant. There is so much concern over this situation that the AICPA has set up a special committee on accountants' liability in order to examine this problem and to ascertain whether anything can be done about it.[79]

The client's view of his CPA is quite an improvement over that of stockholders and the general public. One survey of executives of six hundred manufacturing companies found them to hold highly favorable opinions of their auditors.[80]

The image that the academic community has of public accounting is very weak, suffering from a general lack of knowledge about it. In examining types of organizational administration of various occupations, the noted social scientist Bertrand Gross does not appear to be familiar with the structure and rules of the public accounting profession. He classifies all accounting as a nonprofession because it does not contain a body of organized knowledge, a code of ethics, and a professional organization.[81] In the literature covering automation, technology, and information services, one can find numerous other examples that do not

78. In a speech given at the Graduate School of Business Administration, New York University, February 18, 1965.

79. These points are mentioned in Carey, *The CPA Plans*, p. 412, and in an article in the *Wall Street Journal*, May 24, 1965.

80. Elmo Roper, "As Others See You," *Journal of Accountancy* 117:33 (January 1964). The companies ranged in size from 20 to 249 employees. Seventy-four percent of the companies used a CPA or a CPA firm.

81. Bertrand Gross, *The Managing of Organizations,* 2 vols. (New York: The Free Press, 1964), 2:823.

present an adequate view of accounting. Most of them display a lack of awareness of the existence of, or the size and importance of, public accounting as a profession. The only exceptions are among those who have some close association with the profession or who specialize in the study of occupations and professions.

Another factor that concerned CPAs mention as hindering image projection is the complexity of the image. As an auditor, the CPA is an independent attestor to financial data; as a tax specialist he is an advocate; and as a management advisor he is basically a problem solver.[82] Further, he may detract from his own image by careless practices, such as the "negative myths" he perpetuates by inferring that certain broad concepts that he uses ("cost," "objective," "realized," "conservative") do not involve the use of judgment or economic evaluation.[83] Concern with image is carried to the extreme when an outside consultant tells the AICPA that calling a staff room a "bull pen" and using such words as "semi-senior" are not consistent with the terminology of a learned profession. However, in at least one "learned" profession—law—such terms are used regularly.[84]

Other public accountants mention the necessity for CPAs to carry out their professional tasks regardless of their effect on "image." The CPA must take a "show me" attitude, a conservative measure to counterbalance the optimism of the client management.[85] And other public accountants warn of an attitude of smugness because accounting is presently so well established in comparison to its past. Contrary to the belief held by many CPAs and other financially sophisticated persons that "the auditors have arrived,"[86] one CPA has written that the greatest challenge to public accounting today may be that public accountants have come to believe that they *have* arrived.[87] Some members of the profession believe that computerization and the consulting services must be integrated within the profession; otherwise, other professions will step in to accomplish these tasks themselves.

The role of accounting associations in educating their members, clients, and the general public as to the purpose and functions of the associations is seen by

82. John L. Carey, "The Integrated Accounting Service," *Journal of Accountancy* 120:62 (November 1965).

83. Harold Bierman, Jr., "Myths and Accountants," *Accounting Review* 40:554 (July 1965).

84. See Smigel, *The Wall Street Lawyer*, p. 210. The consultant's statement is mentioned by John L. Carey, *The CPA Plans*, p. 298.

85. Grady, *Inventory of GAAP*, p. 36.

86. The title of the article in *Fortune* magazine by Wise, "The Auditors Have Arrived," which was the first analysis of the Big Eight to appear in a large-circulation publication.

87. Robert E. Witschey, "Is Accounting a Status-quo Profession?" *The CPA* (September 1963), pp. 4-5.

large-firm accountants as an important attribute of professionalization (see table 9). Publications, meetings, and active participation in committees give evidence that professional organizations of public accountants, especially the AICPA, are a strong force in professionalization in public accounting. Just as important, the AICPA is responsible for developing and maintaining a professionalism that touches on all other attributes. Encouraging the CPA to make the greatest possible contribution to the public welfare,[88] protecting the free enterprise system, asserting that management services are rightfully within the province of public accounting, emphasizing the high personal standards and sterling character of the CPA, and the like—all are part of the job of the professional association.

Personal Qualities

Personal qualities beyond technical competence are considered very important by large-firm accountants for distinguishing public accounting as a profession. Perhaps the most important personal quality is to have good judgment. Good judgment for the public accountant—and for any professional, for that matter—means making choices based on technical knowledge *and* wisdom, to the benefit of all parties concerned. The great men of any profession utilize the breadth of human thought, and they consider the interests of many groups and individuals. Consistently good judgment, of course, enhances the name of the firm. It is one of the best sources that public accountants have for building upon their image, because advertising restrictions limit their public and prospective-client contacts almost to nil. Good judgment is an intangible quality that develops with experience, but all men do not possess its ingredients. CPAs consider these ingredients to be integrity, stability, pertinacity, perspicacity, and so forth.

Integrity is given first place by most accountants. It is so important that lack of it can mean a person's job. A manager of one Big Eight firm, working in the personnel department, stressed:

> Integrity is an unwritten rule that's important in *any* situation with a CPA. For example, a person told me in a job interview that he was fourth out of 400 in his graduating class. It impressed me as a good accomplishment. Then, a little later I found he was about 398th out of 400. After that, we had to let him go. How could you have him work with you after that?

If a man cannot be trusted, he cannot very well enter in good faith into the modified type of social exchange that the professional engages in when dealing with his clients. Social exchange involves unspecified obligations and gratitude

---

88. As stated in the "Objectives" of the AICPA.

and trust. Economic exchange does not. Unlike economic exchanges, the professional services that are to be performed are not specified in detail in advance.[89] The element of *trust* in social exchange is very important to the roles of all parties involved in the accounting function. There is the trust that the CPA must place in the client's employees that the transactions were honestly recorded. There is the trust of the stockholder in the CPA's forthrightness in dealing with materiality when conducting his examination of the client's records. There is the client's trust that his CPA will maintain secrecy, and his trust in the CPA's judgment and skill.[90] These roles of social exchange are in many cases becoming institutionalized, that is, formalized, regularized, and established;[91] there is "legitimated directionality of behavior."[92]

Unwritten Rules

In all occupations, institutionalization is manifested in the form of formal and informal rules. The informal rules are the norms, and the formal rules are the codes or law. Generally, for the professions, a greater number of the rules remain informal than for nonprofessional occupations. They remain unwritten; they are "informally" formalized—"there is a behavior *norm* covering every standard interpersonal situation likely to recur in professional life."[93] Only about half the questionnaire sample of this study (table 9) felt that unwritten rules were important in distinguishing public accounting as a profession, probably because their existence is not perceived; they have become part of the behavior pattern of the socialized CPA. The weeding-out process of promotion, itself a set of unwritten rules, has seen to this. The complete acceptance of these rules and the lack of awareness of them were quite evident when questions were asked about unwritten rules during interviews. Once discussion clarified what was being looked for, the many types of unwritten rules were called to mind by the respondents. Several of their examples would normally be found as written rules in nonprofessional organizations. Also, several respondents admitted that by thinking about their habits as informal rules, they brought out inflexible, rigid, informal rules to their consciousness for the first time. (Table 10 gives the result of these questions.)

89. This modified type is discussed by Peter M. Blau, *Exchange and Power in Social Life* (New York: Wiley, 1964), pp. 93-94.

90. The client's trust in the professional's skill and judgment is emphasized by Everett C. Hughes, "Professions," *Daedalus* 92:657 (Fall 1963).

91. Robert Bierstedt, *The Social Order: An Introduction to Sociology* (2d ed.; New York: McGraw-Hill, 1963), p. 342.

92. Talcott Parsons, *Structure and Process in Modern Societies* (New York: The Free Press, 1960), p. 177.

93. Greenwood, Attributes of a Profession," p. 52.

TABLE 10

Unwritten Rules Mentioned by Large
Firm Accountants (N=139)

Response	No. of Responses	%
Professional Image: Support firm's position in all its pronouncements—5; Protect the firm's name—2; You represent your firm at all times—1; Maintain a professional appearance—7; Keep firm's shortcomings within it—1; Keep weaknesses of profession to self—1; Be prepared to defend your position to client—2; Conservatism—1; Conservatism in dress—3; Rules on dress—7; Conservatism in dress and social behavior—2; Political conservatism—1	32	16
The Individual in the Work Situation: Don't complain about work assignments—2; Show interest in your work—1; Expect extra demands of job on personal life—1; Try to keep normal working hours—1; Be time conscious—1; Show initiative on the job—1; Emphasis on imagination and adaptability—2; Stick to your guns even if in minority—1; Give critical judgment from facts at hand—2; Honesty and integrity—2; Informality is stressed—3; Maintain social contacts as possible leads to clients—1; Job security—1	19	9
Social Organization: Opinion of firm must be collective answer of most qualified partners—2; Responsibility spread through all levels of firm—1; Strict adherence to chain of command—1; Respect seniority—1; Deference to superiors—1; Keeping superiors advised of changes—1; Audit partners are "the establishment"—1; Set number of years to make partnership—1; Autonomy of partners—2; Emphasis on utilizating meetings for interchange of ideas—2; Concept of integrated audit—3; Placement of personnel of firm into industry—1	17	8
Client Relations: Service attitude—8; Service attitude beyond auditing—3; Develop good client relations—1; Extra emphasis on maintaining independence—2; Bend with the client to the point of materiality—1; Do a good job regardless of fee charged—1; Give service beyond the fee charged, if necessary—1	17	8
Interpretation of Written and Unwritten Rules: Extra emphasis on adherence to accounting principles and auditing standards—5; Extra emphasis on staff training—4; Extra emphasis on maintaining technical competence—1; Strict adherence to ethics—1; Use judgment re written rules—1; Common sense—1; Don't infringe on legal profession—1; Conservative interpretation of tax rules—1; Consider nation's revenue needs in tax decisions—1	17	8

TABLE 10 (continued)

Response	No. of Responses	%
Relations with Other Accountants: Don't knock other accountants—2; Don't knock other firms—3; Don't offend the small firm by implying large firm domination—2; Maintain strict ethical standards in relations with small firms—2; Snub the small firm—1; Extra care in dealing with clients of other firms—1; Don't criticize the client's accounting staff—1; High degree of interdependence among large firms—2	14	7
Colleague Relations: Help colleagues—6; Colleague debate—2; Emphasis on interchange of ideas—3; Assist subordinates—2	13	6
Professional Attitude: Participation in professional and civic activities—2; Don't let personality interfere with professional work—2; Public accounting is more challenging and vital than private accounting—2; Don't date client's employees—1; Maintain friendly but professional relations with client at all levels—2	9	4
Respondent Stated a Written Rule:	7	3
"Large" is Not a Descriminating Variable:	5[a]	2
Too New with Firm to Discern Unwritten Rules:	4	2
There Are No Unwritten Rules: None—12; Can't discern any—9; All rules are written in our manuals—2; Most rules are in AICPA code of ethics—1	24[a]	12
No answer given on the Questionnaire:	24	12
No Time to Ask Respondent during Interview:	6	3
Total Responses	206[b]	100

[a]The answers of interviewed respondents were nearly consistent with the answers of questionnaire respondents with these exceptions. The low number of "none" for interviews (N=3) probably reflects the effect of the presence of the interviewer and his persistence. Yet five questionnaire respondents gave the thoughtful answer about size not being a factor.

[b]Total responses are greater than total N, because some respondents listed more than one rule.

Professionalization is a process of interrelated attributes. No single attribute stands by itself over time as the only important factor affecting professional growth. Nor do attributes change of their own accord. It takes people with ideas and professional ideologies to move a profession, to give it direction and change. It is clients and colleagues, rather than the general public, who define the professional. However, having the public on your side in the battle for professional recognition is a tremendous protection against unfair criticisms and other hindrances in the struggle for power and prestige.[94] Perhaps this is why the AICPA pays lip service to the service ideal, even though its large-firm members do not see it as especially important to the profession.

In other cases, their perceptions do not equate so well. In the case of licensing, there is more talk than action by the members of the profession; whereas with symbolism it is just the opposite. The former is a situation of professionalism. The latter exists but is generally not recognized as important by members—a negative professionalism. In comparing occupations in terms of degree of professionalization, observers tend to accept benchmarks of professionalization (for example, date of licensure, written code of ethics) before any of the groundwork on ideology has been completed. As a result, one researcher concludes that certified public accounting is a higher profession, along with law, medicine, architecture, and engineering.[95] However, to one of the profession's leading spokesmen, it is not yet one of the "great" professions, and it must evolve speedily in order to encompass the entire field of information processing and control.[96] In light of our analysis, the latter view is the more accurate one; and at the rate the profession is applying itself, this may not take very long. One of the outstanding features we have noted is that professionalization is being attempted on many fronts in public accounting, especially in those areas where the degree of professionalization is considered high (namely, testing procedure, code of ethics).

There are two major conceptualizations of professional development and its effects on social organization. Emphasizing social exchange theory, Blau feels that in professions and bureaucracies there are fewer exchange transactions (consequently, more institutionalization), because this allows independent judgment (through professional detachment). The rewards of social exchange are lost, so the substitute of colleague approval is needed to take its place.[97] In an

---

94. Marie R. Haug and Marvin B. Sussman, "Professionalization and the Public," *Sociological Inquiry* 39:57-64 (Winter 1969).

95. Wilensky, "The Professionalization of Everyone?" p. 143.

96. Carey, *The Accounting Profession*, pp. 94, 158; Carey, *The CPA Plans*, p. 378.

97. Blau, *Exchange and Power in Social Life*, p. 330.

analysis of social systems, Parsons feels that strong reliance on informal controls (more institutionalization) by professionals results in professional confidence in taking risks. This, in turn, leads to *less* bureaucratization. Colleague approval is interpreted as a cause of debureaucratization, an "informally" formalized rule.[98] We take Parson's position. His informal controls are one type of the external rules of my first hypothesis, which is examined in chapter 5.

The total process of professionalization encompasses the reciprocity of expectations between the profession and all interested parties, the latter including clients, third parties, and the public. The profession produces responsibility in the form of integrity and independence, competence in its intellectual technique, and the obligation of a professional attitude. For this, it receives from the interested parties the prestige of a high position, wealth in the form of salaries and fees, and power to control its body of knowledge.[99] The interested parties provide faith and trust, and in return they receive fair and accurate advice and contributions to the community.[100] This process is largely institutionalized, with only limited "chains" of social exchange taking place. In the relationship *between* professions, expectations are considerably less institutionalized where power and uncertainty are key elements in the process of professionalization. This will be the subject for discussion in chapters 9 and 10.

98. Parsons, *The Social System*, pp. 469-471.

99. In an attempt to empirically measure professionalization more accurately, one study concentrates on the major professional organization of each of five professions, in order to measure the variables of size, wealth, and knowledge, and the structural variables of group cohesion. The authors recognize the limitations of the use of available data. Ronald L. Akers and Richard Quinney, "Differential Organization of Health Professions: A Comparative Analysis," *American Sociological Review* 33:104–121 (February 1968).

100. Parts of this reciprocal arrangement are discussed by John L. Carey, *Professional Ethics of Certified Public Accountants* (New York: AICPA, 1956), pp. 3-5, 12.

PART TWO

Analysis of a Profession in Change

Part One presents a picture of the stability and security of the public accounting profession, especially with regard to its large firms, as a little-known but well-functioning group in American society. In the remaining chapters this picture of collective solidarity is challenged by emphasizing conflict both within the profession and between it and other professions. The basis for this analysis is a theory of organizational change (chapter 6), which links the two hypotheses stated earlier. Chapter 7 explains the rationalizing of parts of the auditing function, and chapter 8 outlines the development of new knowledge in management services as cases in point for the theory. The antagonisms between segments in the profession are the focus of chapter 9, special attention being given to the debate over approaches to "social accounting." One view is largely behaviorist, the other organicist. The concluding chapter deals with the conflict between professions and with the significance of systems analysis for the future of the Big Eight and public accounting in general.

5

Bureaucracy in the Big Firms

The daily work of the profession is directed by a system of rules both formal and informal, as well as internal and external to the large firms. The first hypothesis suggests that the emphasis placed on these rules will to some extent determine the amount of bureaucracy in the routine that is found in these large-scale professional organizations. Examples of these rules will facilitate analysis.

INTERNAL RULES OF LARGE FIRMS

Formal Internal Rules

The internal rules of an organization are the rules that are created by and for the members of that organization only. Formal rules are codified (written) and given legal sanction. Formal internal rules cover all areas of the operation of large public accounting firms. There are the rules of the partnership agreement, which govern the general formal organization of the firm and the sharing of profits. Also, most firms have constructed their own code of ethics dealing with clients, the public, and fellow members of the profession. These are more detailed and rigid than the AICPA code. Usually, a loose-leaf folder will be found containing rules for internal administration. For such large firms, elaborate systems for information flow and record-keeping must be maintained. Versed as they are in matters of internal control systems, large-firm CPAs have provided accurate and carefully designed rules for the efficient functioning of their organizations.

Another major body of formal internal rules covers the profession's body of knowledge. Mostly, these rules are highly specific aspects of the more general formal and informal rules external to the firms—the auditing standards and procedures and the accounting principles and procedures. The listing of these rules in some firms fills several loose-leaf notebooks.

Informal Internal Rules

These rules are the unwritten norms of behavior within the firm. Though they are unwritten, they are nearly all institutionalized; they are responsible for a

93

regularized pattern of behavior, the habitual way of doing things by the members of the firm. Because of the rigid weeding-out process in recruitment and promotion in these large firms, and because the rules are unwritten, they remain to a large extent unrecognized as rules by their followers.[1] Many respondents found it difficult to think of the unwritten rules of their firm. Some could not think of any, and others responded only after considerable pause to point out what parts of their actions were required behavior that was governed by the "common law" of their firm.

But once the question had been raised, amorphous, implicit norms became crystallized,[2] and a wide range of informal internal rules emerged (see table 10). Respondents from each firm listed much the same types of rules—which indicated that there is very little difference in behavior from one firm to the next—even though the rules themselves differed in specific details.

One large firm has formalized several internal rules that have remained largely informal in other firms. Written rules do not automatically signify greater importance, however, and some rules of the firm in question are listed merely as suggestions or hints, with little or no authoritative overtones. One booklet of rules contains such items as:

> Be wary of taking part in controversial discussion on such subjects as politics and religion. This can be fatal to further usefulness in that client's office.
>
> As a general rule, you are not expected to entertain the client or his employees.
>
> If discussion takes place in a client's office, take care that you are not overheard by persons not entitled to be informed on the subject.

A few items with a little more teeth to them:

> Do *not* cash your personal or the firm's check at the office of a client, and under no circumstances borrow money from a client.
>
> You have received instructions for preparing time and expense reports. . . . We must be scrupulous in charging our client with only the time spent on his affairs.

1. Socialization through the "screening-out" process and adherence to internal and external rules in public accounting firms has been discussed by two CPAs: John J. Willingham and D. R. Carmichael, "The Professional Auditing Subculture," *Abacus* 4:153-163 (December 1968).

2. Aaron V. Cicourel, *Method and Measurement in Sociology* (New York: The Free Press, 1964), p. 221 discusses how norms become explicit.

Professions construct, maintain, and police a much more elaborate and systematic set of external rules than do nonprofessional occupations. The more autonomous professions such as public accounting and law have more elaborate and systematic external rules than other professions where the majority of members are employed by nonprofessional organizations, e.g., social work, engineering.

The first hypothesis of this thesis holds that these external professional rules operate to keep large organizations of professionals nonbureaucratic by lessening routine and red tape. This hypothesis has been challenged elsewhere, by this statement: "The actual codification of rules in the professions has had little effect on the mechanisms of social control. The writer would suggest that there is widespread disagreement within professions on the desired content of such codes, if the conflicts over fee-splitting, group practice and advertising are any indication. In fact, there is little in the way of behavior control that distinguishes professions from other occupations."[3] An answer to this statement is given by testing the first hypothesis by means of observation and interview of the sample.

Formal External Rules

In the words of one accountant, "Accounting action is continually being undertaken by acknowledgement of preconceived rules or laws."[4] These rules are both written and unwritten and are external to the work organizations of professionals. Those rules external to the firms, which are common to the professions of law, medicine, and certified public accountancy, are the codes of ethics. The AICPA code of ethics has existed in writing since 1907, and its evolution since then has been marked by constant revisions,[5] the latest occurring in 1965.

Other formal external rules of public accounting have already been discussed in the preceding two chapters. In 1948 the certified public accounting profession, through the AICPA, published a statement of "generally accepted auditing standards," an ancestor several generations removed from the 1963 statement,

---

3. William G. Rothstein, "Engineers: Case and Theory in the Sociology of Professions" (Ph.D. diss., Cornell University, 1965), p. 441. In a more recent personal communication, Rothstein emphasized that he intended this point to be concerned with the conduct of professional associations, that private professional firms were not considered per se.

4. Edward J. Burke, "Objectivity and Accounting," *Accounting Review* 39:845 (October 1964).

5. Darwin J. Casler, "The Evolution of the Code of Professional Ethics of the American Institute of Certified Public Accountants" (D.B.A. diss., Michigan State University, 1962), who gives a historical analysis of the code.

Auditing Standards and Procedures. The technical base for accounting practitioners—"generally accepted accounting principles"—also has existed in writing for many years, but has been scattered throughout hundreds of unconnected books, journals, and AICPA releases. Only within the last few years has an effort been made to codify them and thus further formalize them for more efficient rational use.[6]

Informal External Rules

Both informal and external professional rules are becoming limited in number now that accounting principles are in the process of codification. Before the inventory of principles was compiled in Accounting Research Study No. 7, GAAP were informal external rules of the profession. With the research study, they are now in the process of becoming formalized; they are not yet accepted as a *set* of rules binding the AICPA membership. In questions to the interview sample, GAAP were considered as informal external rules.

Rules governing the other two major areas of CPA practice—taxes and management services—are now in their initial stages of formalization. As of 1967, the AICPA division of federal taxation had five written statements, and the committee on management services had two.

Other more informal external rules include those pertaining to the professional's responsibility and his commitment to his profession. The precepts of presenting a good image to the public and of contributing time and energies to the professional associations are continually mentioned orally and in accounting publications.

THE RULES AS MECHANISMS OF SOCIAL CONTROL

Interviews with large-firm CPAs concerning adherence to the code of ethics of their profession led to discussions in which examples of rule-breaking were cited (see the Code of Ethics, chapter 4). Despite this, the large majority of respondents felt that the rules were well adhered to in the profession as a whole. Only a few felt that there was much bending of rules to the desires of clients. One Big Eight partner, a member for several years of the New York State Professional Conduct Committee, noted that there were no cases involving the Big Eight firms during all the time that he was a member. But there are doubts in the

6. Maurice Moonitz and Robert T. Sprouse, *A Tentative Set of Broad Accounting Principles for Business Enterprises* (Accounting Research Study No. 3) (New York: AICPA, 1962); Paul Grady, *Inventory of Generally Accepted Accounting Principles for Business Enterprises* (Accounting Research Study No. 7) (New York: AICPA, 1965).

minds of many practitioners about the true amount of malpractice taking place. An executive partner of one Big Eight firm feels that many violations exist but that they remain undetected because of the confidentiality of the CPA's work. And CPAs of other firms feel that several of the largest accounting firms are thoroughly corrupt.

But there are too many parties interested and anxious about the work of certified public accountants for the profession to constantly hoodwink all of them all of the time. Some students of the professions fail to consider the question of whether there is a *vital* interest of parties to a profession's services. Certainly, if there is no vital interest—that is, something that seriously affects the well-being of large portions of a society, then there is not as substantial a need for maintaining a reciprocity of expectations that involve trust. The "modified social exchange" of the client-professional relationship would not exist; pure economic exchanges would suffice. Control over a vital public service makes the CPA a "strategic elite" by definition.[7] But in order to remain free of regulation and retain his autonomy, the public accountant *must* adhere faithfully to the rules in order to maintain the confidence of the public and the client.

Interested parties, to a considerable extent, force a conformity of internal formal and informal rules on large accounting firms. For those stockholders who in more than nine hundred corporations elect their auditors, the pressure that they could conceivably bring to bear on an errant auditor would be tremendous. Clients, through their influence on stockholders and the threat of suit, can effect the same kind of pressure on their auditors. One example is the difficult situation that Peat, Marwick, Mitchell & Co. faced, a situation brought on by numerous suits against the firm as a result of the illegal financial practices of several of its clients. Several of the firm's most respectable clients (such as General Electric Co. and the First National City Bank of New York) felt impelled to explain or to defend to their stockholders the retention of Peat Marwick as their auditors.[8]

Even under the pressures of the responsibility that is directed toward them, large accounting firms have a notable lack of red tape and formal procedure with which they must deal. The internal rules are there, but personnel of the firms are unaware of all but the most important of them. For the individual, socialization within his firm, through the weeding-out process of recruitment and promotion, accomplishes an internalization of these rules. Also, the major body representing CPAs—the AICPA—serves as the center where the mélange of the codes and standards of individual firms collect, congeal, and are codified and enforced throughout the membership. The rules external to the firms also serve as a base

7. Suzanne Keller, *Beyond the Ruling Class: Strategic Elites in Modern Society* (New York: Random House, 1963), pp. 4, 20 develops the concept and defines it.

8. T. A. Wise, "The Very Private World of Peat, Marwick, Mitchell," *Fortune* 74:90-91 (July 1, 1966).

for their more specific internal rules, some of which are more stringent, others of which merely explain the external rules. Nearly to a man, interview respondents felt that formal external rules were the most important rules governing their respective firms; these were followed by informal external rules, then formal internal rules, and, lastly, informal internal rules. The response was almost identical for rules governing the profession as a whole. As one partner of a Big Eight firm observed on this question:

> We automatically abide by the external rules. They're the standard for the profession. Then the firm obviously builds on these rules; they're [the firm's rules are] the more stringent rules. As for the profession, the external rules are the most important. To the extent the public is aware of accounting rules, it is aware of the external rules, and the courts apply them.

The codes and standards are binding only on the members of the AICPA, who constitute only slightly more than half the total number of CPAs in the United States. However, as has already been noted, more jurisdictions that grant CPA certificates have rules resembling those of the AICPA, since these jurisdictions have been influenced by and have influenced the AICPA rules. The important point is that these external rules allow large firms to devote less time to the internal formulation and administration of the major body of rules that must govern them and to spend that time in professional practice. The direct questions on rules posed to the sample indicate the importance of professionalization to the lessening of routine and rigidity in the firm.

The social control of professional bodies by means of external rules is a *pattern* of bureaucracy known as *professional* bureaucracy.[9] Change in the pattern of professional bureaucracy in a profession will depend on variations in the extent and specificity of rules external to the professional firms, the number of group practices, and, to some extent, the size of these firms. There is no doubt that in public accounting the control is significant and extensive; also the fact that so many segments of American society are concerned about the public services of the CPA insures that his private interests are curbed to the point where they will not injure and may even aid the public's interest (as variously defined). Such action clearly differentiates several professions, including public accounting, from other occupations in terms of behavior control. Whether he wants it or not, the CPA is limited in his personal interests at work by rules constructed by his colleagues, whereas the plumber (or any other tradesman), personally or through his union, will attempt to acquire what the market will bear, subject only to the local or national governmental qualifications.

---

9. The term "professional bureaucracy" is used in an analysis of large law firms by Erwin O. Smigel, *The Wall Street Lawyer: Professional Organization Man?* (New York: The Free Press, 1964), pp. 275-286.

For the firms under study, there was no significant difference between large and small firms in the proportion of time devoted to administrative work. The average in the New York offices of Big Eight firms was 13 percent. The average of the medium-sized firm was 11 percent. Only about 2 percent of the professional staff of a Big Eight firm are engaged solely in administrative work. In a few firms, the percentage is a little higher because of the policy of transferring the majority of administrative tasks to a few professionals rather than spreading them through the entire staff. The main purpose in either case is to allow the professional to remain at his work. The managing partner of one firm remarked:

> It's very seldom a man in our firm stays away from the technical end for very long, because if he does, he becomes a "kept accountant." He loses his professional abilities and becomes a weight on the firm in terms of contributing professionally. One administrative-type job goes by the title of "the broom." He's the man on the big job [two hundred or more public accountants] who prepares everything in the morning before work starts and ties up the loose ends at night and at the end of the job or when some men go off the job. But this isn't a full-time job. Neither is work in personnel a permanent position. We rotate a man after a few years.

In addition to the small administrative component, the Big Eight are highly centralized. The pattern is unusual, because normally, in both professional and nonprofessional bureaucracies, professionalization and centralization are incompatible. The division of labor furthers the development of centralization, whereas professionalization detracts from that development; that is to say, "a professional staff is usually accompanied by a large and dispersed managerial component."[10]

This unusual pattern is found in an extreme form in the largest professional organizations—in the largest accounting firms, for example, administrative authority is centralized in the senior partner and the managing committee, only a few percent of the entire professional staff. There is, as was pointed out in chapter 3, personal and office autonomy in the professional work of the firm; and, ideally, in the partnership it is one man, one vote. But in practice, the firm's general administration is formed and voted on by the small executive group at the top.

Although many studies have been made on the relationship between an organization's size and its administrative component, the conclusions that they have reached have been inconsistent, because the administrators comprise many occupational types. A single "class" of occupations must be dealt with in order

10. Peter M. Blau, Wolf V. Heydebrand, and Robert E. Stauffer, "The Structure of Small Bureaucracies," *American Sociological Review* 31:185-186, 191 (April 1966).

for meaningful comparisions to be made.[11] Working within these limitations, there is one other study of large-firm professionals that allows comparison to the accounting firms—an analysis of public personnel agencies, which was directed by Peter Blau.[12] Three variables are measured in this study:

> The administrative apparatus ratio is *low* when the proportion of clerks among the total staff is less than 60 percent; *high* when it is 60 percent or more.

> The managerial hierarchy is *centralized* when the ratio of non-clerical personnel in managerial positions to non-clerical personnel in non-supervisory positions, excluding those listed as neither, is less than one to three; it is *dispersed* when the ratio is one to three or more.

> Professionalization is *low* when the proportion of the operating staff (excluding managers as well as clerks) who are required to have, at least, a college degree with a specified major, is less than 50 percent; *high* when it is 50 percent of more.[13]

Using these measurement bases in order to make the comparison, the largest personnel agencies and the largest accounting firms display a high degree of professionalization, high centralization, and a small administrative component. The relationship is changed for the medium-sized agencies (approximately two hundred personnel) and the medium-sized accounting firms (also about two hundred): both have a high degree of professionalization and low centralization, whatever the administrative ratio. All twelve accounting firms studied—eight large and four medium-sized ones—follow the pattern of the majority of personnel agencies of like size. More important, the Big Eight show a much higher measurement on the three variables than do the personnel agencies. They all have an administrative ratio of less than 30 percent, are centralized at a ratio of less than one to six if all partners are included as managerial personnel, and are 100 percent professional.

I have shown that the determining variable in this relationship is professionalization. Blau traces the cause to internal rules developed by the administration—substitute methods, such as detailed statistical records of performance which check on the work of subordinates and obtain information on operations without frequent direct supervison.[14] In public accounting the external rules that have been developed by the professional association, which allow a minimum of administration, are the substitute methods. It appears that the less

11. William A. Rushing, "Organizational Size and Administration: The Problems of Causal Homogeneity and a Heterogeneous Category," *Pacific Sociological Review* 9:100-108 (Fall 1966).

12. Blau, Heydebrand, and Stauffer, "The Structure of Small Bureaucracies."

13. Ibid., p. 183.

14. Peter M. Blau, *The Dynamics of Bureaucracy* (rev. ed.; Chicago: University of Chicago Press, 1963), chap. 3; Blau, Heydebrand, and Stauffer, "The Structure of Small Bureaucracies," p. 185.

professionalized personnel agencies have to depend more on internal substitutes and consequently larger administration (but still small compared to nonprofessional organizations of like size) than do the accounting firms. The latter comprise a true professional bureaucracy, as do the twenty largest law firms in the United States.[15]

This comparative analysis gives one answer to the question, "Is there an inverse relationship between the extent to which a . . . profession establishes a set of rules and the necessity for an organization to create its own formal internal rules?"[16] For the largest professional organizations in existence, yes, there is an inverse relationship, but it is becoming limited by increasing size and differentiation.

ADVANTAGES AND DISADVANTAGES OF SIZE:
COMPARISON OF LARGE AND MEDIUM-SIZED FIRMS

Big Eight accountants did comment on several problem areas brought about by their increased size which were not evident in the medium-sized firms visited. One problem that was mentioned frequently was the loss of personal contact between the hierarchical levels of the firm; this results in some loss in efficiency due to the increased impersonal character of the firm. With this loss came less loyalty to the firm—less espirit de corps; several partners mentioned its adverse effect on employee relations and turnover. According to the senior partner of one medium-sized firm, some of the advantages of firms of his size are that "in the smaller firm the partner is closer to the men in the field. He's at the job more often and there aren't the levels of supervision you get in the large firms." In the large firm the partner no longer knows all the men in the firm, not even all the partners in his firm. From the beginning, in the firm's training program, the formal programs are broken down into regional schools. One managing partner of a Big Eight firm noted that fifteen years ago he could sit down at a party and have a drink with every partner in the office, a physical impossibility today. He hastened to add: "Professionally [technically], I still know the capabilities of every partner—it's my job to know. But socially, with a good many, all that can be maintained is a nodding acquaintance." Not that this is a new problem for the Big Eight. A 1918 article in the *Haskins & Sells Journal* reported that someone was brought into the firm to "serve as counselor and guide to its members in matters technical, educational, and professional . . . [because] it has been increasingly difficult to keep in close touch with the staff."[17]

15. Smigel, "*The Wall Street Lawyer.*"

16. Ibid., p. 286.

17. "Introducing the Department of Professional Training," *Haskins & Sells Bulletin* 1:2 (March 15, 1918).

There are problems that are brought on by geography alone. One Big Eight partner noted during an interview that

> the national and international scope of the large firms brings up the problem of uniformity of practice within the firm, especially in those firms which have merged with the local firm in a particular area. For example, Jones & Jones wants to enter Syracuse, New York, and so merges with a local firm there. That firm doesn't want to change its ways so radically, so some allowance has to be made for their methods of practice. If their work has to be used in coordination with other work, the combining of the two is at times a problem. Also, exchange of personnel between offices presents a problem.

This problem of uniformity of practice was mentioned as "most serious" by people in three of the Big Eight firms. The less the uniformity, the less the reliance that can be placed on the most important product of the CPA's work, the opinion.

Large firms handle the largest clients. Assignments to these clients bring about problems peculiar to that situation. The young newer people are worried about too much routine work and overspecialization. At the conclusion of my observation of a recruitment interview at one firm, I wrote a summary to capture the main points of the entire meeting:

> The candidates were visibly nervous for the first hour but loosened up after having the session with the junior [employee of the firm recruiting]. Their main questions to the junior covered the type of work he had done in his first year, the length of time on each type of work, and whether the junior was ever noticed by the senior staff members. Also, there were questions on the amount of overtime and when it was incurred, and a short discussion of promotion, especially with regard to placement outside the firm.
>
> In the interview with the senior, their main concern was with the type of work to which he had progressed. Did he still do detail work? How many different areas did he work in? Did he keep the same client? Then the question regarding promotion was asked; and mentioned again by the senior were the facts that placement could be obtained outside the firm if one didn't fit for one reason or another and that there was a great advantage in having public accounting experience.

The perceived bureaucracy is much greater at the lower levels. In an examination of twenty-four branch offices of four of the Big Eight, Sorensen found a conflict between professional and bureaucratic modes of orientation in the individual, although the amount of discrepancy between ideals and perceived reality for these two modes decreased with increase in rank. As a result, younger firm members are often dissatisfied with their jobs because high professional

102

expectations are unfulfilled.18 In a study of physicians similar conclusions were drawn.19

The problems of specialization are apparent at all levels. Recently, most large firms have instituted the position of managing or administrative partner. Price Waterhouse did so in 1961. In some cases, this position has been added for each of a firm's largest offices or areas. The same practice has occurred in the largest law firms, but not with nearly as much frequency.20 These administrative positions are initiated in order to coordinate the increasing number and size of specialty areas in the firm. But the situation of having different bodies of specialized technical knowledge, side-by-side but for the most part segregated, can be a handicap. Many respondents remarked on the gap in knowledge and communications created by this specialization: "Unfortunately, with the larger clients the audit man relies on a tax expert." "More and more, for some decisions, we have to run to management services to find the answers." "At the present time, the CPA leaves the whole matter [a nonauditing problem that the client has presented to the auditing firm] up to the management services expert and doesn't even participate in the final presentation to management." A management services associate who is a CPA compared the largest accounting firms to the largest law firms with regard to size and specialization:

> We're more formal than the law firms because of our size. We rely on outsiders more than law firms. Our communications experts are journalists; our personnel experts are CPAs but do little or no CPA work.
>
> We have a hierarchy broken down into more layers than the law firm. We're more molded than the lawyers in terms of obeying the internal rules. We control our people more tightly *because* of size.

In effect, each firm has two semi-autonomous hierarchies, one composed of CPAs and the other of mostly non-CPA professionals. In some firms the title of "principal" is a position for non-CPAs; it is given equal rank with partner except that the principal is not a partner in the firm. As a result, his status approaches but never reaches that of a partner. In the normal situation (that is, auditing),

18. James E. Sorensen, "Professional and Bureaucratic Organization in the Public Accounting Firm," *Accounting Review* 42:553-565 (July 1967).

19. Gloria V. Engel, "The Effect of Bureaucracy on the Professional Autonomy of the Physician," *Journal of Health and Social Behavior* 10:38 (March 1969).

20. One publication, written for lawyers by personnel of Price Waterhouse & Co., notes the need for one man to be responsible for law-firm administration and finances. Clark Sloat and Richard D. Fitzgerald, *Administrative and Financial Management in a Law Firm,* Economics of Law Practice Series, Pamphlet 10 (New York: The Standing Committee on Economics of Law Practice of the American Bar Association, 1965), p. 1. Smigel, "The Wall Street Lawyer," p. 239 notes that in some of the twenty largest law firms the duties of recruitment are added to the responsibilities of the managing partner. See also John C. Biegler, "Problems in the Administration of Professional Firms," *Price Waterhouse Review* 8:6-15 (Winter 1963).

the authority of the firm's administrators is based on their technical knowledge and experience. But where nonaccounting experts are part of the professional organization, as in the large accounting firms, administrative authority will tend to be legitimated in terms of incumbency of office. In this situation, obedience tends to be stressed as an end in itself, because the CPA as administrator is not able to judge the nonaccountant expert on the basis of that expert's knowledge. Gouldner calls this a pattern of "punishment-centered" bureaucracy, where rules are initiated by one party only.[21]

The pattern of professional bureaucracy is the dominant force; but because of the infusion of non-CPA experts into the firms, inroads are being made by another pattern, that of punishment-centered bureaucracy. Both the sizeable staff of experts who are not guided solely by the external formal rules of the profession and the sheer size of these firms create the need for stronger internal formal controls. This was apparent in questionnaire and interview responses to the question, "In a sentence or two, state what you think is tne main reason your firm functions effectively, that is, effectively enough to maintain its position competitively." More than one-quarter of the respondents volunteered an answer that was related to administrative efficiency. Just the opposite emphasis was given by large law firms, which are, on the average, less than one-third the size of the New York City offices of the Big Eight. Of the lawyer sample of 188, 27 percent voluntarily mentioned that "looseness of organization" was responsible for effective functioning of the firm,[22] whereas only 5 percent of the accountants did.

Size has advantages that tend to partially compensate for the problems it creates. One partner of a Big Eight firm summed up a lot of what was said on this point:

> Size hasn't affected me adversely one bit. As a matter of fact, it has helped a lot. Today, my work is easier because I can parcel out more of it. Because we have more offices, I don't have to run around so much any more. It [size] hasn't added any red tape. Internal office reports are more complicated, it's true, but we're [partners] not specializing more and more. We, as partners, are responsible for everything that goes on with the client; we have to be broad in *all* areas, including the new ones of management services.

Also, inherent in bigness is less concern with regulation and enforcement of rules that are external to the firm. The largest firms are less susceptible to the wills of clients and can be more objective in their work. First, they *have* to be, because they are pressured by stockholders and other interested parties. Second,

21. Alvin W. Gouldner, "Organizational Analysis," in *Sociology Today: Problems and Prospects,* ed. Robert K. Merton, Leonard Broom, and Leonard S. Cottrell, Jr., (New York: Basic Books, 1959), p. 403.

22. Smigel, *The Wall Street Lawyer,* p. 250.

they can *afford* to be—loss of a client because of the firm's strict adherence to ethical codes does not endanger the life of the large firm; also, the costs of suits by clients or third parties can be more easily absorbed by the largest firms.

Another advantage of larger size that was mentioned often was that it allows the firm to give more attention to its younger people through formal training programs.[23] As one audit supervisor mentioned, this training helps the individual to grow in professional competence, enabling him to assume greater responsibility, and it "accomplishes the [administrative] task of weeding out individuals without this ability."

On the problem of impersonality, several partners did not feel that relations between hierarchical levels were adversely affected because of increased size. One noted that "in the old days the partners were more formal and aloof to begin with, so the situation really isn't much different." To combat the problems of personal communications due to bigness, several Big Eight firms have instituted an open-door policy or a first-name policy between staff and partners. A partner of a medium-sized firm explained that things were no better in the smaller firms: "The average junior here feels the way he does with the big firm, regarding separation from partners. He may be even better off with the big firm than with us even though we have the same benefits as the big boys, because in the big firms there's more time for socializing."

Size offers all the advantages afforded by specialization. The largest accounting firms have a greater division of labor than the medium-sized ones. There are more specialty fields and, as a result, more committees and subcommittees to house them. Any Big Eight firm would list around twenty committees of audit specialization, covering all the major areas of corporate business, small business, government agency examinations, and nonprofit organizations. Each of the other two areas—taxes and management services—would have its own committees or specialists represented on the audit committees. A typical Big Eight specialties list might include:

Acquisitions & Mergers	Investment Trusts
Associations	Machinery
Banks	Mining
Chemicals	Petroleum
Cooperatives	Pharmaceuticals
Educational Institutions	Public Utilities
Electronic Equipment	Publishing
Foodstuffs	Railroads

23. In their accidental sample of accounting firms, Robert H. Roy and James H. MacNeill, *Horizons for a Profession* (New York: AICPA, 1967), p. 160 reported that some form of internal program for staff training was administered in 20 percent of those firms of size 2 to 5; 48 percent of those firms of size 6 to 15; 74 percent of those firms of size 16 to 35; and 95 percent of those firms of size 36 and over.

Hospitals	Small Businesses
Insurance	Steel
Internal Control Systems	Textiles
International Accounting	Transportation

Where a Big Eight firm would have a committee for a particular industry group, a medium-sized firm would have one individual. In some specialties the medium-sized firm would have no one at all; instead it would concentrate its efforts on only the major industry groups. A Big Eight firm that does the auditing for a large number of clients classified under one of these specialty groups might break down the specialization even further. For example, "Metals" might include committees on the steel industry, the copper industry, and several others. Or, "Transportation" might be separated into railroads, pipelines, airlines, waterways, and highways, if the number of clients warranted it. Besides these committees, there is the executive group, which decides which specialists will serve which clients. Specific problems that may arise are directed to the proper departments. As one Big Eight firm's information booklet for clients states:

> Depending on the nature of the problem, this might be someone from our accounting and auditing staff experienced in a particular industry. . . . a tax man especially skilled in some complex aspect of income, estate, or foreign taxes . . . or any cne of a wide range of specialists in our management services division. . . .

These are many good reasons why it is well for a prospective client to choose one of the largest accounting firms as an auditor. They have the experts in the many areas that relate to finance, accounting, and administration. It is even more important that one choose a large (a Big Eight or a medium-sized) firm that is familiar with a specific industry. If a large merchandiser should decide that he was going to compete with the biggest firms in his field, he would certainly include Touche Ross among the list of auditors to be considered. That firm audits many of the largest merchandising firms, including Macy's and Gimbels, the two largest. The auditor's knowledge of special cost savings, which is the result of his long and concentrated auditing experience, would be invaluable. That the auditor can maintain a satisfactory level of client confidence even when auditing competitors is evidenced by the great number of competing enterprises that are audited by the same accounting firm, as is the case with the merchandisers mentioned.

Of course, this can and does become a situation where specialization breeds specialization, because as the auditor becomes better known for his specialties, more work in those areas comes to him. In one case, that of Allied Stores, a special committee of a board of directors was engaged to select auditors for its corporation. After extensive study, the committee chose to change auditors from one Big Eight firm to another, primarily because one of the chosen firm's industry specialties matched that of the corporation. The chairman of this committee reported that the committee

> made a very thorough study of all of the audit firms of the size and nature capable of handling a company of our size and composition and complexity, and studies Ernst & Ernst and Touche, Ross, and a number of others, ... analyzed them in terms of the ... background of the various firms, ... in terms of the specialty functions that are available to meet the special need of ours, such as this accounts receivable financing we have been talking about and other ... specialty functions, and ... came to the conclusion ... that the best firm ... in the interest of the Company and its stockholders, was Touche, Ross. ...

> Questioner: Well, I wouldn't say that Ernst & Ernst was a small firm incapable of doing this work which it has done for years.

> Chairman: Nor I.

> Questioner: And secondly, were there any differences [of opinion between Allied and Ernst & Ernst] which existed which in any way brought this situation about?

> Chairman: None whatsoever.[24]

What about the accountant in the medium-sized firm? Where does he get his business and how does he keep it? Does he specialize? How does he compete with the giant firms? The answers were not long in coming from senior partners of medium-sized firms. One commented:

> The middle-sized client is our mainstay. We do more than an audit for them. To give business advice to these clients who have little or no accounting personnel is our job.

> The public accounting profession is divided into two professions, the national firms give the audit, tax advice, and management services. They have the mid- to large-sized clients who have professional accountants inside their organizations. Also, in many cases the large CPA firm will take only certified audits. The other profession is the small firm which serves as an itinerant controller. The small client wants somebody over and above the audit. They want somebody who they can call for advice. Peat Marwick would not even consider taking a client to a bank to obtain a loan. But this is an expected and accepted part of our service.

Another senior partner listed the differences between large and small firms by number, as:

> 1. They've got the clients; we've got to go out and get them.

24. Lewis D. and John J. Gilbert, *Twenty-Sixth Annual Report of Stockholder Activities at Corporation Meetings During 1965* (New York: L. D. and J. J. Gilbert, 1966), pp. 253-254.

2. We have different backgrounds, ethnically and economically.

3. We do the detail work and we have all along. We learned the feeling for the little numbers. The big thing is the mass of little things. The big firms start at the top and work down. We work from the bottom up, from the small things to the big things. In the case of materiality, the small bits are immaterial, but put together they become material. With us, you're guilty until proven innocent.

4. We're hard-driving, tense, nervous workers. The men in the big firms are more leisurely in their day. One time, we—myself and the head of another medium firm—went to a committee meeting of the AICPA to try to resolve an issue. The big-firm men were all leaving by 5 P.M. the latest, to catch their trains to the suburbs. When my friend and I were practically the only ones left we took a taxi back to our offices for more work.

Another senior partner listed reasons for advantages of the local or regional firm over the largest firms in a speech before a state society of CPAs:[25]

1. Close personal partner contact with clients.

2. Clients of a size that are generally without in-house specialists either in the management services or the tax areas [are better served by the local or regional firm].

3. Better possibilities for communication both within and outside the firm.

4. Less turnover of recruits—40 percent of Big Eight recruits are not there after five years.

5. Flexibility of operation—the bigger you get the harder it is to change—and therefore [you have] less ability to plan effectively for the future.

In order to combat such disadvantages, several of the Big Eight have concentrated on developing local-office autonomy and personal autonomy. The "home" or "executive" office gives only general direction and policy to each local office; daily administration is the complete responsibility of each office. A partner is assigned full and final responsibility for the client. His work is reviewed, but usually not thoroughly until after the opinion for his client has been issued.

Specialization in the Big Eight, then, does have its brighter sides. As one audit senior commented when asked why his firm competed effectively: "Size itself. By that I mean the efficiency which size creates in terms of specialty." Size allows for specialization into committees within and outside the firm. These committees are the focus for much creative activity for personnel, and they

---

25. George S. Olive, Jr., "The CPA Firm of the Future," speech before the Minnesota Society of CPAs, September 28, 1965.

allow for expression of individual interests. Specialization carries far in public relations—committee work and representation is one of the few ways that a firm can publicize its expertise. To give added impetus, some firms offer cash awards of several hundred dollars for the better articles and speeches. Specialists in the various industry groups provide an efficiency of operation that only large organizations can offer.

Even with all the emphasis on specialization, a breakdown of how the Big Eight accountant spends his time does not show any overall extreme development. As table 11 indicates, the most specialized area is management services; almost a third of those who devote time to that area do so nearly full-time. And unlike the majority of the staff, very few persons spend only a moderate amount of time in management services, a clear sign of a higher degree of specialization.

An important generalization from this table is that despite the large number of specialties and the high division of labor, the Big Eight are only moderately specialized for the size of their firms. Their ability to spend most of their time in professional work is combined with both the desire and the necessity to remain "generalists" in their work. This is necessary because of the large number and different sizes of clients served by the audit teams. These groups are only temporary, and much shifting of personnel has to be done. At the same time, specialists must be available on demand, and they must be welded into an efficient unit on the job. A partner must have a wide background of experience in order to coordinate such efforts. This is desirable because they feel that job integration and enlargement is a distinct possibility in the profession. Some gave instances where this was already being practiced to a limited extent. The statement that "every man is a general partner" was continually repeated in Big Eight firms. It was seen as a responsibility of the partnership to its clients and to itself to gain the knowledge necessary for making the broad decisions required in today's complex economic institutions. The concept of a "total audit" or "operations audit," which integrates the tax and management-advising services into the annual audit, is being stressed by several firms. This enlargement of jobs and integration of services at the higher levels allows for increased specialization at lower levels. This is just the opposite of the logical conclusion that job enlargement is related in inverse proportion to job specialization. In an analysis of this relationship, Faunce specified that "the accessibility of larger amounts of more accurate information makes it possible to manage organizations of increasing size without increasing the differentiation of organizational structure."[26] This relationship is expected to occur in public accounting to the point where, with no change in size or with increasing size, entire levels of a firm will be eliminated due to increased accuracy and amounts of information. It is expected

26. William A. Faunce, "Automation and the Division of Labor," *Social Problems* 8:159 (Fall 1965).

TABLE 11

Degree of Specialization in Big Eight Firms (N=111)

Area of Work	% of Sample Working in Area	% of Firm Time Devoted to Area	Degree of Specialization of that Time by Tenths (in Percent)									
			100	90	80	70	60	50	40	30	20	10
Auditing	73	52	33	12	11	12	5	10	6	2	–	9
Taxes	48	18	23	8	2	–	2	–	1	–	15	49
Management Services	43	20	29	1	1	1	1	1	1	1	2	42
Administration	40	8	–	–	2	–	2	7	2	14	16	57
Other	17	2	–	–	–	–	–	–	5	–	21	74

that much of the "detail work" that is done today by the juniors and semi-seniors will be made obsolete by electronic data processing and will require the young accountant to handle the audit of whole systems. Junior and semi–senior levels will be gradually phased out by a combination of automation (allowing job enlargement) and job integration. The decrease in organizational complexity will at the same time ease the administrative task.

The efficiency inherent in specialization is powerful enough that many medium-sized accounting firms have found it in their interest to join into regional or national confederations in order to compete with the Big Eight in its nationwide services in audit, taxes, and management services, and in internal management areas such as job recruiting and training programs. Three confederations of smaller firms are now in existence: The American Group of CPA Firms, which was founded in 1963, with the joining of ten established regional firms, and is composed of a total of 83 partners; CPA Associates, which was founded in 1957, with the joining of 24 smaller firms from most parts of the U.S.; and a looser confederation formed in the mid 1950s, which is known as Group Ten. One drawback of confederations that is mentioned frequently is the lack of central control over all the firms in a confederation. This permits divergent opinions to sway operations enough so that firms do not coordinate and cooperate to the extent that is necessary in order to compete with the large firms. William Black, the recently retired senior partner of Peat Marwick, commented on the need for limited autonomy:

> ... in a CPA operation, like anything else, there inevitably has to be a single boss—someone to say that's the way we're going to go. In a confederation, all the firms have more or less equal status. There's no central authority usually to enforce the plan of operations.[27]

Consolidation is another alternative open to these smaller firms. This is the way many of the largest firms expanded.[28] It may be the way that several more firms will become giants of the profession, though they still have a long way to go. Because they have reached the saturation point in terms of representation, consolidations by national firms have been declining recently, whereas those by regional and local firms have been rising.

However, despite the smaller firms' concern about severe competition coming from the giant firms, they have effectively competed in at least one highly competitive area where interstate practice is not restricted. When examined, the

27. As quoted in an article in the *Wall Street Journal*, May 24, 1965.

28. For example, in 1962, Lybrand, Ross Bros. & Montgomery acquired Scovell Wellington & Company; this is believed to be the largest single merger in the history of the profession. This increased Lybrand by 29 partners in 12 U.S. cities. As a former part-time employee of the acquired firm, I also recall that the firm was international in its scope of operations. The particulars of the merger are reported in the *Lybrand Journal*, vol. 43, supplement no. 1 (1962).

offices of 61 local and 27 national firms in several metropolitan California areas revealed that the local firms are holding their own.[29]

Throughout these chapters, organizational factors of large accounting firms have been compared to those of large law firms in the study by Smigel. It is appropriate at this point to summarize the major similarities and differences between them. Table 12 does this, in each case giving reasons for the differences and the likenesses.

TABLE 12

Comparison of Organizational Features of the
Eight Largest Public Accounting Firms
and the Twenty Largest Law Firms

RECRUITMENT:

(a) Formal Education

Similarities: Only college graduates with high grade-point averages.

Differences: Law firms recruit from graduate professional schools only.

Reason Why: The largest firms of the two professions require top quality, well-trained people to instill confidence in their clients that the best experts are serving them. However, accounting has not established graduate professional schools in public accounting, so it must recruit from a broad selection of more than one hundred schools.

(b) Going Rate for Recruits

Similarities: Ll. B.—$9,000; M.A. in accounting—$8,000.

Reason Why: These are the highest offers in their respective fields, to draw the best graduates.

SIZE:

(a) Number of Personnel

Differences: Average law firm has a staff of 100. Average accounting firm has a staff of 1,500 people, increased to 3,000 nationally.

Reason Why: Public accounting is smaller in terms of number of licensed practitioners (90,000 as compared to 300,000 for lawyers) but is more centralized in terms of firms vs. individual practitioners and large firms vs. small firms. Also, the nature of their work (on-site observation of inventories, fixed assets, etc.) requires geographical diversity.

(b) Geographical Distribution

Differences: Accounting firms are national and international in location of offices. Law firms are limited to New York City.

Reason Why: Up to the decentralization of U.S. industry after World War II, the largest accounting firms and largest law firms differed little in size and geographical location. At that time a few from each profession had offices internationally. As

29. Reported by John L. Carey, ed., *The Accounting Profession: Where Is It Headed?* (New York: AICPA, 1962), pp. 132-133.

TABLE 12 (continued)

explained in (a) above, decentralization was a key factor in the growth of public accounting firms. However, the requirements for annual audit in an expanding economy were even more important factors for growth in accounting firms. With the secure base of an annual fee from clients in a local area, the branch office could search out private companies and individuals for audits and for tax and management services.

DIVISION OF LABOR:

(a) Job Segmentation

Similarities: A high degree of segmentation of lower levels of the firms.

Reason Why: The size of the client and the complexity of the engagement are such that the work must be partitioned and then later integrated by the partners.

(b) Job Specialization

Differences: Greater specialization by accounting firms.

Reason Why: Larger size allows it. Very important also is the solid base of the yearly audit. It provides a constancy and uniformity of practice in a firm over a wide area of accountancy. Practitioners are able to branch out into new services and to specialize in old services.

(c) Ratio of Professional Staff to Nonprofessional Staff

Differences: Law firms—40% professionals. Personnel agencies (Blau, Heydebrand, and Stauffer, "The Structure of Small Bureaucracies")—more than 40%. Accounting firms—80%.

Reason Why: The nature of the professional's work in large part determines the size of nonprofessional staff.

(d) Size of Administrative Component

Similarities: Law firms—10%. Accounting firms—12%.

Differences: In the spread of that administration.

Reason Why: As size continues to increase in professional organizations, the administrative component does not increase. Professional rules external to the firms in part delimit the need for increased administration. Much of the new routine and administration of rules in the Big Eight are handled by individual partners. Of Big Eight professionals, 40% devote some time to administration; only 4 percent devote more than 50% of their time to administration (see table 11). In the law firms, only the executive group is involved in administration.

Summary Theoretical Statement on Organizational Factors of Size and Division of Labor: In professional organizations size tends to be directly related to complexity and centralization of administration, and inversely related to size of administrative component.

(e) Hierarchy of Positions

Similarities and Differences:

Year	Law Firm	Accounting Firm
1		junior (All firms.
2	junior (only	Two firms have two levels
3	a few firms)	of juniors.)

113

TABLE 12 (continued)

Year	Law Firm	Accounting Firm
4	— — — — — — — — — — — — — — — — —	
5		senior
6	middle-range	— — — — — — — — — — —
7	associate	supervisor (Two firms
8	— — — — — — — — — — — — —	have this level.) — — —
9	senior associate	
10	— — — — — — — — — — — — —	manager
11	junior partner	
12		
13		— — — — — — — — —
14		partner
—		
—		
20	middle partner	
—		
27	senior partner	

Reason Why: In general, there are four major positions for both firms: (junior–junior) (middle–range associate–senior) (senior associate–manager) (partner–partner). In the law firms, partnership is made at 10 years, as opposed to 14 for the accounting firms. However, some managers are equal to junior partners of law firms in terms of responsibility delegated to them and in terms of status and earnings.

Only 10% of professionals in accounting firms are partners, compared to 31% for law firms. Again, the junior partner-manager similarity accounts for part of this. But the major reason is centralization of functions in the accounting firms. They are much larger and more bureaucratized in terms of internal rules, and administrative and technical decision-making is centralized. That is, it is more authoritarian vs. the more democratic process of law firms at their top level. Small group experiments have pointed to the increased efficiency of authoritarian-type decision processes, in terms of quantitative productivity.

FORMAL ORGANIZATION:

(a) Work Organization with Client

Similarities: A simple team system with supporting "services" departments of specialists.

Reason Why: This provides a more personalized relationship with the client. Also, assignment to several different types of clients gives breadth of experience to the individual.

(b) Executive Group

Differences: For the smaller law firms, there is a governing coalition (Smigel, *The Wall Street Lawyer*, pp. 236-238). For accounting firms, there is a leader (the senior partner) of the executive group.

Reason Why: The smaller of the large law firms have a more loosely structured internal hierarchy at the top. The firm is run by a coalition of powerful individuals (members of the executive group), each of whom is there by virtue of the power he controls. In the accounting firms, the power is institutionalized into positions at these highest levels, including that of "president," the senior partner.

114

TABLE 12 (continued)

(c) Turnover per year

Differences: Law firms—about 10% turnover. Accounting firms—20% turnover, with a range from 15% to 40% through the eight firms.

Reason Why: The high degree of competitiveness of the up-or-out policy of promotion. Also the enticing positions offered by private industry (usually a client), which offer more security at earlier stages of the career.

FORMAL EXTERNAL PROFESSIONAL RULES:

(a) Code of Ethics

Similarities: Both professions have a well-developed code.

Differences: The legal code carries heavier sanctions for deviants.

Reason Why: Legal proceedings generally have more direct bearing on the general public than those of public accounting. However, public accounting is now entering a period of intense public exposure and may also receive (or may itself develop) heavier regulation and stiffer penalties in its codes. Membership in professional organization (60% of 90,000 for AICPA; 40% of 300,000 for ABA) may be one indication of interest in the development of the profession by its members. The legal profession is established. Public accounting is not as well established.

(b) Who Determines Which Laws and Methods for Applying the Body of Knowledge

Similarities: They are determined external to the practitioners, for the most part. Law is based on court precedent. Accounting methods are based on general acceptance, as determined by the SEC, the practices of business entities, AICPA committees, and CPA literature.

Reason Why: This limits the legal responsibility and accountability of the professional.

Because the accounting firms are larger, they are an answer to what the law firms and other large professional organizations might expect with increasing size and specialization. The pattern of professional bureaucracy could be shifted by the effects of increased size, thereby lessening the importance of external professional rules. Of course, the universality of the degree of adherence to the codes of the profession would affect this pattern. Also, the work of a profession may be peculiar enough to affect the pattern. The nature of their work keeps CPAs in small groups, which creates little need for a complex system of internal administration. This tends to compensate for the more complicated set of administrative rules needed to cover a large number of unrelated specialties over a wide geographic area.

SUMMARY

The first hypothesis has been explained in a discussion of the types of rules governing the large accounting firms—formal and informal rules, and external and internal rules, as well as their relationship to one another in these expanding professional organizations. To the extent that they replace internal rules of the firms and the administrators of them, external rules reduce the bureaucracy of formalism, ritualism, and routine. Changes that affect the pattern of professional bureaucracy, such as new professional functions and size of firm, influence the degree of professionalization in public accounting, because they affect and are affected by the attributes of a profession.

As depicted in table 11, administration has not become a specialized function in these firms. Rules external to the firm play a large enough role in guiding professional behavior, and professionals are able to share the load in the tangential work of administration. This minimizes the impact of administration on the organization of the firm without disregarding its importance. At the present time, Keller's speculation that "the larger the size the larger *should be* the administrative component,"[30] does not hold for the large public accounting firms. These firms have to, and they can afford to, follow rules that are external to their firms; they have little need for the elaborate and rigid system of internal rules that exists in a nonprofessional organization of comparable size. But with increasing size, internal rules begin to be stressed more; and with increasing non-CPA professionals in proportion to CPAs, authority for rule enforcement changes from an external to an internal source. The importance of external rules begins to decrease and a punishment-centered pattern of bureaucracy fills the gap.

What may lie in the future for these firms one cannot determine by unilinearly extending present trends of size and organization. In the words of one Big Eight managing partner: "If, fifteen years ago, my predecessor was asked if his office would be able to expand to today's size, he would have believed it impossible. And, if somebody could tell me the size of this office fifteen years from now, I'd probably say the same thing."

30. Keller, *Beyond the Ruling Class*, p. 86.

6

Power and The Dynamics of Organizational Change

THE DYNAMICS OF BUREAUCRATIC ORGANIZATIONS

The extreme rationalization created by the bureaucratic form of organization results in a high degree of predictability of the system of action within its direct sphere of influence. Yet, no matter how bureaucratic the organization, there remain areas of uncertainty, areas as yet unnoticed or too difficult for bureaucratization. These are areas where influence of an individual or group within the organization can be expanded, because control over the source of uncertainty means control over all positions affected by this uncertainty. The attainment of power over others resulting from control over uncertainty is accomplished in part by risk-taking. The power of a group (or subgroup, segment, or individual) wanes when the group's source of uncertainty has been rationalized (bureaucratized, that is, increasing the extent of the characteristics of bureaucracy), especially with regard to the amount, specificity, and extent of rules. In order to gain new power to replace this lost power, a group will demand change, which brings new sources of uncertainty. Groups are reciprocally dependent on power relations, power being ever-present in the organization because of "the impossibility of eliminating uncertainty in the context of bounded rationality which is ours."[1] The mobilization of power is central to the bureaucratic organization,[2] and the exercise of that power begets conflict and change.[3] Care must be taken that too much or too little uncertainty (through change) is not generated in the social system. The former would result in situations too unpredictable for

---

1. Major parts of this theory have been culled from a book by Michel Crozier, *The Bureaucratic Phenomenon* (Chicago: The University of Chicago Press, 1964). The quote is found on page 158. The statement concerning risk-taking stems from a discussion by Frank H. Knight, *Risk, Uncertainty and Profit* (Boston: Houghton Mifflin, 1933), especially pp. 238-239, and Peter M. Blau, *Exchange and Power in Social Life* (New York: Wiley, 1964), pp. 135-137.

2. Talcott Parsons, *Structure and Process in Modern Societies* (New York: The Free Press, 1960), p. 41; S. Eisenstadt, "Bureaucracy and Bureaucratization," *Current Sociology* 7:111 (1958).

3. See the Introduction by Robert L. Kahn in *Power and Conflict in Organizations*, ed. Robert L. Kahn and Elise Boulding (New York: Basic Books, 1964), especially pp. 1-3.

risk-taking, thus leading to increasing conformity and rigidity and loss of flexibility; the latter would result in situations of detailed rules and consequent rigidity.[4]

This theoretical statement integrates my two hypotheses. The second hypothesis will be evaluated as part of the testing of the entire theory in chapters 7 through 10. Before going ahead, it is necessary to review and analyze concepts that touch directly on the theory. This will define its bases and serve as a conceptual framework for discussion.

POWER, DECISION-MAKING, AUTHORITY, RESPONSIBILITY

Power is a form of influence that produces intended effects on other men.[5] The individual or group recurrently affects the situation in order to "change the probabilities that others will respond in certain ways to specified stimuli."[6] As related to the theory of uncertainty in bureaucratic organizations, "people have power over other people insofar as the latter's behavior is narrowly limited by rules whereas their own behavior is not."[7]

Power is exercised through decision-making. Decision-making is the group's or the individual's selecting what it (he) considers to be the best course of action from among a number of alternatives after determining consequences of these alternatives. The exercising of choice (selection) is not action,[8] but it constitutes the impetus behind the action. The origin of action is choice. This choice can be rational or irrational. It affects or can be affected by coercion, inducement, and constraint.[9] The standards for making selections in order to reach satisfactory solutions are cultural elements of an object, or values.[10] The complexity of the

4. Crozier, *The Bureaucratic Phenomenon,* p. 186. An interesting biological analogy is made by G. Ledyard Stebbins, "Pitfalls and Guideposts in Comparing Organic and Social Evolution," *Pacific Sociological Review* 8:9 (Spring 1965), in discussing the effect of rules on the cultural system.

5. Bertrand Russell, *Power: A New Social Analysis* (New York: W. W. Norton, 1938), p. 35. The restriction to the human species is made by Dennis H. Wrong in lectures at New York University in February 1964.

6. The quote is from Abraham Kaplan, "Power in Perspective," in *Power and Conflict in Organizations,* ed. Kahn and Boulding, p. 12. "Recurrence" is emphasized by Talcott Parsons, "On the Concept of Political Power," *Proceedings of the American Philosophical Society* 107:237-238 (June 1963).

7. Crozier, *The Bureaucratic Phenomenon,* p. 158.

8. Joseph Frankel, "Towards a Decision-Making Model in Foreign Policy," *Political Studies* 7:1-2 (February 1959).

9. The relation of power to coercion, inducement, and constraint is analyzed by Harold D. Lasswell and Abraham Kaplan, *Power and Society* (New Haven: Yale University Press, 1950), pp. 97-99, 201.

10. Talcott Parsons, *The Social System* (New York: The Free Press, 1951), pp. 12, 14.

decision-making process becomes apparent when it is realized that not only do values influence choice,[11] but that choice influences values as well. A certain choice will lead to internalization of specific values, attitudes, and behavioral patterns.[12]

The process of decision-making encounters semantic difficulties, because so many words are used interchangeably to describe it—decision, choice, selection, judgment. In order to distinguish between these terms, the word "decisioning" will be used to describe the interaction between prior values and choices before the final moment when a selection (synonymous with choice and decision) is made among alternatives of action.[13] Judgment is choosing when there is only a small amount of knowledge of the alternatives available.[14] The gaps in knowledge are filled by making assumptions concerning past, present, and future events, based on value standards. These are the areas of uncertainty (lack of knowledge) that are attacked by the individual or group. It is the man whose value standards fit with his group (or client) and the application of which brings the group wealth, prestige, or power who is considered to have good judgment, or wisdom. Because there is no "perfect" certainty, a choice is always in part the result of judgment. The amount of judgment in decisioning will depend on the amount of knowledge available for the particular problem to be solved.

The entire process of decisioning and choice constitutes the process known as decision-making. Decisioning and choosing can take place on many levels. What is a choice at one level will be only a small part of the decisioning at another more general level, where many choices of several groups will be involved in making a single choice.

Power that is formalized is authority.[15] This formalization is accomplished

11. Clyde Kluckhohn et al., "Values and Value-Orientations in the Theory of Action: An Exploration in Definition and Classification," in *Toward a General Theory of Action*, ed. Talcott Parsons and Edward A. Shils (Cambridge: Harvard University Press, 1951), p. 395.

12. Morris Rosenberg, *Occupations and Values* (New York: The Free Press, 1957), p. 7. The author discusses the influence of values on choice (and vice versa) and anticipatory socialization.

13. The term "decisioning" and parts of its definition are taken from Craig C. Lundberg, "Administrative Decision: A Scheme for Analysis," *Journal of the Academy of Management* 5:169 (August 1962). The term is synomymous with what Chester Barnard called the "processes of decision" in his *The Functions of the Executive* (Cambridge: Harvard University Press, 1938), p. 14.

14. "Conscious" judgment is the meeting of uncertainty, the exercise of responsibility. Knight, *Risk, Uncertainty and Profit*, pp. 294-295. For a discussion of judgment, see also C. West Churchman, *Prediction and Optimal Decision: Philosophical Issues of a Science of Values* (Englewood Cliffs, N.J.: Prentice-Hall, 1961), p. 293.

15. Lasswell and Kaplan, *Power and Society*, p. 133; Robert Bierstedt, "An Analysis of Social Power," *American Sociological Review* 15:733 (December 1950); Parsons, *Structure and Process*, pp. 39, 197.

by legitimation, "the appraisal of action in terms of shared or common values."[16] Those in positions of authority assume responsibility, "the formal commitment to practices in behalf of specified interests."[17] One in a position of responsibility is trusted and held accountable for the consequences of his judgment and choice.[18] Authority is itself a source of power,[19] because those in positions of authority assign responsibility. They have power over others, because they control and apportion areas of uncertainty in which risk-taking is involved. This apportionment can filter down through the various levels of an organization, because responsibility for uncertainty is not confined only to the top of organizations but exists throughout their hierarchies.[20] A new form of accounting, responsibility accounting, recognizes this concept and is organized around it. The "accountability" nature of responsibility accentuates the partial dependence of those who are in authority to those who are administered. This point is emphasized by nearly all students of political science. Gross, in particular, points to the reciprocal triangular relationship between power, authority, and responsibility.[21]

CERTAINTY, RISK, UNCERTAINTY, AND RATIONALITY

Central to the theory of the dynamics of bureaucratic organization is the uncertainty produced in social interaction. A concentrated but uncoordinated effort has been made by economists, mathematicians, statisticians, and psychologists, and in a few cases by sociologists and students of administrative science, to simulate uncertainty in bureaucracy, thus making it "certain."[22] Researchers have constructed static models of rational behavior, defending them as the only

16. Parsons, *Structure and Process,* p. 175.

17. Lasswell and Kaplan, *Power and Society,* p. 161.

18. Responsibility means accountability, says Robert T. Harris, *Social Ethics* (Philadelphia: Lippincott, 1962), as quoted by John L. Carey, *The CPA Plans for the Future* (New York: AICPA, 1965), p. 18. The relationship of accountability to choice and judgment is made by E. T. Hiller, *Social Relations and Structures* (New York: Harper & Bros., 1947), p. 366.

19. Blau, *Exchange and Power in Social Life,* p. 211.

20. Ibid., p. 219. "Risk is an essential element in responsibility, that is, assuming responsibilities entails making decisions whose outcome is uncertain" (p. 218). "The individual's ability to stand uncertainty for extended periods of time governs the level of responsibility he can easily assume" (p. 217).

21. Bertrand Gross, *The Managing of Organizations,* 2 Vols. (New York: The Free Press, 1964), 1:280-302.

22. A summary of some of these areas is found in John R. Raser, *Simulation and Society* (Boston: Allyn and Bacon, 1969).

logical and feasible move before attempting to build a dynamic model incorporating nonrational behavior.[23] The static model presents the normative choices made in decision-making, that is, what should be or ought to be. Preferences from among alternatives from which a choice is made are consistent, because the consequences of each possible choice are known by the decision-maker, and he will choose according to the utility of the consequence. Past experience and expectations of future action are considered in the process. The decision-maker "maximizes expected utility" by choosing the alternative that has a utility "larger" than all others. The mathematical model of this theory, known as game theory, assumes that the utilities of all consequences can be placed on a cardinal scale. There is an "as if" determinism: "Given that a subject's preferences can be represented by a linear utility function, then *he behaves as if he were a maximizer of expected values of utility.*"[24]

On this basis, decision-making occurs in three different situations: (1) *Certainty:* the consequence of each action is known; (2) *risk:* the probability distribution of possible consequences of each action is known; (3) *uncertainty:* the probability distribution of possible consequences is unknown or not meaningful.[25]

More recently, the question of emotions and irrational behavior has stimulated further examination of the model so as to include in it the concept of subjective probability, essentially a combination of risk and uncertainty. Rough probability estimates are given to situations of uncertainty because the judgment inherent in uncertain situations is not as arbitrary or as free as it seems.[26] To get away from the static model of perfect rationality, the notion of "stochastic transitivity" is invoked.[27] Basically, this is a model of irrational behavior, for example, boredom or playfulness, where irrationality does not usually completely cancel an individual's choice but only alters it. For example, some events may

23. John von Neumann and Oskar Morgenstern, *Theory of Games and Economic Behavior* 3d ed.; Princeton, N.J.: Princeton University Press, 1953), p. 44; R. Duncan Luce and Howard Raiffa, *Games and Decisions* (New York: Wiley, 1957), p. 7.

24. Luce and Raiffa, *Games and Decisions*, p. 31.

25. Ibid., p. 13.

26. *Foundations of Statistical Inference*, a discussion opened by Leonard J. Savage at a meeting of the Joint Statistics Seminar, Birkbeck and Imperial Colleges, in the University of London (London: Methuen & Co., Ltd; and New York: Wiley, 1962), pp. 9-10. Yet Savage warns that all probabilities are to some extent metaphysical and that "the theory of subjective probability describes ideally consistent behavior and ought not, therefore, to be taken too literally" (pp. 62-70). The same qualification is presented by Luce and Raiffa, *Games and Decisions*, app. 1, "A Probabilistic Theory of Utility," especially pp. 372-373. See also the summary of John Cohen, *Behavior in Uncertainty* (London: George Allen & Unwin, 1964), chap. 7.

27. Robert P. Abelson, "The Choice of Choice Theories," in *Decision and Choice: Contributions of Sidney Siegel,* ed. Samuel Messick and Arthur H. Brayfield (New York: McGraw-Hill, 1964), p. 259.

create an increase or decrease of a person's economic power on the market, but he will still have more or fewer alternatives of choice available; his dollar always counts. But in a collectivity, a vote does not contribute to a choice if it is cast in favor of the minority representative. Here, irrationality (the minority voter is considered irrational by the majority) negates stochastic choice—the "solution for response probability" is either one or zero.[28] This is one striking example of the differences between individual and group decision-making that prevents a direct transplant of some psychological findings to sociology and vice versa.

Another unusual interpretation of the decision-making process is offered by the British economist George Shackle, who makes a distinction between "distributional uncertainty" (probability) and "nondistributional uncertainty" (judgment of possibilities).[29] He contends that we cannot assume, as Descartes did, that the individual would put off making a decision until all necessary evidence was collected, nor can we substitute Laplacian or Von Misean probability in place of the missing evidence. Instead, available ends are not given but created. Probability becomes, in principle, inappropriate. Instead, a possibility estimate is made by the decision-maker in which he keeps in focus only the extremes of the alternatives of choices of ends (the extent of these extremes depending on his knowledge and imagination). This provides him with an orderly environment. The nonrepeatable, unitary decision, which is common to the business world, limits the decision-maker to the use of subjective probability. In making a judgment, there are degrees of possibility (surprise) ranging from perfect possibility (no surprise) to impossibility (maximum surprise). Thus, what is "right" (probability of one) is completely different in meaning from what has no surprise (possibility of one).[30]

Shackle's theory has been strongly criticized for its emphasis on subjectivity; but along with other theories, it has helped to stimulate further thought on the theory of probability and prediction of action in the social sciences. The whole question of certainty in scientific prediction is raised in this issue; it occupies a large area of the philosophy of science. One of the major concerns in this area is that dealing with the relationship of science to certainty.[31]

28. Stochastic choice allows the response probability to be something other than zero or one. Ibid., p. 269. The example of voting choice is discussed by Bruce Leoni, "The Meaning of 'Political' in Political Decisions," *Political Studies* 5:236 (October 1957).

29. G. L. S. Shackle, *Decision Order and Time in Human Affairs* (Cambridge, England: Cambridge University Press, 1961), p. 47. Essentially the same breakdown is given by Knight, *Risk, Uncertainty and Profit*, pp. 233-235.

30. Shackle's view is largely existentialist. His "solitary moment" of the present resembles the "discontinuous ranges of separately identifiable qualities of surprise" of J. W. N. Watkins, "Decisions and Uncertainty," in *Uncertainty and Business Decisions,* ed. C. F. Carter, G. P. Meredith, and G. L. S. Shackle (Liverpool, England: Liverpool University Press, 1957), pp. 120-121.

31. An excellent summary, with a slightly different emphasis from the one presented here, is given by John R. Raser, *Simulation and Society.*

Certain conclusions can be drawn from the discussion thus far and from philosophical arguments pertaining to it. I have noted that the constructing of theory (much of which involves prediction) involves both probability, on the basis of previous observation, and possibility, on the basis of expectations. Hence a certain degree of uncertainty is present; the more comprehensive the theory, the more the uncertainty and the more the risk (in the sense of the number of chances of being refuted) involved as to the truth of the theory. Yet "if it takes no such risks, its scientific content is zero—it has no scientific content, it is metaphysical."[32]

Perfect certainty is unattainable in the world of empirical knowledge.[33] "It does not follow that for a fact to be known it must be such that no one could be mistaken about it or such that it could not have been otherwise."[34] Yet, there can be no science without faith that nature is subject to law.[35] These laws, governed by the principle of probability, will never measure "absolute" certainty but will only give degrees of security.[36] Thus, our knowledge of reality is what is referred to by the "many highly inferential concepts of the sciences;"[37] it is culturally determined.

The norms of social organization also attempt to impress uniformity of behavior on its members. But in addition to operating so as to attain a degree of predictability, rules of social life are teleological in that they have the purpose of maximizing expected utility as any particular group defines utility. Unfortunately, game theory ignores the limitations of the knowledge of available alternatives and power plays that are brought about by social factors. We are not informed whether *"all* possible consequences" is intended for the model of rational behavior, or just "possible consequences." As March and Simon have noted,

32. Karl R. Popper, *Conjectures and Refutations* (New York: Basic Books, 1962), p. 334.

33. The phrase "perfect certainty" is logically tautological. Certainty is "perfect." Some scientists do use the phrase, however, to identify logical, nonrefutable, a priori, ideal-type certainty from its empirical meaning.

34. A. J. Ayer, *The Problem of Knowledge* (Baltimore: Pelican Books, 1956), p. 25.

35. Norbert Wiener, *The Human Use of Human Beings* (Boston: Houghton Mifflin, 1950), p. 193.

36. John Dewey, *The Quest for Certainty* (New York: Minton, Balch & Co., 1929). p. 290.

37. Herbert Feigl, "Philosophy of Science," in *Philosophy* (Englewood Cliffs, N.J.: Prentice-Hall, 1964), p. 530. Graham Wallas, *Social Judgment* (New York: Harcourt, Brace, 1935), p. 30, comments that our descriptions of reality are warped by our artificial models of them, but social judgment attempts to fill this gap.

models that do limit the extent of rational behavior have already been introduced.[38] And, one sociologist has suggested three kinds of uncertainty in the context of an analysis of medical students: first, limitations in the body of knowledge (perfect certainty cannot be attained); second, incomplete or imperfect mastery of available knowledge; third, the difficulty in distinguishing between the first two.[39]

We might view this perspective on a continuum of information. Perfect information is certainty, predictability, and it implies control of the future. The other end of the continuum is the lack of any information—that is, uncertainty, chaos, or entropy.[40] Those areas in between include subjective probability and risk, the former being closer to uncertainty, the latter to certainty. More simply, the greater the certainty, the less probability is involved, and vice versa.[41] Even the difference between the objective and subjective worlds has become fused together with the advent of modern probability theory.[42] The "subjective value of the expected outcome" is also considered in the total estimate of probability.[43] There is confusion in the use of the terms "risk" and "uncertainty" here. Actually, on the continuum most real situations are situations of imperfect information that require risk-taking, situations of dealing with the unknown, including the areas of subjective uncertainty. Therefore, to distinguish between the two terms: risk is choosing on the part of individuals or groups; it is always tied to social structure and process. Uncertainty is an analytic concept describing areas of lack of knowledge of the social and physical environment.

This continuum of uncertainty from least certain to most certain is inherent in the work of many earlier writers. Barnard categorized classes of material that

38. James G. March and Herbert A. Simon, *Organizations* (New York: Wiley, 1958), p. 169. The serious drawbacks of "gaming" as simulation are listed by Raser, *Simulation and Society*. Criticisms are found throughout the social-science literature and are too numerous to mention here.

39. Renée C. Fox, "Training for Uncertainty," in *The Student Physician*, ed. Robert K. Merton, George G. Reader, and Patricia L. Kendall (Cambridge, Mass.: Harvard University Press, 1957), p. 208.

40. Raser, *Simulation and Society*, p. 20. The comment on control is made by Rudolph E. Hirsch, "The Value of Information," *Journal of Accountancy* 125:41 (June 1968).

41. This arrangement of probability on a continuum is hinted at by reviewers of the literature: Ward Edwards, "The Theory of Decision-Making," *Psychological Bulletin* 51:391 (1954); Lucien Foldes, "Uncertainty, Probability and Potential Surprise," *Economica* 25:254 (August 1958).

42. Pitirim A. Sorokin, *Fads and Foibles in Modern Sociology and Related Sciences* (Chicago: Regnery, 1956), p. 295. One accountant-author theorized that cycles or periods of subjective and then objective civilization evolve through history, bearing some resemblance to Sorokin's irregular fluctuations of ideational and sensate cultures. See DR Scott, *The Cultural Significance of Accounts* (New York: Henry Holt & Co., 1931).

43. Considered nonlinear in relation to the estimate of (objective) probability by Charles Wilson and Marcus Alexis, "Basic Frameworks for Decision," *Journal of the Academy of Management* 5:150-164 (August 1962).

the mind works with, going from "precise information" to "hybrid material" to "speculative material," and corresponding to the occupations of appellate lawyer, accountant, and politician, respectively.[44] Drucker related uncertainty specifically to cost accounting, listing four stages of uncertainty from most certain (replacement, obsolescence) to least certain (risk proper, uncertainty).[45] The senior partner of one Big Eight firm utilizes uncertainty implicitly in describing the accrual basis of accounting:

> Judgments as to accountability of . . . risks (and uncertainties) must be made. . . . The method has as its central objective the transferring or apportioning of the financial effect of transactions and events from the period in which they occur to the period or periods to which they may be appropriately related. It attempts to match revenues with related costs where a physical relationship is identifiable and to establish a logical, systematic, and objective method of apportionment where the direct connection cannot be established.

The "cost recovery accounting approach" is used where risks and uncertainties of the future are so high that corporate income is applied to reduce the investment cost at least to its minimum salvage value.[46]

More recently, the principles of information theory were used to analyze the general accounting process. Using the concept of "uncertainty reduction," Lee and Bedford state that "the amount of information from an accounting measurement of a single economic event is a function of an observer's subjective probability distribution as to the magnitude of the event's effect."[47] Where the specific event is to be placed on a continuum of information will depend to some extent on the amount of rationality exercised by the group.

A bureaucracy reacts to phenomena of potential power by attempting to rationalize it. This is a quest for certainty or power. As Aron has said, "The rationality of knowledge makes for greater power."[48] He should have added "for those who are in control of that knowledge." And the scientific method is the most successful technique for gaining that knowledge from areas of uncertainty.[49] An extremely rational organization (or a highly organized occupation)

44. Barnard, *Functions of the Executive*, pp. 309-320.

45. Peter F. Drucker, *The New Society* (New York: Harper & Bros., 1950), pp. 52-59.

46. Herman W. Bevis, *Corporate Financial Reporting in a Competitive Economy* (New York: Macmillan, 1965), p. 35; the quote is on p. 31. Also by the same author, "Contingencies and Probabilities in Financial Statements," *Journal of Accountancy* 126:37-45 (October 1968).

47. Lucy C. Lee and Norton M. Bedford, "An Information Theory Analysis of the Accounting Process," *Accounting Review* 44:274 (April 1969).

48. Raymond Aron, *The Industrial Society* (New York: Simon & Schuster, 1967), p. 70.

49. Harold Sackman, *Computers, System Science and Evolving Society* (New York: John Wiley & Sons, Inc., 1967), p. 14.

would contain a complex system of rules to cover the multiplicity of uncertainties that it had experienced. This extreme rationalization, as our theory points out, results in the loss of power over the rationalized knowledge; in time it becomes part of the "public domain." Thus, new areas of uncertainty must be sought out and captured in order for the organization or occupation to maintain its power position relative to competing groups and collectivities.

Technical and organizational changes create ever-new areas of uncertainty. The risk-bearing entrepreneurs of the past—the Fords, Carnegies, Edisons, and so forth—are now the corporation, governmental, and university research complexes, pooling their knowledge to reduce uncertainty. However, many areas of risk and uncertainty remain, even for those who deal with the administrative element. The managements of large organizations deal mostly with people, not things; they are necessarily involved with change in programs, not with execution of them. Their aspirations are geared to and demand innovation.[50] Decisions have to be made with regard to recruitment; replacement of managerial positions; community relations; philanthropy; new technical inventions; company acquisitions, mergers, and consolidations; and the like. These decisions generally contain a great deal of uncertainty, and they require careful judgment —all in a highly bureaucratized structure. Public accountants, one among a number of types of experts that serve the managements of economic organizations, have traditionally concerned themselves with the check on the basic financial statements of these organizations. But within the last two decades, this tradition has changed as public accountants have expanded into many types of economic information services; this expansion is manifested in the growth of the functions of tax and management services. CPAs, especially those in large accounting firms, have come to assume several of the areas of managerial uncertainty within the orbit of their advisory capacity. The struggles within the profession to attain the power that lies in this uncertainty, and its meaning for the hypotheses, is taken up in chapter 7, which deals with accounting and auditing, and chapter 8, which covers management services. Also, the developing power struggle between public accounting and other professions for this uncertainty will be examined, utilizing the same theory of bureaucratic organizations.

Besides the sample interviews and questionnaires, a content analysis was performed[51] of the recent literature on the profession contained both in the major accounting journals and in books in order to uncover views and evidence

50. Herbert A. Simon, "The Role of Expectations in an Adaptive or Behavioristic Model," in *Expectations, Uncertainty, and Business Behavior,* ed. M. J. Bowman (New York: Social Science Research Council, 1958), p. 56.

51. Content categories are so broad as to preclude a purely quantified analysis. The general character of the information is the focus instead.

that both supports and refutes the theory. This examination encompasses four levels of analysis: (1) segments of public accounting (and its firms); (2) groups of firms (Big Eight versus medium-sized); (3) firms as a whole (versus firms as a whole of other professions); and (4) public accounting as a whole, compared to other professions. Information for the first three levels is derived mostly from the sample data; for the last level, from the accounting literature.

7

Uncertainty In Accounting

With regard to the body of knowledge in public accounting, members of the profession have generally taken opposing views, which are based on a division of strain found in all professions—that between the practical and the theoretical.[1] The ideological boundaries are clearly set and well recognized by those within the profession. To make a very broad generalization, the practitioner is the more conservative in viewpoint, less willing to accept rapid change, and more inclined to build his future on the inductive logic of experience. The theorist, on the other hand, is desirous of further developing an intellectual discipline by utilizing the deductive method of science on accounting events, inducing abrupt change onto accounting practice. As might be expected, very few members populate the extremes of these two positions. In their own formulations most members combine ideas that are representative of both sides.

But the ideologies are there. They extend to the professional associations,[2] and they can therefore be expected to influence the type of literature emanating from these sources. And, naturally, an ideology of practicality is found in the large firms—where, as one manager put it, "Decisions are made with a knowledge of firing-line business conditions, not with a pure or academic knowledge." Again, the lines between theorist and practitioner are hazy, and they are continually crossed; but the large-firm accountant necessarily is the practical realist like his client, the American businessman. He sees accounting as an art, and he sees himself as the artist shaping the financial picture.

AUDITING JUDGMENTS: THE QUESTION OF MATERIALITY

No two auditors will agree exactly on the monetary value of most items listed on the financial statements of a client. The latitude given to them in their work is allowed because it has to be allowed. Even if a fixed and unvarying value would be placed on physical goods, it would be impossible to know the exact status of these goods at most stages of their processing in an organization. Even when an unusually thorough examination of the accounts of any modern

1. The point of strain between the two is emphasized by Everett C. Hughes, "Professions," *Daedalus* 92:661 (Fall 1963).

2. Realizing their wide differences, Robert K. Mautz emphasizes some of the similarities of two major professional associations, the AAA and the AICPA, in his article, "The Practitioner and the Professor," *Journal of Accountancy* 120:64-66 (October 1965).

economic organization is conducted, it is physically impossible to check all the transactions that have taken place. In addition, there are legitimate alternatives available to the accountant for fixing the value on financial items. The method will vary, consideration ultimately being given in most cases to the maximization of the client's profits. There are, however, restrictions on the use of some methods of valuation in one financial area, if at the same time certain methods are used in another, or on inconsistent changes of method from period to period. The various methods are permitted, basically, to allow for and account for different modes of operation, different cycles of operation, different processes or products, changes within the process, and so forth.

The results of this diversity in accounting valuation, which are necessitated by uncertainty (lack of perfect knowledge of goods and services) and incompatibility (differences between and changes within organizations), are "informed opinions," or "judgments." When asked the question, "In what area of his work do you feel the CPA utilizes the most judgment?" the most common response was: "In all areas." This was to emphasize the importance of judgment in his work, because most respondents would then describe the accuracy of reporting the values of cash and securities as opposed to reporting the values of inventories, goods-in-process, depreciation, and the like. An executive partner of one Big Eight firm gave an example of the result of judgment in these areas of high uncertainty: "On a million dollar inventory, if six CPAs were to each judge it separately, there would be a range of judgment of plus or minus 10 percent of that million dollars."

If the judgment of the auditor does not coincide with that of his client, there may be a question of materiality. Whether an item were material or not would depend on whether the disclosure of or the method of treating it would influence significantly—that is, "make a difference in"—the judgment or conduct of a reasonable person.[3] One example given by an audit senior:

> The CPA utilizes very much judgment in reporting the materiality of the situation. For example, in a company with net sales of $60,000,000 annually, we know we're off $50,000 on one account. The question is, are we going to spend months, or more than a year finding it? No, because it's immaterial. However, if there were to be a question of whether to report $7,000,000 in profit or in retained earnings, this is material.

There are no accepted rules on materiality other than the definition above, so the auditor has to determine materiality for each situation as it arises. Thus, he judges the value of items and judges whether his judgment of the valuation is materially different from that of his client—two separate stages of judgment in

3. Based on definitions by James L. Dohr, "Materiality—What Does It Mean in Accounting?" *Journal of Accountancy* 90:54-56 (July 1950); and Paul Grady, *Inventory of Generally Accepted Accounting Principles for Business Enterprises* (Accounting Research Study No. 7) (New York: AICPA, 1965), p. 40.

the audit procedure. In terms of information theory this means that if there is a decrease in the number of cases where materiality must be determined (because of increase in knowledge and rules for selection from among alternatives in these areas), then there is a decrease in judgment. Also, questions of materiality can be computerized if the situations that go into making up the question can be quantified.[4]

THE ACCOUNTING PRINCIPLES DEBATE:
EXTERNAL RULES LIMITING POWER

Spurred by a general public distrust of financial statements, in the early 1930s the AICPA (at that time the AIA) listed five basic principles that it considered necessary for a business to follow in order to attain "general acceptance" of its reporting. During the following decades a cumulative series of Accounting Research Bulletins were disseminated by the institute to members and interested parties as guides to general acceptance. Few of these were given over to the limitation of alternative methods of accounting, to the nearly constant concern of some CPAs, both practitioners and theorists.[5]

The question of codifying the principles, increasing their specificity, and limiting the alternatives again came into the public accounting spotlight recently. In discussing alternatives, one view is that almost every audit is different enough that alternative methods should not be abolished for the sake of uniformity. This is the official position of the AICPA, set forth in its pamphlet *Audits by Certified Public Accountants* (1950), although there is a large minority of dissenters, who encompass a range from slight to complete disagreement. The dissenters argue that the lack of uniformity in reporting procedures (external rules) will not earn the confidence of investors, stockholders, and the general public. In turn, this will drastically affect the stature of public accounting as a profession; and what is worse, this may forfeit the attest function to the federal government or some other group. Leonard Spacek, senior partner of Arthur Andersen & Co., has pointed to the major inconsistencies created in accounting reports due to the wide choice of available alternatives. For example, one steel company reports a profit increase nearly twice as great as that of another steel company, due solely to a different method of accounting for investment credit.[6]

4. These points are discussed by Warren Reininga, "The Unknown Materiality Concept," *Journal of Accountancy* 125:30-35 (February 1968).

5. A concise history of the principles debate is given by Reed K. Storey, *The Search for Accounting Principles: Today's Problems in Perspective* (New York: AICPA, 1964). A summary and interpretation of the more recent debate is presented by Robert N. Anthony, "Showdown on Accounting Principles," *Harvard Business Review* 41:99-106 (May-June 1963). Also, T. A. Wise, *The Insiders* (Garden City, N.Y.: Doubleday, 1962), pt. 1 and app.

6. Leonard Spacek, in a speech at the Graduate School of Business Administration, New York University, February 18, 1965.

Large profit adjustments are made by oil companies due to acceptable alternative methods of charging intangible drilling costs.[7] One accountant points out that a recent edition of *Accounting Trends and Techniques*, a research report issued annually by the AICPA which lists the alternative methods used by six hundred large U.S. corporations, shows that more than twenty different methods of inventory valuation were in use in 1963.[8] A partner in one medium-sized firm noted, "When the client sees this, he pressures you to use those methods which will present him in the best light, whether they are consistent or not with the total accounting and audit program."

Over the last decade, much publicity has arisen because of scandals involving publicly held corporations. Billy Sol Estes and the salad-oil swindle are common knowledge in America today. And one does not have to be a sophisticated analyst to detect the more frequent irregularities that show up in business reporting. The news media give good coverage to such incidents. The lack of specificity of rules for applying principles to the client organization was exposed in the Yale Express and Atlas Plywood stories, printed in *Fortune* magazine.[9] The former describes the entirely justified (according to present standards) "massive adjustments" and write-offs that the auditors made, which resulted in a $1,140,000 profit in 1963 being restated in 1965 at a $1,880,000 loss.

Whether or not these kinds of events were a major incentive for attempts at clarification of accounting principles and methods, beginning in 1961, the first of a number of Accounting Research Studies was published by the AICPA. These studies have started the task of clarifying in writing the basic assumptions of accounting, the principles stemming from these assumptions, and in some cases the specific rules and guides for applying these principles. After issuance of the first study, of which the list of basic assumptions is a summary statement (see The Nature and Scope of the Public Accountant's Work, Chapter II), a rash of articles in accounting journals debated the benefits and defects of "postulates" and "principles." Two later Accounting Research Studies each presented a set of principles: ARS No. 3 is an ideal set, and ARS No. 7 is compiled primarily from the accumulated experience of AICPA research bulletins and committee opinions.[10]

7. T. A. Wise, "The Auditors Have Arrived" (Part I), *Fortune* 62:148, 239 (November 1960).

8. Robert T. Sprouse, "Historical Costs and Current Assets: Traditional and Treacherous," *Accounting Review* 48:691 (October 1963).

9. Richard J. Whalen, "The Big Skid at Yale Express," *Fortune* 72:146-149, 226-236 (November 1965); "The Mess at Atlas Plywood," *Fortune* 57:118-119, 234, 236 (January 1958).

10. Maurice Moonitz, *The Basic Postulates of Accounting* (ARS No. 1) (New York: AICPA, 1961); Maurice Moonitz and Robert T. Sprouse, *A Tentative Set of Broad Accounting Principles for Business Enterprises* (ARS No. 3) (New York: AICPA, 1962); Grady, *Inventory*.

The latter study was the first comprehensive codification of existing accounting literature pertaining to principles of accounting. There are also many other researches being conducted on related areas of uncertainty, for example, on terminology directly or indirectly related to principles. What does the phrase "generally accepted accounting principles" mean, according to the definition of "general" and "accepted"? What is the difference between "variations" and "alternatives"?[11] Another study delves into the problem of terminology that surrounds the concept of cash flow.[12] And others are contributing to clarification of terms, levels of approach to accounting thought, and procedures in this thought.[13]

The end result of all this work is to increase the external professional rules with regard to number, specificity, and extent. The task of doing so has gained momentum in public accounting recently through the debate on principles, and it may continue at an increasingly rapid pace. The Code of Professional Ethics has continually been revised and strengthened, and *Auditing Standards and Procedures* has for some time been a general, though very flexible, set of rules for the process and conduct of the audit. Rationality is beginning to be realized at the expense of decreased uncertainty, as many statements in the profession's literature testify, at least by implication. I decided to directly confront large-firm accountants with this question in my interviews, and to add to it the really inseparable consideration of the effects of computerization. The question was worded as follows:

> Because accounting and auditing procedures are becoming more computerized and because their principles and procedures are becoming more formally spelled out, the judgment function of CPAs is being considerably weakened. Therefore, CPAs will utilize other areas of greater judgment potential—that of management services and its related forms—to carry on, professionally strong. Does this sound plausible to you? Why, or why not?

Few disagreed entirely; few agreed completely. Most argued that judgment was not and most likely would not be reduced by computerization. There was less criticism of the remainder of the question. A sample of comments that are representative of the range of answers of members of Big Eight firms aids in pointing out the awareness of large-firm accountants to these problems. One specialist in management services on the senior level commented:

11. *Report of Special Committee on Opinions of the Accounting Principles Board* (New York: AICPA, 1965), pp. 13-16.

12. Perry Mason, *"Cash Flow" Analysis—and the Funds Statement* (ARS No. 2) (New York: AICPA, 1961).

13. Among the many good examples: R. J. Chambers, "Why Bother with Postulates?" *Journal of Accounting Research* 1:3-15 (Spring 1963); Frank J. Imke, "Relationships in Accounting Theory," *Accounting Review* 41:318-322 (April 1966); Howard J. Snavely, "Accounting Information Criteria," *Accounting Review* 42:223-232 (April 1967).

I disagree on the formalizing of auditing procedures. Perhaps this could be done regarding receivables and in observing inventories. But the rest, as to scope, that is, determining the audit approach and the kind of program of audit—that's all up to the auditor.

Management services is only an aspect of internal control [of the client], so, is only part of the auditing attest of financial statements. Take an example—a large consumer products manufacturer who is highly computerized. We have to ask ourselves whether we really understand his computerized system of operations. We conduct an annual review, utilizing our management services men, examining the flow of computer information as it goes through its steps. We have to ask if the data are computerized properly. This is all for the audit.

The response of an audit junior:

The judgment area may be narrowing with the increase in AICPA rules and regulations. However, with the computer, things are made easier and you're more sure of yourself because of less human intervention. But, it does not eliminate auditing work. There's an increase in reliability but not a decrease in judgment. The CPA still has to analyze the output of the computer. And, management services will grow, but accounting and auditing will be the largest and most important part of our work.

An administrative partner:

If generally accepted accounting principles are set up exactly in mechanical methods, you may get a decrease in the judgment factor. But then, how in the world would you ever get exact rules, for example, on deferred development costs? There are so many questions here depending on the situation of the company, the business it's in, whether and how the public affects the costs over the years, etc. Judgment will not disappear in situations like this unless everything is rigidly specified.

As for the rest of your hypothesis, I'm not so sure we as a profession are moving into management services because we can't make it without it, that is, because we have to move into it, but because it's a way for us to expand our services to our client in a creative way.

An administrative partner of another firm:

You're fifty years ahead of your time. Judgment will not be taken over yet by the computer. It is serving to give data, and these data will be more sophisticated in time, but not for a while. As for accounting principles, they're in their infancy. In Washington [D.C.], today, this very minute, there is controversy on a newly written tax principle. Just as law is now beginning to computerize in some areas, the computerization of the CPA field will soon take place, but ours will come faster because our client is already in the midst of it. But there won't be a major loss of judgment.

A tax manager:

> With your conclusion, I agree. With the first half [judgment loss due to computerization and formalization], I have serious reservations. The CPA judgment function is expanding due to the computer. As for accounting principles, they're not going to limit the CPA's judgment. In trying to express them formally, we will see how vast the field is. As accountants realize this, they see how they can expand their services, especially in management services.
>
> With regard to the whole concept of judgment control, rulings usually *increase* judgment. For example, there are now opinions on tax responsibilities passed by the Federal Tax Committee of the AICPA which will now bring more judgment. It [tax services] will virtually be felt as an audit, opening a world of judgment.

Regarding routine and red tape, answers to the several interview questions on accounting and auditing judgment indicated that the increase in numbers, specificity, and extent of external professional rules does tend to *reduce* the work and worry about these rules within the firm, but only if the increase does not overextend itself. Because, except for the bitter controversy that extreme regulation would engender, much more of the firm's time would necessarily be spent in recording and interpreting rules in their daily application. The answers also pointed out quite clearly that the large-firm practitioner feels that increase in external rules does *increase* the rationality of the body of knowledge. More certainty results from this increase, they say, but there are some forms of uncertainty (areas where risk and judgment exist) that devolve from the increased rationality, especially in computerization. There were spontaneous and voluntary comments by one-quarter of the interview sample to the effect that the computer can only do what it is told to do, that is, what is programmed for measurement. But with computers it works both ways. In the latest stage of development, hypotheses can be generated and chosen by the computer on the basis of their correspondence to the logic of the environment, thus suggesting improvements in goal-seeking behavior. One such example is the computer simulation of the evolution of sequences of symbols, which generates a pattern of survival of "best" combinations. Rather than providing the exact nature of the problem, the programmer only specifies the exact nature of the goal desired.[14] It may not be very long before the machine will take over minor judgment functions of financial organization and control.

The other frequent comment by large-firm accountants (one-third of the interview sample) is that with specificity of rules in public accounting, CPAs are

14. Lawrence J. Fogel, Alvin J. Owens, and Michael J. Walsh, "Intelligent Decision Making Through a Simulation of Evolution," *Behavioral Science* 11:253-272 (July 1966). Also, John R. Quinlan and Earl B. Hunt, "The FORTRAN Deductive System," *Behavioral Science* 14:74 (January 1969).

looking to new areas of "creativity" and "innovation." Several recent studies of the future of the profession suggest that public accounting must be aware of and must generate new areas of uncertainty.[15] One example of this quest for uncertainty involved the question of specification of accounting methods for investment credit. Known as the investment credit issue, this protracted argument among accountants and between accountants and the federal government can be examined as a conflict between elements that advocate a logically deductive approach to accounting as against those that advocate general "acceptability" and "external consensus" by business, governmental, and accounting experience. The former would lead to increasing rationality (certainty, information) of the present body of knowledge, and the latter attempts to preserve the uncertainty of the body of knowledge in a status quo. The two sides of the conflict are not formed according to the practitioner-theorist dichotomy. For example, four of the Big Eight firms represented on the Accounting Principles Board of the AICPA were against limiting to one method the apportioning of tax savings from the credit: Price Waterhouse; Haskins & Sells, Ernst & Ernst, and Peat Marwick.[16] They were in favor of the wisdom of experience, that is, what is generally acceptable—that alternative methods be allowed with regard to investment credit.[17] But the majority of the profession was for the limitation.

Thus the basic controversy goes beyond the theory-practitioner split to the division of certainty-uncertainty. As Marvin L. Stone, president of the AICPA in 1968, said in a summary of the investment credit issue: theoretically, either way can be justified, but in fact, big business realizes that "rationalizing the whole body of corporate accounting practices will serve the best long-range interests of their organizations."[18]

The argument of deductive logic versus inductive analysis continues, mostly in the art versus science approaches to viewing accounting as an intellectual discipline.

15. Robert H. Roy and James H. MacNeill, *Horizons for a Profession* (New York: AICPA, 1967), p. 33.

16. "A Matter of Principle Splits CPAs," *Business Week,* January 26, 1963, p. 55.

17. A partial summary can be gleaned of the investment credit debate as related to theory-acceptability in Grady, *Inventory,* pp. 33, 55. The CPA's responsibilities with regard to external consensus are discussed by Herman W. Bevis, *Corporate Financial Reporting in a Competitive Economy* (New York: Macmillan, 1965), p. 187. An article by Maurice Moonitz, then Director of Research at the AICPA, gives a general analysis and details of the major events of the investment credit issue. Moonitz corroborates my interpretation of this debate regarding the creativity and deduction by the Accounting Principles Board. See Maurice Moonitz, "Some Reflections on Investment Credit Experience," *Journal of Accounting Research* 4:47-61 (Spring 1966).

18. Marvin L. Stone, "Public Confidence in Private Enterprise: Let's Keep It," an address before the Economic Club of Detroit, March 11, 1968, reprinted in *Journal of Accountancy* 125:52-57 (April 1968). The author includes a summary of the investment credit debate.

ACCOUNTING ART AND ACCOUNTING SCIENCE

All through its modern history, accounting has been called an art by some and a science by others. In his first edition of *Auditing Theory and Practice*, Robert Montgomery called it a science; he said that "it should be possible to present its underlying principles so that they may be comprehensible to the average mind."[19] Others have considered accountancy as primarily an art,[20] and still others have emphasized that it contains elements of both art and science. Art is here signified to be creative judgment, that is, where, at best, only rough probability estimates can be made concerning the action in question. A high degree of uncertainty is present. Those who discuss accounting as a science view it as a science that is based either on the inductive method or the deductive method, or a combination of both operating in close coordination.[21] The principles and procedures of accounting that are derived from the experience of accounting are championed by those who follow the inductive method of logical analysis, those who consider the method of accounting to be one of artistic analysis.

If the method is the construction of ideas and the attempted refutation of these ideas through logic *and* practice and not merely validation of conventions handed down by business practice, then accounting becomes a science, even if it only uses the comparative method of ideal types, which is comfortable to the social sciences, and not the more specified, narrow natural-science method of

19. Robert H. Montgomery, *Auditing Theory and Practice* (New York: Ronald Press, 1912), p. 7.

20. *Accounting Terminology Bulletin No. 1* (New York: AICPA, 1953).

21. Most accountants believe that a theory is constructed by the inductive process, says Vahe Baladouni, "The Accounting Perspective Re-Examined," *Accounting Review* 41:215-216 (April 1966). The primary exponent of induction in accounting is usually quoted as A. C. Littleton, although earlier in his writing he did include deduction as part of theory construction. Cf. his article "Fixed Assets and Accounting Theory," *Illinois Certified Public Accountant* 10:12 (March 1948). The deductive method is espoused especially by Edward J. Burke, "Objectivity and Accounting," *Accounting Review* 39:837-849 (October 1964), and by John W. Buckley, Paul Kircher, and Russell L. Mathews, "Methodology in Accounting Theory," *Accounting Review* 43:274-283 (April 1968); it is mentioned by Colin Park, "Thought Processes in Creative Accounting," *Accounting Review* 33:441-444 (July 1958). A combination of induction and deduction is suggested by William J. Vatter, "Postulates and Principles," *Journal of Accounting Research* 1:196 (Autumn 1963), and Imke, "Relationships in Accounting Theory," p. 322. A good summary of the theorist-practitioner division is drawn by Earl A. Spiller, Jr., "Theory and Practice in the Development of Accounting," *Accounting Review* 39:851 (October 1964): In accounting theory, business transactions and events are dealt with by abstraction, in terms of assumptions, which are the basis for deduction, which leads to conclusions. Whereas in accounting practice they are dealt with in problems, in terms of procedures, which are the basis for induction, which leads to generalizations.

experimentation.[22] The theory is the deduction, a set of logically interrelated hypotheses. Analysis of classes of events takes place; it is only through attempted refutation that the empirical value of an idea can be verified. The deduction, the idea, necessarily interacts with inductions, which build up to and lead from that idea.[23]

Several glaring problems of public accounting that directly affect the largest firms are related to this discussion. One recent example concerns the use of logical analysis in accounting. In October 1964 the Council of the AICPA ruled unanimously that departures from opinions of the Accounting Principles Board, as well as Accounting Research Bulletins, be disclosed either in footnotes to financial statements or in the auditor's report. The recommendations of this ruling state in part that:

1. "Generally accepted accounting principles" are those principles which have substantial authoritative support.
2. Opinions of the Accounting Principles Board constitute "substantial authoritative support."
3. "Substantial authoritative support" can exist for accounting principles that differ from Opinions of the Accounting Principles Board.[24]

The logic is obviously weak, for it leaves open to the user all accepted accounting principles, not just those that are "generally acceptable," that is, those that have "substantial authoritative support." In a private letter, the senior partner of one Big Eight firm has noted in more technical language the same error in logic.[25]

The entire concept of "acceptance" or "general acceptance" is directly opposed to innovation. Accepted accounting principles are principles having substantial authoritative support. Evidence of this support is found in "opinions of committees of the Institute to which authority for dealing with accounting

22. Views of accounting as an art, as contrasted to natural science, are given by Marvin L. Stone, "Public Confidence in Private Enterprise," and John Lawler, "The Quest for Accounting Philosophers," in *Empirical Research in Accounting: Selected Studies, 1967*, Supplement to vol. 5 of the *Journal of Accounting Research* (Chicago: Institute of Professional Accounting, Graduate School of Business, University of Chicago, 1968), p. 88.

23. Karl R. Popper, *The Poverty of Historicism* (London: Routledge & Kegal Paul, 1957). References to Popper's hypothetico-deductive method are occuring with increasing frequency in accounting literature, e.g., Daniel L. McDonald, "Feasibility Criteria for Accounting Measures," *Accounting Review* 42:622-679 (October 1967). Popper's method does *not* disagree with that of inductivists—see Barney G. Glaser and Anselm L. Strauss, *The Discovery of Grounded Theory* (Chicago: Aldine Publishing Co., 1967), pp. 5-6.

24. *Disclosure of Departures from Opinions of Accounting Principles Board*, Special Bulletin of Special Committee on Opinions of Accounting Principles Board (New York: AICPA, October 1964).

25. A summary and analysis of the statements is given by Marshall S. Armstrong, a member of the Accounting Principles Board, "Some Thoughts on Substantial Authoritative Support," *Journal of Accountancy* 127:44-50 (April 1969).

has been delegated by Council, the Securities and Exchange Commission, certain regulatory commissions, to the extent that their rulings are not in conflict with accepted accounting principles from other sources, textbooks of recognized standing, experienced and competent CPAs and in the practices commonly followed by business entities."[26] An accounting innovation, by definition, would lack this acceptability, as was shown clearly in the analysis of the AICPA rejection of a U.S. Steel innovation.[27] Furthermore, control that rests on a basis of acceptable variations (alternative methods) allows public accounting to make presentations that are in accordance with the ideological bent of the controlling interests. The senior partner of Arthur Andersen has recently commented on this issue:

> To illustrate the absurdity of allowing control to rest in the sterile hand of the so-called "acceptance" of accounting variations, one needs only to imagine what the government policy would be if acceptance also controlled decisions in civil rights cases, regardless of the merits of the issues.[28]

In the accounting literature, several suggestions and a few attempts have been made to integrate accounting thought to social-science concepts and theory. The attempts, as written by accountants,[29] are mostly sociologically oriented, and they have met with heavy criticism from practitioners. A partner of one medium-sized firm commented on the approach taken by accounting theoreticians: "The problem is, 'What is the problem?' It's not the answers given so easily in *The Accounting Review* [which presents primarily the academic point of view]. They think it's easy to define the problem, but it's not. Most of the time they don't define it correctly and are miles from the problem itself." This may or may not be true. In any case, the practitioner is just as guilty for misunderstanding the purpose of science. The May 1966 editorial in *The Journal of Accountancy* (presenting primarily the practitioner's point of view) equates the empirical verity of science with the a priori truth of formal logic. Then it takes issue with "social science jargon," as used by accountants, for writing about what "is so obvious, that, if put in plain English, it wouldn't be worth saying." Which has so many times been answered by analyses that prove the obvious to be incorrect. Not to mention that the obvious in social science must

---

26. Grady, *Inventory*, p. 16.

27. Richard Leo Smith, "A Case Analysis of External Accounting Influence over Managerial Decisions" (Ph.D. diss., Graduate School of Business Administration, Harvard University, 1955), pp. 283-286. See also the comments of R. J. Chambers, "A Matter of Principle," *Accounting Review* 41:445 (July 1966).

28. Spacek, speech of February 18, 1965.

29. For example, John J. Willingham, "The Accounting Entity: A Conceptual Model," *Accounting Review* 49:543-552 (July 1964); Bunji Aoyagi, "Sociological Accounting," *Journal of Accountancy* 106:51-55 (July 1958).

be categorically tested, because it *is* science, that is, it has become part of the scientific analysis. Also, "jargon" is abundant in science, because one of the principles of science is parsimony, an economy of concepts to promote precision and even to suggest new research problems.[30] What may be considered jargon is very often necessary technical terminology for the specialist in his field, and results will not be written up in "straightforward" language.

The debate of art versus science invades the whole area of change in public accounting. The sides taken by parties do not necessarily break down to the theorist-practitioner division. There is much overlap, as has been demonstrated. The question of science or art has been muddled by a lack of understanding of the two concepts, especially the former. But underlying the entire conflict is the growing concern about increasing certainty and the consequent loss of judgment. The advocates of science foresee that there will be increased prestige for accounting as a science and increased self-control over its domain of services and the power that comes with it. Those who wish to maintain the status quo are afraid of the certainty that science brings to experts, for, unconsciously, they are aware that "as science invades the domain of the experts, those aspects of their rules which it affects decrease in importance."[31] This is reason enough to fear the incisiveness that is characteristic of science.

Areas of uncertainty in traditional accounting and auditing are under continuous attack by modes of rationalizing, especially those of science and the applications of science found in computerization. The more conservative view feels, however, that uncertainty, in the form of judgment, will prevail in accounting, even though "ground rules" are being established, and no matter how sophisticated the system of mechanics may be.[32] This view also finds that the more liberal interpretation reflects "unwarranted fears that the independent auditing and reporting function may become obsolete."[33] They argue that there are new and changing definitions of and areas of profit, assets, and so forth. In exploratory stages of development, the whole being of a company is in flux, as one audit manager put it. The leeway that an auditor has in questions of

30. These points are defended by Paul F. Lazarsfeld and Robert K. Merton, "Friendship as Social Process: A Substantive and Methodological Analysis," in *Freedom and Control in Modern Society,* ed. Morroe Berger, Theodore Abel, and Charles H. Page (New York: Octagon Books, 1964), pp. 24-25.

Problems stemming from the lack of a scientific attitude in accounting are discussed by David Green, Jr., "Evaluating the Accounting Literature," *Accounting Review* 41:52-64 (January 1966).

31. Michel Crozier, *The Bureaucratic Phenomenon* (Chicago: University of Chicago Press, 1964), p. 300.

32. *Accounting Education,* AICPA Committee on Relations with Universities (New York: AICPA, 1963), p. 38.

33. Paul Grady, "The Independent Auditing and Reporting Function of the CPA," *Journal of Accountancy* 120:67 (November 1965); James M. Fremgen, "Utility and Accounting Principles," *Accounting Review* 42:457-467 (July 1967).

materiality here is very wide. In other new areas of business thought and practice, it is the same. One audit senior pointed to the broad scope of judgment used in lease-back arrangements: "One sees it as a purchase, another as a rental. Depending on how you record it, it will change the profits figure." The entire question of which auditing and accounting procedures are to be used greatly affects the outcome of the audit. In fact, the differences created by the type of method chosen can be large enough to determine the success or failure of the business enterprise. The liberal element, on the other hand, feels that the new services of scientific decisioning and decision-making, much of it automated, will someday find the CPA without a job, unless they move into these new services.[34] They often cite the case of the reduction of a corporate accounting division to the status of a department and the simultaneous introduction of an information services division.[35]

There is no clear picture that emerges from the debate in accounting as to whether the traditional audit is becoming an "annual nuisance," but our analysis indicates there is a strong shift toward developing new areas of knowledge. Public accountants are not sure; but they are not taking any chances, and so they are exploring new possibilities in auditing (the focus of chapter 9) and have moved strongly into management services, an area of management decisioning that is fraught with uncertainty. Traditional accounting (and its auditing) is an accounting for the past and the present only. This fact, which has often been repeated in the last twenty years,[36] may be starting to change under the pressures of increasing certainty and the demands of clients. As the director of management services in one medium-sized firm, himself a partner, commented:

> Until very recently, public accounting has not taken the initiative to move into data processing. But it now realizes that the relative importance of the auditing required diminishes because of better internal control methods and data processing. Business has found out that from this it can reasonably predict the future for some cases. As a result, it is less

---

34. Thomas W. McRae, "Looking Backward—The Decline and Fall of the Accounting Profession," *The Quarterly/Touche, Ross, Bailey & Smart* 8:27-30 (June 1962), reprinted from *Accountancy,* the Journal of the Institute of Chartered Accountants in England and Wales, 72:670-671 (November 1961); Sidney Davidson, "The Day of Reckoning: Managerial Analysis and Accounting Theory," *Journal of Accounting Research* 1:117-126 (Autumn 1963); Carey, *The CPA Plans For the Future* (New York: AICPA, 1965), pp. 239 ff.

35. Sexton Adams and Doyle Z. Williams, "Information Technology and the Accounting Organization," *Management Services* 3:15-23 (September-October 1966).

36. Peter F. Drucker, *The New Society* (New York: Harper & Bros., 1950), p. 208; C. West Churchman, *Prediction and Optimal Decision: Philosophical Issues of a Science of Values* (Englewood Cliffs, N.J.: Prentice-Hall, 1961), p. 322; Bevis, *Corporate Financial Reporting,* p. 68.

interested in the distant past, and is concerned more with the recent past and especially in changing the future. Also, data processing creates a more accurate record of the past than an accountant; its built-in checks are superior.

This view can be placed in the more general language of sociological theory, specifically, to the power-uncertainty relationship: "As soon as the progress of scientific management or of economic stabilization has made one kind of difficulty liable, at least to a certain degree, to rational prediction, the power of the group whose role it is to cope with this kind of difficulty, and of the people who represent it, will tend to decrease."[37] If the large-firm accountant is considered a kind of entrepreneur, he is investing his time to produce institutional change in his firm with prospects of adequate return for uncertainties encountered. To borrow from macroeconomic theory, as Easterbrook remarks, in our advanced economy of rapid institutional change, change is frequently accomplished by external expansion rather than by internal adjustments.[38] In public accounting firms today, expansion is external, into the area of management services. It is to this important area that we now turn.

37. Crozier, *The Bureaucratic Phenomenon*, p. 164.

38. W. T. Easterbrook, "The Entrepreneurial Function in Relation to Technological and Economic Change," in *Industrialization and Society*, ed. Bert F. Hoselitz and Wilbert E. Moore (The International Social Science Council, 1963), pp. 57-73.

8

Uncertainty In Management Services

The data processing accomplished by modern electronic computers has brought the realization to large business enterprises and to public accountants that a "total information system" can be constructed with the aid of these computers in order to give a more accurate view of the going concern. Although this system presently contains only the basic financial data that can be programmed onto the computer, other separate information, especially in the areas of management decisioning, is being included in the public accountant's total examination and evaluation of his client. CPAs are engaging more and more in "management accounting," or "managerial accounting." They assist management in "establishing a plan for reasonable economic objectives and in the making of rational decisions."[1] This entire field of advisory services in public accounting is covered by the term "management services."

WHAT THEY SAY ABOUT MANAGEMENT SERVICES

Several research surveys of this field present a general outline of the types of specialties in it and the amount of time devoted to each. In one nationwide survey,[2] 160 active Chamber of Commerce businessmen reported that they used the services of their public accountants in the following areas:

Area of Service	% of Sample Using CPA
Budgets	6
Cost analysis or controls	23
Insurance coverage	24
Pension or profit-sharing plans	33
Dividend policy	16
Investment of idle funds	18

1. The quote is from a report of the AAA Committee on Management Accounting, in *The Accounting Review* 24:210 (April 1959). Managerial accounting is discussed by Robert M. Trueblood, "The New Frontier of Financial Executives," *The Quarterly / Touche, Ross, Bailey & Smart* 9:40 (March 1963).

2. John Ashworth, "Some Further Data on the Image of the CPA: An Interim Report," *Journal of Accountancy* 115:53 (February 1963). See also the chart by Elmo Roper, "As Others See You," *Journal of Accountancy* 117:35 (January 1964).

Area of Service	% of Sample Using CPA
Mergers and acquisitions	29
Office management procedures	41
Dissolutions	14
Personnel	26
Working capital requirements	35

A survey sponsored by 33 medium-sized firms,[3] with an average of six partners in each firm, located in 23 states gave the following information on major groups of management services:

Group	Activity Index[a]
(1) Finance	79
(2) General Management and Administration	74
(3) Office Management	71
(4) Purchasing	64
(5) Other Professional Services	50
(6) Personnel	36
(7) Research and Development	21
(8) Traffic and Transportation	20
(9) Production	18
(10) Sales	16

[a]The activity index would be 100 if each accounting firm had rendered all the types of services in each group.

From the 42 specific classes of services from which the respondent could choose, the 5 highest activities were:

Group Class		Example	Activity Index
(2)	Use of other experts	Advice as to use of an attorney, appraiser, or other specialists	96
(2)	Special investigations	Purchase or sale of business	95
(3)	Office equipment	Advice as to machine bookkeeping	93
(1)	Cost accounting	Development of cost methods, standard costs, and so forth	89

3. "Management Services by CPAs," *Journal of Accountancy* 103:43-45 (June 1957). Another similar study is James E. Hammond, "Statistics on the Accounting Profession," *Journal of Accountancy* 104:42-49 (November 1957).

Group Class		Example	Activity Index
(1)	Business organization and reorganization	Advice for organization, sources of capital, securities to be issued, provisions of contracts and agreements	88

The 5 least active were:

Group Class		Example	Activity Index
(8)	Traffic management	Surveys of traffic management	12
(10)	Packaging and shipping	Survey of shipping methods and costs	11
(9)	Production methods and standards	Time and motion studies, development of production standards, survey and evaluation of production methods	10
(6)	Industrial relations	Advice as to labor-union contracts, guaranteed annual wage agreements, other fringe benefits, and so forth	9
(10)	Market research	Conducting market research for products and services	7

The questionnaire sample of the Big Eight firms (see table 5) devoted 20 percent of its time to one form or another of management services. Table 13 gives a breakdown of these services. Because the dividing line between auditing work and management services work is unclear, the first two of the three major sections of specialties in table 13 would contain much overlap of the two work areas. The amount of overlap would be difficult to determine, because different firms (and different individuals) have varying definitions of where management services end and where auditing advice begins. Based on several detailed responses on this point, I estimate that approximately 50 percent of the first section and 25 percent of the second section could be classified more as accounting services than management services. This would tend to lower the total management services time of the sample by a few percent if the conservative definition of management services is used. However, this decrease is not large enough to significantly affect conclusions based on these figures.

When the entire sample was asked of what importance these services were to the growth of public accounting as a higher profession, the response was

TABLE 13

Apportionment of Big Eight Time in Management
Services Specialties (N=111) in Percentage

Specialty		Time Spent	
Finance and Accounting:			
(e.g., advice on inventory valuation policies, depreciation procedures, expensing of repairs, business organization and reorganization, credit policies, cash management)			30
Systems and Procedures *Directly* Related to Finance and Accounting:			
(e.g., development of cost systems, design of internal financial statements, advice on machine bookkeeping)			25
Systems and Procedures Related to Finance and Accounting:			
(a) General management and administration			
Investigations on purchase or sale of business	8		
Management information and evaluation systems			
(total information flow, budgeting, work simplification)	6		
Advice on use of special counsel or specialists	2	16	
(b) Other			
Management sciences (EDP, linear programming, statistical sampling)	10		
Analysis of internal control systems	5		
Production (development of production standards, survey of methods, time & motion studies, factory layout)	4		
Personnel (advice on labor contracts, wage agreements, fringe benefits, psychological testing)	3		
Sales (market research, shipping methods and costs, public-opinion polls)	2		
Purchasing	2		
Transportation (traffic-management surveys)	1		
Research and Development	1		
Other	1	29	45
Total			100

generally highly positive: extremely important, 48 percent; very important, 27 percent; important, 14 percent; not very important, 9 percent; unimportant, 2 percent. These proportions were basically the same for all firms. Nor did they vary significantly by position in the firm and major area of work. The reason these services are important to this growth can be summarized into four major areas of opinion, according to response from the same sample: services to client, 33 percent; necessary for growth of profession, 24 percent; a natural area for CPAs, 14 percent; produce innovation, 7 percent.

The increase in the amount of management services by CPAs has been considerable in the past several years, the mean increase (excluding the Big Eight) is 7 percent of total services.[4] And for the near future, the position of management services in large firms seems assured. The importance of management services, when related to whether this importance might change (see table 14), is one indication. Only 6 of the 140 respondents can foresee a decrease in importance. Totaling the nine cells of the upper left-hand corner of table 14,

TABLE 14

Importance of Management Services Presently, as
Related to Importance for the Future (N=140)

Importance for the Future	Importance Presently						
	Extremely Important	Very Important	Important	Not Very Important	Unimportant	No Time	Totals
Extremely Important	49	22	2				73
Very Important	4	8	7	5			24
Important	2		6	2			10
Not Very Important				2			2
Unimportant					1		1
No Time			1			1	2
Can't Tell	2	6	3	3	2		16
No Answer	8	3	1				12
Totals	65	39	20	12	3	1	140

4. According to a recent AICPA survey, reported by John L. Carey, *The CPA Plans for the Future* (New York: AICPA, 1965), p. 236. No information was given on the number of years covered by the survey.

fully three-quarters of the sample see them as important both now and in the future. Inquiries to 75 prominent CPAs from firms, education, industry, and government, in a 1963 survey,[5] elicited the following predictions of changes in the annual billings of public accounting firms in 1985:

	Audit Attest	Taxes	Management Services
Increase	9	19	57
Decrease	39	24	5
No change	11	17	1
No answer	6	5	2

Estimates of why these services will become so important were offered by 73 of the 140 respondents to the sample (see table 15). They emphasize the

TABLE 15

Answers to the Question: "Why do you think management
services will be an aid to the growth of public
accounting as a 'higher' profession in the future?"
(N=73)

Response	No. of Responses
Due to the complexity of business information e.g., computerization	28
They give better services to the client	9
Client will realize the CPA is qualified to perform them	6
Client will expect these services	5
They will create a good public image	3
They increase professionalization, especially through giving full services	7
Their innovative qualities improve the status of the profession	9
Better services to the client because of the independent position of the auditor in relation to the client	5
Audit may be replaced by the function of consultation	2
These services give technical expertise only	3
Total Responses	77[a]

[a]Four responses were coded under two categories, for a total of 73 respondents.

5. *Accounting Education,* AICPA Committee on Relations with Universities (New York: AICPA, 1963), p. 66. Sixty-five persons answered and returned the questionnaire.

importance of areas of uncertainty—areas of complexity and areas that demand innovation. It is thought by some public accountants that much of this increase will be in management science techniques, for example, computer simulation, work measurement techniques, sampling, and linear programming. One estimate (for the total number of public accounting firms) sees an increase of management sciences from the present 5 percent of a firm's services to more than 30 percent by 1985.[6] Table 13 shows that it was 10 percent for Big Eight firms in 1965.

THE LARGE-FIRM ACCOUNTANT AS ADVISOR AND DECISION-MAKER

Public accountants in large accounting firms conduct examinations in a wide range of business and related activities: these examinations go beyond the construction and auditing of financial statements. The broad definition of accounting, which includes auditing and management services, has been extended to cover nearly *all* economic activity, not only in regard to recording, classifying, and interpreting information, but in some cases in regard to suggesting organizational goals and assisting in their implementation. The context within which this activity of the large-firm accountant (and other experts) takes place has been the subject of debate under various headings: influence versus decision-making, advice versus decision-making, initiation versus approval, influence versus authority, and expertise versus policy decisions. The most common answer given is that the expert's influence is limited to suggestion and opinion and that the acid test for determining who makes the decision lies with the party who holds final responsibility for the decision—which, in the case of large-firm accountants, is the client.

However, like power, responsibility is found at various levels of the organizational hierarchy; it is collected in "pockets." Responsibility is assigned to those who have a part in making the decisions for the organization; varying degrees of it are found through the entire decisioning process. Whether it is accepted by those to whom it is assigned is another question.

Responsibility is found where a person observes and transmits information. The way in which he perceives and symbolizes reality will affect the decision-making process, depending on the importance of the information in that process. The importance itself is to a considerable degree determined by how it is perceived and transmitted. The accounting firm is charged with the responsibility of accounting for reality as defined by the organization that engages it for this service.

Not all information is transmitted. From among the chaos of events of

6. H. Justin Davidson, "Management Sciences in Accounting: Some Predictions," *The Quarterly / Touche, Ross, Bailey & Smart* 11:33-39 (June 1965).

reality, certain events are selected for transmission. In the case of prediction, the same procedure holds. From among the total number of known possibilities, a consultant to an organization's management will choose certain alternative courses of action. The responsibility of the expert is to present relevant alternatives accurately. It is for him to *judge* which alternatives are relevant.

The allocation of such amounts of responsibility to experts confers a great amount of power with it, for they intentionally or unintentionally limit alternatives. This kind of power is manifested in the decisioning process—what takes place before the final selection. But the power of expertise can be great enough to control the final selection. The expert's responsibility is not to give orders but to select alternatives, yet he commands power in the organization because of the unusual dependence of the management on him. His power is more than the term *"power* subject" signifies. By the default of management, he not only initiates decisions but approves them in a good number of instances, management holding a veto power but "not a capacity . . . to plan implementation without the competence of the expert."[7]

The public accountant's ideology shies away from this interpretation of the expert's power. The CPA projects his own role as one ot assistance, the content of which is governed largely by management's standards.[8] The recruitment brochure of Haskins & Sells discusses its operations in management services:

> Our basic objective in conducting management advisory services work is to function as consultants in assisting client managements to develop more effective—and more profitable—operations through improved management controls and other management techniques. This involves working closely and in collaboration with members of the client's organization in defining problems, developing solutions, and making recommendations rather than working on problems unilaterally or assuming management's responsibility for final decisions.

Another example of this careful delineation of the public accountant's role is given by the management services director of Arthur Young, in which he cites the method of incremental costing by the accountant, which allows management

7. Talcott Parsons, *Structure and Process in Modern Societies* (New York: The Free Press, 1960), pp. 66-67.

8. For example, see Robert M. Trueblood, "The Management Services Function in Public Accounting," *Journal of Accountancy* 110:42-43 (July 1961); Joseph S. Glickauf, "New Dimensions in Management Decision-Making," *Arthur Andersen Chronicle* 22:7-18 (October 1962); A. W. Patrick and C. L. Quittmeyer, "The CPA and Management Services," *Accounting Review* 38:109-117 (January 1963); Kenneth S. Axelson, "Are Consulting and Auditing Incompatible?" *Journal of Accountancy* 115:54-58 (April 1963); James Wesley Deskins, "Management Services and Management Decisions," *Journal of Accountancy* 119:50-54 (January 1965); Felix Kaufman, "Professional Consulting by CPAs," *Accounting Review* 42:713-720 (October 1967); Henry DeVos and Alan H. Mandelker, "Management Services–Why?" *Journal of Accountancy* 127:92-93 (May 1969).

to choose from alternatives with regard to what is to be produced or not produced.[9]

It is often pointed out that the CPA's assistance in implementing decisions is not as frequent with the more sophisticated large clients. However, through their costing procedure they have an important influence on business behavior.[10] Wherever there is a large amount of accountant perception and transmission —that is, selection of which alternatives to present his client, or choice of the alternative itself—wherever you find these accountant controls over uncertainty operating consistently, there will be a considerable influence on the client's course of action. Furthermore, clients often desire to assign some of their responsibility for financial representations and decision-making to the CPA in order to relieve some of the pressures that investors' and stockholders' criticisms exert on management's operations.[11] The reasoning behind this action is that it infers that the best possible financial course was followed by management.

Realizing their influential position as advisors, public accountants have been careful to define this influence as a power of persuasion, emphasizing that they have no authority to coerce a client.[12] For if a CPA is too closely associated with the decision-making process of his client, he will not be seen as independent. In such areas as management services and management audit (the latter is examined in chapter 9), this becomes a knotty problem. Advising in formulating goals and in implementing them blurs the fine line of distinction between advising and decision-making.

How blurred this line is in the large accounting firms is indicated in responses that the interview sample gave to the question: "Do clients request that you make decisions for them over and above the advice you give?" Of the thirty responses, seven answered "frequently," twelve "sometimes," four "rarely," and seven "never." Actual comments further clarified the concern of the CPA. An administrative partner of one Big Eight firm countered: "I would rather phrase the question, 'Do you make decisions for the client?' This answer is no. We tell our auditors that ours is a position of advice. We tell our management services people to spread out the facts but not to make decisions." But, after further discussion of actual cases of his firm's advising, he commented: "It's a tricky thing to say who makes the decision. In the total decision process, how do you tell who out of the group 'makes' the decisions, the one who is top dog and says,

9. Ralph F. Lewis, *Management Uses of Accounting: Planning and Control for Profits* (New York: Harper & Bros., 1961), p. 73.

10. Robert A. Gordon, *Business Leadership in the Large Corporation* (Washington, D.C.: The Brookings Institution, 1945), p. 265.

11. John L. Carey, ed., *The Accounting Profession: Where Is It Headed?* (New York: AICPA, 1962), pp. 45-46.

12. Herman W. Bevis, *Corporate Financial Accounting in a Competitive Economy* (New York: Macmillan, 1965), p. 187.

'We'll do *this!*' or the one or more who've influenced him?" An audit partner of a medium-sized firm said:

> Clyde [the client] wants to do something. We will make him see the situation in a different light. Then, this affects his decision. In some cases this is necessary because the client doesn't want to make the decision on his own.
>
> There is a narrow line between advice and decision-making. In certain cases a piece of advice is in effect a decision. Also, I consider advice a part of reaching a decision.

One Big Eight management services specialist (senior level) commented: "The client doesn't say, 'Please tell us what to do.' But you still feel they're going to do what you say. In most cases, you try to refrain from being direct in your answer." Another from the same specialty level said:

> Some people [public accountants] enjoy this problem [of making decisions]. But it's poor consulting. They've [the client] got to run their own house. One client of mine wants me to do the whole job, that is, his internal administration. They don't question our results; they have confidence in us, sometimes too much. They buy a study.

A good many respondents noted that decisions were made more often for smaller clients than for larger ones, the latter being knowledgeable enough about the alternatives presented to them to make the final choice themselves. A Big Eight tax manager noted:

> In taxes, it depends on the client whether we're going to be making a decision. He may call and ask the CPA about something, and in the case of the larger client, he'll call his lawyer too. This is pure advice. With the smaller client, they want us to hold their hand. At certain times we do make decisions, which we can't help, but in the majority of cases, he [the CPA tax specialist] is usually an expert giving advice.

The CPA, in effect, acts as a controller for the smaller client.

Several respondents did emphasize the shrewdness and wisdom of big business executives and administrators in handling the information of experts from various fields of knowledge. Indeed, some consider the power that scientist experts have over managers and administrators nothing more than myth.[13] However, the evidence is that large-firm accountants have acquired more responsibility in the decision-making process of their clients, if only because they have accepted a larger share of that process. This can and does extend to the "final" decision. For when the public accountant presents his reports, they are usually accepted as correct, especially in highly technical cases—an "anticipatory approval" of the CPA's work and advice by the client.

13. Daniel S. Greenberg, "The Myth of the Scientific Elite," *Public Interest* 1:51-62 (Fall 1965).

Because large-firm CPAs see that more responsibility is being assumed, most do not acknowledge it, because they feel that by doing so their independence will be threatened. However, conflict of interest is not necessarily inherent in responsibility for decision-making where that responsibility is attached to power and not authority. The public accountant has always had some interest in his client other than an altruistic one, as was argued in chapter 4. It is to the distinct advantage of any professional to bring his client "success" in whatever form that may be—health, wealth, or happiness—and to maintain that success better than any competitor within or without the profession. An ethical code sanctions and delimits the extremes to which he may go in attaining this success for his client, and licensure protects him from outside interference. As many public accountants have stated, complete independence of the professional from the client is an impossibility unless the professional fee is eliminated. This conflict of interest has always existed, but because more responsibility for decisions is now entailed in the practitioner-client relationship, it does not necessarily increase the interest of the practitioner. The practitioner has always realized that his fortunes would depend almost entirely on his ability to serve "success." Success for the CPA's client is wealth and, increasingly, with or without the profit motive, health and happiness through economy. Financial investment that is related to a client would certainly magnify the practitioner's interest to the point where no satisfactory amount of disinterested practice could be carried on for third parties. This is the reason for the strict regulations by the profession on independence regarding financial interest in clients.

But in most management services work the responsibility of the CPA is not a "final" one. The CPA has the *ability* and *opportunity* to decide for the client, but he does not have the *right*. Without this right he cannot command, no matter how many final decisions of his have been anticipatorily approved by his client. He does not have the responsibility for the final outcome of the decisions he has made or influenced, although some CPAs feel that they should assist in the implementation of the decisions—a further step towards that responsibility. Technically, without the right to command (authority), the CPA is not involved in a conflict of interest—he does not hold substantial enough control of a client to affect his own ability to report objectively to third parties. If he did, he would be in direct control of the company's fortunes. His interest would center on company growth and the presenting of the best picture possible of the organization, to the ultimate benefit of the CPA in the form of increased fees, but to the temporary and even long-term detriment of third parties.

But where do you draw the "responsibility" line in determining what is a conflict of interest, when more and more of the decision-making process in finances and the processes of management decisioning itself are entering the bailiwick of the large accounting firm? With "perceived independence"? With "actual independence"? The problem will soon have to be faced, and it will become more urgent if the predictions of hoped-for expansions in public accounting are fulfilled.

COMPUTERIZATION

The rapid technological development of electronic data processing equipment in the past decade has greatly affected the shape of the work force of the clients of public accountants. The change has come mostly at the lower levels of their hierarchical structure, where simple repetitive tasks, commonly accomplished by hand or mind, were taken over by the machine. With the advent of high-speed, miniaturized, and centralized computer systems of the last few years, more complex decisioning processes have been relegated to their high-capacity, split-second processes. In nearly all types of large-scale organizations, these new electronic data processing systems are now replacing functions that have been performed by lower and middle management persons, as well as functions of the outside experts who serve these organizations. Hospitals are employing computers for diagnosis. There is serious experimentation with electronic retrieval of legal precedents and with automated psychotherapy, in which the computer interprets speech and reacts with an appropriate precoded message.[14] Computers can draft alternative combinations of engineering designs, and they can prepare balance sheets and income-and-expense statements, fully backed by detailed performance accounts.[15]

This latter computerized area has sounded a warning to the public accounting profession, for with the ability to easily and cheaply attain such detailed information, a limited amount of "automated auditing" may already take place with very little aid from the public accountant.[16] One public accountant confronts his colleagues with this question: "The computer doesn't need your traditional fiscal tide tables. As managers gradually become aware of this, will you have new oracles ready for them?"[17] For a good many individual practitioners and firms, the answer is yes, and the oracle is management services. For others, the answer is no: This was indicated when the AICPA reported that 25 percent of "an AICPA membership sample" said that they could have acquired additional clients if they had been able to offer EDP services.[18] "The trend in

14. John Mann, *Changing Human Behavior* (New York: Scribner's, 1965), p. 173.

15. Automation of accounting functions is discussed by Edwin T. Boyle, "What the Computer Means to the Accounting Profession," *Journal of Accountancy* 121:57 (January 1966).

16. S. Leland Dill and Donald L. Adams, "Automated Auditing," *Journal of Accountancy* 117:54-59 (May 1964).

17. Thomas J. Whistler, "The Manager and the Computer," *Journal of Accountancy* 119:32 (January 1965).

18. From an editorial in *The Journal of Accountancy*, 121:21 (February 1966).

auditing," commented a CPA in management services on the supervisor level of a Big Eight firm, "is to reduce the amount of work performed and to make what remains more regulated and therefore automatic. Growth in value and stature of the profession can occur only in tax advice and management counseling." A tax manager of one Big Eight firm has stated:

> The traditional function of the "worksheet auditor" is in the process of being eliminated through automation. The partner responsibility of making decisions on presentation [of the opinion] remains, of course, but the current "staff" will be replaced by persons capable of checking the input and programming of EDP systems.

> Historical cost accounting will continue to serve a useful (protective) role, but its economic utility is diminishing. The accounting firm which is not in a position to help the business improve profits as well as issue traditional reports will not be able to compete effectively.

Once the public accounting firm has set up a strong management services program, it has entered an area of considerable uncertainty in which much creative work can be accomplished. For although mathematical programming will increase the amount of certainty of the situation,[19] judgment as to the importance of this information and interpretation of how it should be used is still necessary. In a good many situations the knowledge of possible outcomes is extremely limited; they are situations in which considerable judgment potential is necessary.

The full impact of computerization is yet to be felt in public accounting. Although computers have been used in business for more than fifteen years, it was only during the period 1966 through 1968 that more than half the computers in existence have been installed, and the number is expected double again during the next three years.[20] More important, the development of software—that is, new programs in organizational structure and information technology—has not kept pace with the development of hardware. This is now rapidly changing as more sophisticated methods are developed, such as real-time systems, shared computers, overlapping programs, and unwritten electronic

19. Representative statements that refer to this result in accounting can be found in Nicholas Dopuch, "Mathematical Programming and Accounting Approaches to Incremental Cost Analysis," *Accounting Review* 48:746 (October 1963); Clark Sloat and Arthur B. Toan, Jr., "Decision-Making Art—or Science?" (Part II), *Management Services* 1:27–31 (May–June 1964); Arthur B. Toan, Jr., "Management Science . . . Its Impact on Management Thinking," *Price Waterhouse Review* 9:10 (Winter 1964).

20. Gordon B. Davis, "The Auditor and the Computer," *Journal of Accountancy* 125:47 (March 1968).

input.[21] Essentially, the CPA must be able to program a tight internal control system for the computer if a computerized information system is to be utilized effectively to prevent mistakes and fraud.[22] With the exception of the large firms, especially the Big Eight, the accounting profession has not been preparing for these changes. Educational programs and systematic development of literature has been slow to start. Only the largest firms, which develop their own educational programs and do specialized work in management services, are innovating in the field. For example, IBM goes to Touche Ross for advice on new applications for the computer;[23] certainly a testimony to Big Eight skills and capabilities in the field.

THE PARADOX OF UNCERTAINTY

The traditional audit still requires that a good deal of personal judgment be applied at many stages, yet a growing number of public accountants see the need for increasing the judgment potential of their profession by expanding into management services. They feel that if auditing procedures and accounting principles are to be refined and alternative methods are to be limited, then it is important to gain control over new areas of uncertainty. The ultimate fear of rationality in auditing is the loss of power that goes with privileged knowledge, as is the case in any occupational area. Thus,

> as the technical engineer's success in the fight for power comes from the lack of rationalization of his field of action, so it is this lack which gives him the strategic advantage of controlling the only source of uncertainty in an otherwise routinized setup. . . . [He is] never trying to make progress in the control and predictability of his own field.[24]

Computerization acts as a catalyst for the development of information systems, which is a large part of the work of management services.[25] It therefore

21. Robert Beyer, "Top Management in the 1970's . . . and Beyond," *The Quarterly/ Touche, Ross, Bailey & Smart* 12:2 (March 1966); Neil C. Churchill and Andrew C. Stedry, "Extending the Dimensions of Accounting Measurement," *Management Services* 4:15-22 (March-April 1967); John W. Wagner, "EDP and the Auditor of the 1970's," *Accounting Review* 44:600-604 (July 1969).

22. Phillip T. May, Jr., "System Control: Computers the Weak Link?" *Accounting Review* 44:583-592 (July 1969).

23. The lack of preparation is discussed by Harold Weiss in a book review in the November 1966 issue of *Datamation* (pp. 115-119). The IBM example is given in an article, "Are CPA Firms Taking Over Management Consulting?" in *Forbes* magazine, October 1, 1966.

24. Michel Crozier, *The Bureaucratic Phenomenon* (Chicago: University of Chicago Press, 1964), p. 131.

25. Kaufman, "Professional Consulting by CPAs," p. 715.

has a twofold effect on the changing body of knowledge; it helps to rationalize some of the more routine audit steps, and at the same time it opens up new possibilities for innovation in operations auditing and management services.

As the body of knowledge with regard to management services has developed, large firms have had to construct both formal and informal rules within their firms in order to formalize relations between CPAs and non-CPA professionals and to interpret the ethical behavior of these new professional types with the clients of accounting firms. At the same time, these new areas of knowledge that are coming under the control of CPAs provide a power base for them. Management services widen the scope of possibilities in decisioning, thus requiring more judgment by the auditor.

In sum, in these large firms there is an increase in the bureaucracy of routine and a decrease in the bureaucracy of rationality as management services gain in prominence in public accounting. This supports my second hypothesis. The paradox is that rationality of auditing has been overcome by the introduction of management services, only to be replaced by the routine produced by the latter. Rules of knowledge are being replaced by rules of operation.

Management services are a boon to public accounting, but they have given pause to the thinking accountant. He is chary of the consequences of new power, in fact he generally does not search it out. As one analyst put it: "Few experts wish to prevail, to *become* the power—indeed their temperament and inclination are usually otherwise—but their function demands that they should wish their ideas to prevail."[26] So, in this new role, there is concern that overextension, either in one direction (certainty) or the other (uncertainty), will endanger the status of the profession. This brings to mind Wilensky's suggestion that "there may be an optimal base for professional practice—neither too vague nor too precise, too broad nor too narrow," that professional knowledge is to some extent tacit knowledge, which gives the established profession its aura of mystery.[27] Either extreme will produce conformity and rigidity, the former because reality is too difficult to cope with, the latter because it is no longer a challenge.[28] There is, then, some attempt on the part of its members to regulate change in the profession. The accountant's expertise is itself judged by the presence of change. As one accounting theorist states, "The significance of accounting data tends to be justified by the existence and occurrence of the conditions of uncertainty and risk, following the assumption of constant

26. George A. Kelley, "The Expert as Historical Actor," *Daedalus* vol. 92 (Summer 1963).

27. Harold Wilensky, "The Professionalization of Everyone?" *American Journal of Sociology* 70:148-149 (September 1964).

28. Crozier, *The Bureaucratic Phenomenon*, p. 186.

change."29 Once these data become accurate and once they are absorbed by society as general knowledge, the profession's "quest for uncertainty" is renewed. The "fate" of management services and new quests in public accounting are new developments; they are now examined in order to trace further the historical process of this profession.

29. Nicholas Dopuch, "Metaphysics of Pragmatism and Accountancy," *Accounting Review* 37:256 (April 1962).

9

A Profession In Conflict:
New Debates In Public Accounting

SEGMENTATION IN THE PROFESSION

The emphasis in examining the public accounting profession thus far has been to show how well integrated it is—it's cohesion, its consensus, and its homogeneity. This emphasis on consensus is a major perspective in sociological theory. A second is conflict theory, which emphasizes struggle, inequality, power, and coercion.[1] As might be expected, the same dichotomy exists in the sociology of occupations, the so-called Ivy League and Chicago schools.[2] Recently, several theorists have posited a synthesis of the two perspectives and have applied it to social stratification and social problems.[3] When examining a profession—public accounting—a synthesis also emerges. The pervasiveness of conflict and its importance in helping to explain the development of this profession cannot be underestimated.

One of the standard ways to approach an analysis of conflict is to use the concept of subgroups or segments. A segment in a profession is a coalition that is in opposition to other coalitions. A large part of its activity is a power struggle for the possession of institutional arrangements or of some kind of place within them. Professions are "loose amalgamations of segments pursuing different objectives in different manners and more or less delicately held together under a common name at a particular period in history."[4]

The public accounting profession is segmented primarily according to the formal organization of its members. One segment comprises the largest firms, the

1. Walter L. Wallace, ed., *Sociological Theory* (Chicago: Aldine Publishing Co., 1969).

2. R. James McCorkel, "Chicago and Ivy League Sociologies of Occupations: A Comparative Analysis," a paper read at the annual meeting of the Southern Sociological Society, New Orleans, April 11, 1969.

3. On social stratification, see Gerhard Lenski, *Power and Privilege* (New York: McGraw-Hill Book Co., 1966); on social problems, see John M. Martin, Joseph P. Fitzpatrick, and Robert E. Gould, *Analyzing Delinquent Behavior: A New Approach* (Washington, D.C.: U.S. Government Printing Office, 1968). Pierre L. van den Berghe, "Dialectic and Functionalism: Toward a Theoretical Synthesis," *American Sociological Review* 28:695-704 (October 1963), is a key article.

4. This description of segmentation is given by Rue Bucher and Anselm Strauss, "Professions in Process," *American Journal of Sociology* 66:325-334 (January 1961). See also Anselm Strauss et al., *Psychiatric Ideologies and Institutions* (New York: The Free Press, 1964).

Big Eight. Another is made up of medium-sized and small firms. A third, very loosely organized segment, is that of individual practitioners. One place where these coalitions are most evident is in the operations of public accounting's largest professional association, the AICPA. One particularly good example occurred at the 1960 annual meeting of the membership, where the argument over strengthening the code of ethics clearly exposed two factions, the Big Eight and a few semi-national firms against the smaller firms.[5] The model of segments, in discussing the conflicts of values between segments, lists "spurious unity" as one such conflict. What occurred at the AICPA meeting was just that: "established associations become battlegrounds as different emerging segments compete for control. Considered from this viewpoint, such things as codes of ethics and procedures of certification become the historical deposits of certain powerful segments."[6]

Small firms have on many occasions reported their disturbance at the amount of influence wielded by the largest firms. At least one CPA spokesman has commented in print on the constant "possibility of fragmentation" of minority groups.[7] Another point that must be considered in discussing the AICPA is its size. Such a large membership (55,000) requires a complex system of formal organization in order to cover and satisfy the membership. This is a task that few organizations of this size have managed to do without incurring the price of segmentation or, possibly worse, of factionalism and the ultimate destruction of the organization.[8] Thus far, the AICPA has avoided or solved serious conflicts, but its increasing size and the increase in complexity of knowledge may negate this success.

The consensus school views a profession as a community, its major characteristics being:

1. Its members are bound by a sense of identity.
2. Once in it, few leave, so that it is a terminal or continuing status for the most part.
3. Its members share values in common.
4. Its role definitions vis-à-vis both members and nonmembers are agreed upon and are the same for all members.
5. Within the areas of communal action there is a common language, which is understood only partially by outsiders.

5. The event is described by T. A. Wise, "The Auditors Have Arrived" (Part I), *Fortune* vol. 62 (November 1960).

6. Bucher and Strauss, "Professions in Process," pp. 331-332.

7. John L. Carey, ed., *The Accounting Profession: Where Is It Headed?* (New York: AICPA, 1962), p. 153.

8. Kenneth E. Boulding, *Conflict and Defense* (New York: Harper & Bros., 1962), p. 160, remarks that "the larger an organization grows, the more tendency there is for factions and dissident elements to grow within it and for the organization ultimately to split or to fall apart."

6. The community has power over its members.

7. Its limits are reasonably clear, though they are not physical and geographical, but social.

8. Though it does not produce the next generation biologically, it does so socially through its control over the selection of professional trainees, and through its training processes it sends these recruits through an adult socialization process.[9]

The profession of public accounting *is not* a community according to this definition. At the same time there are segments within the profession: the Big Eight are a community, except possibly with regard to characteristic number 2. But they are now experiencing the beginnings of another type of segmentation, one based on technique: This is the expanding area of management services. There has been as yet no successful general formula for effectively interrelating the functions of auditing and management services when a complex economic organization must be served by both functions. Specialization resulting from this complexity has made it impossible for any one individual to master the technical knowledge of both fields, nor is this expected. CPAs will have to accept specialties with their own separate limited autonomy, just as lawyers and doctors have. The differences between public accounting and the other professions, however, are that these specialized segments are operating in unique professional organizations (in terms of size and distribution) and that the specialty is made up primarily of members who come from or who could join another "emerging" profession—management consulting.

Even subspecialties could segment from the many technique sources of management services. Already, groups of actuaries who are employed by or associated with some Big Eight firms number ten, twenty, or more persons. In at least one firm, in order to get around partnership restrictions, the actuaries comprise a separate-but-equal partnership from the parent firm.

To one close observer of the profession, countervailing forces appear to be at work, the first being "divisive, tending to create new professions and subprofessions and to split off specialty groups from the main body."[10] My analysis has shown one of these forces to be specialization. The second force "is cohesive, trying to pull together ... the proliferating groups in the same general areas of knowledge and work."[11] This force would be the desire for autonomy on the part of the professional community as a unit.[12] The loose amalgam of powerful segments, each gaining control over certain areas of the profession, is not yet the case for public accounting as a whole, though recent and expected developments may take it in this direction.

9. William J. Goode, "Community within a Community: The Professions," *American Sociological Review* 22:194 (April 1957).

10. John L. Carey, *The CPA Plans for the Future* (New York: AICPA, 1965), p. 449.

11. Ibid.

12. Goode, "Community within a Community," p. 198.

As the specialties in management service have become more fully developed and accepted as part of the expertise of the normal CPA firm, there has been a call for a code of ethics in this field of operations. The AICPA Committee on Professional Ethics has issued three opinions on this problem, numbers 12, 14, and 17, which have begun to delimit the area of ethical conduct. And the AICPA Committee on Management Advisory Services has issued two statements that specify guidelines on the areas and extent of participation, scope of service, and competence. Still another ruling has been established by British accounting associations for a diploma in management services after a two-part examination has been passed. The first part requires two. years of management services experience, and the second part requires a thesis and an oral examination on that thesis. This may eventually serve as an academic and licensing basis for the area.

Thus the process of externalizing rules begins to take shape in another area in the profession. However, while externalization of rule-making in management services tends to debureaucratize (in terms of routine) firms in this area by limiting the number of internal regulations and the personnel needed to adminis- ter them, at the same time the formalization of rules bureaucratizes (rational- izes) action in the area. That this latter process could occur is the concern of the former Executive Director of the AICPA, who feels that in management services, public accounting should not be too quick to define a structured body of knowledge; so, "rather than carry around a set of technical solutions looking for a problem to which they can be applied, he [the CPA] carries an approach, ability as a problem solver, and essentially sells his judgment."[13]

So the rules paradox still exists in management services in the 1970s, as it did in 1960, only now the routine is on the *decrease* and rationality is on the *increase*. But management services is a broad field with many facets yet to be exploited for new knowledge, and the Big Eight are rapidly moving to incorpo- rate ever-larger and more comprehensive areas of uncertainty. With their back- ground in EDP, this has brought them into the area of information theory.

NEW AREAS OF UNCERTAINTY: THE CONCEPT OF TOTAL INFORMATION SERVICES

Information is knowledge of activity that is measured, stored, and communi- cated. The problems of what information should be measured for storage and how it should be organized in order to communicate it have only begun to be examined. Measurement of the complex information processes of a large indus- trial corporation have required the services of experts from several fields,

13. Carey, *The CPA Plans*, p. 227.

including accountants, industrial engineers, economists, and marketologists. Communication of information has required the services of advertisers, specialists in community and public relations, and internal communications administrators. Storage and retrieval have usually been relegated to the less important positions in the organization, and so these areas manage without experts.

With the new "information revolution" brought about by electronic computers, two major changes in information services have occurred. First, the amount of information that can be measured has increased tremendously. Processes of production and control can now be measured in terms of millions of bits of information per second. Second, the computer has united into one operation the three major stages of information processing. Within a period of seconds after stimuli have been received, the modern digital computer measures, records, and communicates all information for which it is programmed. In order to supply the increased information to the computer, a whole new breed of experts is now beginning to serve large-scale organizations. The machine is "fed," and its disgorged information is interpreted by statisticians, psychologists, econometricians, certified public accountants, and others. New techniques allow information from the different parts of the organization to be integrated within the same program.[14] The system is rapidly becoming "total."

In the job of running an organization, experts are called upon by its operating management to aid, with the use of computers, in decisioning on important matters. In the past, information measurement had been geared to presenting the past and, in some cases, the present. With the advent of probability statistics, coupled with electronic data processing, areas of judgment fell into the realm of electronic prediction. This is an especially important function for business enterprises in competition, and it has even greater significance for the yet more complex relations of purely social and political organizations.

What is to be the role of public accounting in this revolution? Under the impetus of a study by the Long-Range Objective Committee of the AICPA, a number of reports and articles, and at least one book have been directed to this question. The consensus is that public accounting is the natural profession to be in charge of planning, measuring, attesting, and communicating the total information services of an economic nature to its client—the management, owners, and third parties of organizations. That is, this service would encompass the decision of what is to be measured, as well as the interpretation and evaluation of that measurement.[15] This service would be extended to labor-management relations,

14. A. F. Moravec, "Basic Concepts for Planning Advanced EDP Systems," *Accounting and the Computer* (New York: AICPA, 1966), pp. 273-286.

15. This is essentially the conclusion drawn in a report of the Long-Range Objectives Committee. See Paul Lazarsfeld, "Accounting and Social Bookkeeping," in *Accounting in Perspective*, ed. Robert R. Sterling and William F. Bentz (Cincinnati: South-Western, 1971), pp. 88-101.

state and federal government reports, projection reports, management performance reports, and the like, the results of which would appear as an attest.[16] In
order to accomplish this, we must have a "constructive" or creative accounting;
we must invent systems of concepts and techniques.[17]

What is the profession now doing to attain this goal? There has been
increasing pressure for changes to new concepts in accounting, for example, to
price-level adjustments. One result of this Accounting Research Study No. 6,
Reporting the Financial Effects of Price-Level Changes. Closely related to this is
the accrual system of accounting, where the value of a transaction is recorded
immediately; there is no waiting for actual collection or payment. There are also
suggestions for audits that are based on natural cycles and on-going processes,
rather than being limited by the idea of annual-ending reporting.[18] And there is
increasing emphasis in large firms on giving more comprehensive information
services, which sometimes goes by the name of "operations auditing." An audit
partner of one Big Eight firm commented:

> We stress training in our firm, training in the total concept of ac-
> counting; of the wide view, beyond financial accounting to the survey of
> the state of the business in terms of its purposes and goals and the
> efficiency with which they're being reached. I agree with your thesis in
> that public accounting needs something new; it needs something to simu-
> late its recruits, to interest the bright young man into choosing accounting
> and to keep this interest once he has joined us. The first years in a large
> firm can really be grinding and monotonous and a big letdown for the
> young person expecting interesting and stimulating work because he is in a
> profession. And here's where operations auditing may be an answer to this
> problem: it tells a man [CPA], "What's our problem?" and "Why is it a
> problem?" and "What can be done about it?" This is the challenge, and it's
> a big job, and we're letting a few of our younger staff have a go at it.

16. Carey, ed., *The Accounting Profession*, p. 159; David F. Linowes, "The Future of
the Accounting Profession," *Accounting Review* 40:97-104 (January 1965), and "Professional Organization and Growth," *Journal of Accountancy* 120:24-29 (July 1965); *Accounting Education* (AICPA, 1963), especially pp. 10, 22; William F. Campfield, "Critical
Paths for Professional Accountants during the New Management Revolution," *Accounting
Review* 38:521-527 (July 1963).

17. Adolph J. H. Enthoven, "Economic Development and Accountancy," *Journal of
Accountancy* 120:29-35 (August 1965); David F. Linowes, "Government and the Accounting Profession," *Journal of Accountancy* 121:53-57 (May 1966).

18. Cf. Laurence J. Fitzsimmons, "Continuous Auditing," *Arthur Young Journal*
3:12-15 (January 1956); Colin Park and John W. Gladson, *Working Capital* (New York:
Macmillan, 1963), especially pp. 15-18, 52; Joseph L. Roth, "What's Ahead for the
Auditors?" excerpts from a report to the Council of the AICPA, May 6, 1969, in *Journal of
Accountancy* 128:61 (August 1969).

An audit partner of another Big Eight firm noted in passing that "operations" or "procedural" accounting encompasses much more than the traditional audit. It is interested in auditing how well something is being performed according to its estimates of how well it should be performed, whereas traditional accounting audits only the transactions that have occurred through the operations of the company.

By its comprehensiveness, operations auditing includes the management services area,* including electronic data processing. Current problems in computer operations in client accounting and in CPA auditing are being given much attention in the accounting literature, with extensive discussions of auditing the computer programs of clients, loss of information, construction of computerized test models of the accounting system, and employee collusion.[19] There has not yet been any programming of nonrational behavior and the effects of that behavior into a digital-analogue computer model, as has been begun experimentally in the social sciences.[20] But the management sciences people in the large accounting firms are generally aware of these developments.

Another new area, one that goes beyond the general definition of management services to the attest of management itself, is being discussed in public accounting. The attest is made of compliance to certain prearranged standards of management's processes of information gathering, decisioning, and control, not of the results of these processes.[21] Questioning of sixty-five prominent practitioners and educators of public accounting on this point revealed that nearly half thought the profession was ready for this type of attest, but not for areas of *top*

---

* In *Auditing Standards and Procedures: Statement No. 33* (New York: AICPA, 1963), p. 28, the AICPA defines internal control under two subheadings: accounting controls and administrative controls. I previously referred to the synonymous aspects of "management services" and "internal control." Joseph W. Dodwell, "Operational Auditing: A Part of the Basic Audit," *Journal of Accountancy* 121:32 (June 1966), relates "internal control" to management services in this manner.

19. For example: W. Thomas Porter, "Evaluating Internal Controls in EDP Systems," *Journal of Accountancy* 118:34-40 (August 1964); Herbert Arkin, "Computers and the Audit Test," *Journal of Accountancy* 120:44-48 (November 1965); Wayne S. Boutell, "Auditing Through the Computer," *Journal of Accountancy* 120:41-47 (November 1965); John A. Tracy, in a letter to *Journal of Accountancy* 121:19 (February 1966); H. Bruce Joplin, "The Accountant's Role in Management Information Systems," *Journal of Accountancy* 121:43-46 (March 1966); Yuji Ijiri, "Axioms and Structures of Conventional Accounting Measurement," *Accounting Review* 40:36-53 (January 1965); Robert R. Sterling, "Elements of Pure Accounting Theory," *Accounting Review* 42:62-73 (January 1967).

20. John T. and Jeanne E. Gullahorn, "Some Computer Applications in Social Science," *American Sociological Review* 30:353-364 (June 1965); John R. Pierce, "Communications Technology and the Future," *Daedalus* 94:506-517 (Spring 1965).

21. See the comments by Neil C. Churchill and Richard M. Cyert, "An Experiment in Management Auditing," *Journal of Accountancy* 121:42 (February 1966); Carey, *The Accounting Profession*, p. 161.

management operations. Nearly two-thirds of the respondents felt that by 1985 the profession would be able to handle the management attest, and close to one-half answered in the affirmative for top management attest.[22] It is reported that the management attest is being requested by some boards of directors and stockholder groups.[23]

This new field, usually referred to as management auditing, is the broadest term yet applied to work done by public accountants. It includes the area of operations auditing, management accounting, and responsibility accounting. The management audit deals with the future, as well as the past and the present. It reviews formal and informal organizational structure, information systems and flows, and decision patterns, in order to determine management's "optimum arrangements for running an entity." The auditor then evaluates management's effectiveness in organizing and directing these factors.[24] Management accounting provides economic information to managers. This branch of organization theory deals with the future.[25] An effective management accounting system will be the basis for information used to simulate what *should be* produced, as compared to what *is* produced—what is called responsibility accounting.[26]

The management audit would include examination and evaluation of these new forms of accounting, certainly a strategic job for a profession. It will require that present unrelated and undeveloped information systems be organized into what the managing partner of Touche Ross calls a Management Information Services function, a "total systems control."[27] As with accounting principles and management services, there are those in the profession who are against such a projection of the CPA's area of competence, because they see it as a threat to independence.

Another new area developed by the Big Eight, which might be classified as an extension of management services, is actuarial work.[28] Of the fifteen largest firms (as determined by the number of members in the Society of Actuaries) who advise U.S. corporations on the financing of their pension plans, two are Big Eight firms: Peat Marwick is third largest, and Lybrand is fourteenth largest. The

22. Summarized from questionnaire results presented in *Accounting Education*, pp. 67-68.

23. Ibid., p. 10.

24. William L. Campfield, "Trends in Auditing Management Plans and Operations," *Journal of Accountancy* 124:41-46 (July 1967).

25. John E. Field, "Toward a Multi-Level, Multi-Goal Information System," *Accounting Review* 44:596 (July 1969).

26. Clemens A. Erdahl, ed., "Building a Management Accounting System," in the Management Services news section of *Journal of Accountancy* 127:81-84 (April 1969).

27. Robert Beyer, "Top Management in the 1970's . . . and Beyond," *The Quarterly/ Touche, Ross, Bailey & Smart* 12:2 (March 1966).

28. The discussion of actuaries is based on the article by T. A. Wise, "Those Uncertain Actuaries," *Fortune* 73:164-166, 184-186 (January 1966).

importance of pension-funding can be measured in the increasing amount of profits that are tied up in them. Currently, about 9 percent of corporate profits are retained there, with some companies reverting up to 50 percent. The guidelines for costing these plans are so unclear that enormous adjustments can be made to financial statements, depending on the method applied. The questions of refining methods and of ethics have not even been breached yet in this whole new segment.

Another consideration, hardly ever found in print because it directly contradicts the business-oriented ideology of public accounting, deals with the possibilities for public accounting in a socialist economy. Arguments against the profit motive of production have occurred simultaneously with the increasing complexity and interdependence of society. These debates may produce a change from reward being given to management for greater profits to reward given to management for improved economic performance (cost reduction, product improvement, and so forth). In this system, entrepreneurial risks would vanish,[29] but the risks inherent in responsibility would remain. And whether that responsibility would lie ultimately with management or with the federal government, public accounting prognosticators hope that, in either event, CPAs will be prepared technically and intellectually to perform advisory and attest services.

INFORMATION THEORY VS. THE PRINCIPLE OF UNCERTAINTY

The concept of uncertainty has been used in this book to describe a state brought about by new knowledge: namely, that information increases uncertainty (judgment potential). However, as a special branch of systems theory, information (knowledge) is seen only as reducing ignorance and uncertainty. The latter definition deals with the system as it exists. It limits itself to a static level of uncertainty, which is constantly reduced as the amount of information increases. As it pertains to cybernetics: the more the information, the more the certainty; the less the information, the less the structure and the more the entropy, randomness, and uncertainty. This is *information theory*. On the other hand, the *principle of uncertainty* states that no knowledge is indubitably true,[30] that new knowledge is generated in and through the system, a dynamic process of social change. Information theory has to do with reduction of ignorance; the principle of uncertainty concerns the creation of new knowledge.

29. Carey, *The CPA Plans*, p. 210.

30. Ralf Dahrendorf, *Essays in the Theory of Society* (Stanford, Calif.: Stanford University Press, 1968), p. 240.

Large-firm accountants are naturally becoming involved in the application of information theory. In accounting, information is "accounting data evaluated for a specific use. . . . An accounting estimate is improved by reducing the uncertainty under which it is made."[31] This fits very well for some computerized accounting and auditing—the highly rationalized areas that can easily be quantified. But it is becoming a serious block in the development of accounting theory, and ultimately it could affect accounting and auditing practice. The economic theory of information is now being applied to a form of macro-accounting known as social accounting. This is basically a system of accounting for changes in a national, regional, or local noneconomic social system such as a county, state, or city. The result is an equilibrium theory for social action in which individuals are utility maximizers and will expend whatever effort is necessary to maintain the status quo, essentially a consensus-theorist conceptualization.

One of the most ambitious projects in social accounting has been a "systems analysis approach" to Detroit's war on poverty, in which a team from Touche Ross worked with the Mayor's Committee for Human Resource Development. The supervisor of this team stated that "the War on Poverty does not have a profit motive in the business sense; but in all other respects the similarity is striking."[32] A poverty "market" is defined, "market information" is collected, and "performances" of poverty areas are measured through the success of Community Action Programs.[33] On this basis the team "reviews the allocation of resources procedure" and provides "internal management" information, as well as "data which will satisfy public demand."[34] "Performances" of poverty areas are determined by measuring police-department offence complaints, arrests, and youth-bureau information; city welfare relief rolls and stamp operations; clinic venereal disease and tuberculosis cases; health department reports of births, deaths, and stillbirths; dependent children statistics; unemployment and old-age statistics; truancy and dropouts; legal aid requests; and the like.

The assumption behind this social accounting is that all data are sense data and thus are quantifiable.[35] However, as Etzioni has shown, "erroneous accounting, and hence misbased strategies in societal planning, becomes likely

31. Norton M. Bedford and Mohamed Onsi, "Measuring the Value of Information: An Information Theory Approach," *Management Services* 3:15 (January-February 1966). See also Robert R. Sterling, *Theory of the Measurement of Enterprise Income* (Lawrence: University Press of Kansas, 1972), pp.39-63.

32. Jean-Paul A. Ruff, "Poverty Programs: A Business Management Approach," *The Quarterly/Touche, Ross, Bailey & Smart* 12:24-25 (June 1966).

33. William J. Bruns, Jr., and Robert J. Snyder, "Management Information for Community Action Programs," *Management Services* 6:15-22 (July-August 1969).

34. Ruff, "Poverty Programs."

35. David F. Linowes, "Socio-Economic Accounting," *Journal of Accountancy* 126:37-42 (November 1968).

when it is assumed that a concept is measured in its entirety, though, in fact, only a fraction of it [that is, its rational aspect] is measured." For example, reduction in the discharge rates of mental hospitals and the average length of hospitalization might lead to the conclusion that mental illness is becoming less of a problem. However, readmission rates have increased even more—"fewer beds may be needed but the patients keep them warm for each other."[36] At the highest levels, subjective judgments that are normatively and politically motivated must be considered in the measurement strategy.[37] All data may ultimately be quantifiable, but not all data are sense data.

Accountants are found on both sides of the debate. The "rationalists" tend to stick with information theory when dealing with macroaccounting phenomena.[38] There is a tendency for this group to view the nature of accounting as "consensual" and not conflictful, as concerned with the maintenance of the status quo entity and not with "subcoalitions."[39] The Detroit poverty study concludes that a major purpose of the program is to "anticipate trouble before it erupts and to make changes and adjustments as required."[40] The "organicists" have a more qualitative orientation. They view accounting as probabilistic in nature,[41] even that accountants should assume a normative stance, that they

36. Amitai Etzioni and Edward W. Lehman, "Some Dangers in 'Valid' Social Measurement," in *Social Intelligence for America's Future,* ed. Bertram M. Gross (Boston: Allyn and Bacon, Inc., 1969), p. 47. The quote is from Howard E. Freeman and Ozzie G. Simmons, *The Mental Patient Comes Home* (New York: John Wiley and Sons, 1963), p. 3, as quoted in the Etzioni-Lehman article.

37. Amitai Etzioni, *The Active Society* (New York: The Free Press, 1968), p. 266. As the author notes (p. 303), the three major determinants of decision-making are power, knowledge, and normative commitment.

38. For example: Harold W. Jasper, "Future Role of the Accountant," *Management Services* 3:51-56 (January-February 1966); Adolph F. Moravec, "Using Simulation to Design a Management Information System," *Management Services* 3:50-58 (May-June 1966); John W. Dickhaut, "Accounting Information in Decision-Making," *Management Services* 6:49-55 (January-February 1969); Robert Beyer, "The Modern Management Approach to a Program of Social Improvement," *Journal of Accountancy* 127:37-46 (March 1969).

39. Reginald S. Gynther, "Accounting Concepts and Behavioral Hypotheses," *Accounting Review* 42:289 (April 1967).

40. Beyer, "The Modern Management Approach," p. 40.

41. Robert M. Trueblood, quoted in *Journal of Accountancy,* October 1966, p. 12; Robert H. Roy and James H. MacNeill, *Horizons for a Profession* (New York: AICPA, 1967), p. 99; Leon W. Woodfield, "Lessening the Dangers of Uncertainty," *Management Services* 4:51-55 (January-February 1967); Howard F. Stettler, "CPAs/Auditing/2000±," *Journal of Accountancy* 125:55-58 (May 1968); Kermit D. Larson, "Implications of Measurement Theory on Accounting Concept Formulation," *Accounting Review* 64:46 (January 1969).

should be responsible for determining what *should* be rather than what the client has requested.[42]

There is a basic contraposition between the principle of uncertainty and the desirability of completely rationalizing through a total information model in order to find the "one best way," which some accountants espouse. This information model is, ironically, a utopian view, not unlike that of Marx and other utopian socialists who envisaged a "perfect" system, albeit one in which the personal initiative in private industry is the champion. There is a tendency for a value-free technology to be constructed. Affective elements are not considered and are consciously eliminated from any model of system operation. The "free-floating" intellectual and his total ideology, his vision of the future, is being replaced by the "scholar-expert" who does not accept value-laden schemes, but rather wants to use the most rational system of social analysis. In the words of one severe critic, they are becoming intellectual mandarins.[43] The language of organizational theory today reflects the "machine metaphor" (social engineering, equilibrium) and not the "organic metaphor" (open systems, adaptive, developmental).[44] In the process, man becomes dehumanized; there is "action without deliberation."[45]

In contrast, the principle of uncertainty sees no knowledge as indisputably true, no decision as finally right. Therefore, if one does not want to elevate error, one must accept various ideas, particularly contradictory ones, a plurality of decision patterns to interact and compete. "Uncertainty demands variety and competition. From the assumption of a fundamental uncertainty about what is right, there follows the necessity of conflict," of the antagonism of power interests, generated and institutionalized.[46]

There is the real fear that the narrow theory of information will completely envelop accounting, becoming the ideological whip of an Orwellian future. So far, however, the profession is a long way from such a future. As examples in the last three chapters have shown, there is a good deal of conflict, diversity of opinion, and exploration of new ideas within a fairly stable social structure.

42. Norton M. Bedford, "The Nature of Future Accounting Theory," *Accounting Review* 42:84 (January 1967); Sterling, *Theory of the Measurement,* p. 61 and passim.

43. Noam Chomsky, "The Responsibility of Intellectuals," *New York Review,* February 23, 1967.

44. Warren G. Bennis and Philip E. Slater, *The Temporary Society* (New York: Harper & Row, 1968), p. 120.

45. The quote and the rationalist-organicist dichotomy are from a comprehensive analysis by Sheldon S. Wolin, "A Critique of Organizational Theories," in *A Sociological Reader on Complex Organizations,* ed. Amitai Etzioni (2d ed.; New York: Holt, Rinehart & Winston, 1969), pp. 133-149.

46. Dahrendorf, *Essays in the Theory of Society,* pp. 239-253.

The change that has to do with a push toward uncertainty creates a certain amount of conflict between competing individuals and groups in an organization. This is true for accounting firms. The power struggle between the conflicting parties encourages innovation. But the conflict must be legitimated, otherwise it depresses this innovation. Therefore, "other things being equal, the less bureaucratized (monocratic) the organization [in terms of routine and rigidity], the more conflict and uncertainty and the more innovation."[47] For large accounting firms, this statement does not hold. There, uncertainty is not created by a lack of routine but is more the effect of the rationalizing of innovation. Furthermore, the relationship is reversed. The more uncertainty and innovation there is, the less bureaucracy of rationality. The relationship is not a simple one, either. For with increased innovation, the bureaucracy of routine can be multiplied to control the great amount of uncertainty that innovation has produced. This is a reaction to the fear of overextended practice, that is, the desire to maintain the "optimal base" of professional practice.

But in their normal course, the firms pursue change by making conflict normative in the organization. This legitimizes innovation. There is a "creative conformity" that is sponsored by the accounting firms,[48] for they realize (to limited degrees) the danger that they will lose power as the result of increased rationality in areas of professional knowledge. Norms that sponsor independent judgment (the definition of creative conformity) are much in evidence in large accounting firms. Several instances have already been noted of the importance attached to judgment by the large-firm sample. But there is "judgment" (with limited amounts of creativity, for all judgment involves use of the creative process), and there is "creative judgment," a more radical restructuring of reality.[49] To the question of why management services are important to the growth of public accounting, one audit manager responded: "It's one of the few areas where there is creative work, rather than looking over someone's shoulder to check [as an auditor does]. It is an area where clients would seek us out. An auditor is like a dentist—you go to him only if you have to." This kind of judgment, creative judgment, will claim new areas of uncertainty for the firm

47. Victor A. Thompson, "Bureaucracy and Innovation," *Administrative Science Quarterly* 10:4 (June 1965).

48. Erwin O. Smigel, *The Wall Street Lawyer: Professional Organization Man?* (New York: The Free Press, 1964), pp. 314, 322, discusses the norms that maintain conflict for lawyers in large law firms.

49. John Mann, *Changing Human Behavior* (New York: Scribner's, 1965), p. 128: "It [creativity] represents an ability to restructure a limited aspect of psychological, social, or physical reality."

and the profession. The norms that sponsor this judgment are extremely important informal rules of the large firms, for they produce innovation and can bring power to the firm and the profession.

In another sense, uncertainty developed by the profession is the effect of rationality, due to new combinations brought about in a body of knowledge as a result of that rationality. Increased judgment due to computerization is a case in point. Facets of this type of bureaucracy presently can serve as an impetus for a new cycle of professional activity. This further complicates the picture of cycles of activity; the movements in the profession toward professionalization and its bureaucratic trends are so closely interwoven that a simple diagram (see table 16) hardly suffices to explain the complexity of cooperating, competing, and opposing forces. But it may help to clarify the process of professional bureaucracy.

Professionalization and bureaucracy are bound up with attempts by the profession to enter areas of uncertainty. As a new area is absorbed, external rules are instituted to provide technical and ethical guidance. This results in increased emphasis on the code of ethics and the body of knowledge, as in the case of management services. In instances of change, the remaining attributes (of the profession) are all ultimately affected by these two. As the rules of the area become more clearly specified and detailed, the fear of loss of personal judgment (another attribute considered most important by the questionnaire sample) is incentive to push on to another new area of uncertainty. In this manner, professional standing is maintained.

Presently, public accounting is formalizing in the area of auditing, and it is experimenting with the new, nonrationalized areas of operations auditing and the management audit. What this means for the large firm is a continuous limited bureaucracy, as is seen in table 16. It is estimated that management services are midway in the process of being rationalized. (The question comes to mind:

TABLE 16

Professional Bureaucracy in Large Accounting Firms

Action of the Profession	Type of Bureaucracy (in firm)	
	Routine and Red Tape	Rationality
external professional rules increasing in numbers, specificity, and extent	debureaucratization	bureaucratization
push towards uncertainty	bureaucratization	debureaucratization
external professional rules increasing in numbers, specificity, and extent	debureaucratization	bureaucratization

172

Would any profession be able to remain a profession if it did not entertain new ideas and operations? The classic example is the failure of barbers to capitalize on new advances in surgery. Another more recent example might be the failure of social workers to explore, through their professional associations, new philosophies and the social, economic, and political procedures and ramifications of them.) The cycle of action within the accounting profession is repeating itself in the area of management services as it operated (and is still operating) for auditing. Not that management services has gone any considerable distance thus far in rationalizing and externalizing rules in its area. The diversity of knowledge and the techniques that it draws from other disciplines, coupled to the audit function in a total information service or operations audit, leaves room for much highly creative judgment. But even so, new areas of uncertainty related to and beyond management services are being explored by public accountants; and this represents the beginnings of still another movement in the cycle of professional action.

Many cycles of varying importance may overlap in the process of change; for example, management services, management audit, actuarial work, computerization, are at various stages of development. What is important is that, in a relatively stable organization, so much conflict and change can occur. For conflict in areas of theory and practice acts as the impetus for any change in the body of knowledge or rules of the firms and the profession. The function of the professional association and its membership is to increase uncertainty by controlling a body of knowledge (limiting rationality) and by constantly creating new knowledge as the old inevitably becomes circumscribed by rules. The entire process is a power phenomenon that produces conflict, "and conflict between antagonistic interests gives lasting expression to the fundamental uncertainty of human existence, by ever giving rise to new solutions and ever casting doubt on them as soon as they take form."[50] Conflict is necessary to the profession's existence. In many cases it is the key element in cohesion,[51] for without the stimulus of intellectual battle, public accounting would soon atrophy.

In this respect the Big Eight are of inestimable importance to the growth of public accounting. Because of the size of these firms and because of their emphasis on creative conformity, the profession has kept pace with the growth of other professions that are vying for the increasingly important advisory role to nearly all types of formal organization. This has become an area of intense conflict and competition, and today it is perhaps the most significant impetus for change in public accounting.

---

50. Dahrendorf, *Essays in the Theory of Society*, p. 227.

51. Percy S. Cohen, *Modern Social Theory* (New York: Basic Books, 1969), p. 161: "Conflict may be the very stuff of cohesion."

10

Professions in Conflict:
The CPA and the Future

COMPETITION BETWEEN PROFESSIONS:
THE CPA AS GENERALIST

There are several areas in which professions perform services that overlap one another and generate conflict over who is to perform them. Long-established professions usually have clearly defined and restricted areas of knowledge over which they preside, with conflict erupting only at the periphery of their boundaries, where new knowledge has generated areas of uncertainty. One such example is the controversy between lawyers and accountants, ranging from the early 1940s to the late 1950s, on the question of who was to be legally constituted to engage in certain areas of tax work and related consulting.

But in the large unclaimed area of uncertainty the conflicts between emerging professions and between emerging professions and established ones tend to be larger, and these conflicts can cause the downfall of one or more of their professions. Such a conflict is the one involving large public accounting firms and management consulting firms over the area of management services. The argument is continually repeated by public accountants that they are in the key position to give consulting services to management. They are the ones who by training and experience know best the financial status and operations of an organization. They do not have to take the time and money to perform a special study (especially of internal control systems) to gain this knowledge, because they already have collected and analyzed it in their normal audit function. Their work is continuous, year to year, so they have past experience with the client and with other similar clients to go by in their evaluations. Finally, their auditing job is at stake when they consult, whereas a one-shot consulting job carries no such threat. A good example of this last point was made by the senior partner of one medium-sized firm:

> I saw a management consulting firm almost ruin a client of ours. What had happened was that a very fundamental principle of responsibility was ignored—there was no concern with how the new device would operate in the future. After the company was fouled up [by this new device], it took us more than a year to get them back into the black. We had to do work simplification studies, make up monthly reports, hold meetings with their banks, review sales policies, etcetera, etcetera.
>
> Later, when I saw the management consulting firm representative, I asked him why they hadn't gone further into the possible consequences of

175

the new device, and he said to me, "It's a nice day. What are you worried about?"

The competition between public accounting firms and management consulting firms for management services engagements is stiff. But as some accountants were quick to point out, management services in accounting is only a small part of the whole field of management consulting, and management consulting has much room for expansion, for both management consultants and for accountants. One study of management consulting concluded that management consultants appear to be too well established for CPAs "seriously to expect to beat them down competitively," because CPAs have such a poor image, the rules of their profession preclude advertising and direct solicitation, they cannot enter into partnership with non-CPAs, and they have no formal testing of their competence in management services.[1] But already the last two of these reasons are being attacked. In the large accounting firms a separate hierarchical structure has been constructed to accommodate management services people, and in at least one instance a separate working partnership of non-CPA specialists has been constructed as a way around the problem. In 1966 a rigorous examination on management services for accountants was established in Great Britain. Also changing rapidly is the scope and amount of Big Eight management services. One writer reports that Peat Marwick may well be the world's largest management consulting service and that it holds within it the world's largest executive placement agency.[2] Its gross revenues are four times those of the largest architectural firm or management consulting firm, twice those of the largest advertising agency, and ten to fifteen times those of the largest law firms. The article goes on to list some of its activities:

1. Arranging mergers and acquisitions for approximately 250 candidates in 1966.
2. Placement in the past year of 250 executives in corporations, some of them not audit clients, and placement of 300 men from its own firm with client firms.
3. Advising foreign governments: for example, on construction of new industrial projects (India); computation of price and cost values in industry nationalization (England).
4. Management services to the highway departments of ten states with fees ranging from $75,000 to $250,000 for preparation of programs on construction and maintenance costs and management methods.

1. Richard M. Lynch, "Professional Standards for Management Consulting in the United States" (Ph.D. diss., Graduate School of Business Administration, Harvard University, 1959), p. 334.
2. T. A. Wise, "The Very Private World of Peat, Marwick, Mitchell," *Fortune* 74:88-91, 128-130 (July 1, 1966).

Peat Marwick grossed $17.5 million in 1965 from management consulting, whereas Booz, Allen & Hamilton, the largest general management consultant, grossed $20 million. For the Big Eight, management services are expanding at the rate of 15 percent annually. For the 45 "elite" management consulting firms who are members of the Association of Consulting Management Engineers, expansion is approximately 10 percent. For the consulting business in general it is 4 percent.[3]

The rapid development of EDP—electronic data processing—involves *all* professions that engage directly in information services in a struggle, if they are a little unwary, for the status and prestige that results from EDP's power. Lazarsfeld has commented on this phenomenon to public accountants, as paraphrased from an interview:

> The computer is invading all divisions of business and this raises the issue of who should control the computer. A power fight could develop between accountants and other groups, for the division which controls the computer also controls the investments of the company. The stakes are high in this conflict or collaboration issue, for the status and prestige of the various professions will be dependent upon the outcome.[4]

One area of computer competition is already under way between CPAs and banking professionals.[5] It would be surprising if even greater competition did not develop with management consulting firms in the near future, as information analysis in many areas of expertise is a central part of their work. Also, in the concept of *total* information services, as applied in operations auditing, large firms will find a conflict with the legal profession and with other experts who are involved in counseling the leadership of large-scale organizations. For example, if a top executive needs advice on an acquisition, a merger, a reorganization, or a purchase or sale of securities, he is more apt to call his auditor, if he is aware that his auditor can supply this service, to ask him what he feels is the best move. Subsequently, the large body of legal work will be handled by the lawyers. Even if the auditor's counsel occupied only ten minutes on the phone, it is the counsel of a power position. This type of advice was given on four different occasions during my interviews with partners and managers. As a supervising senior of one Big Eight firm put it: "We will be going outside the

3. "Are CPA Firms Taking Over Management Consulting?" *Forbes*, October 1, 1966.

4. Paul F. Lazarsfeld, *Profile of the Profession, 1975 from the Viewpoint of a Sociologist* (New York: AICPA, 1964), p. 12.

5. Cf. Maurice B. T. Davies, "The Impact of Electronic Data Processing on Relations between Banks and CPAs," *Journal of Accountancy* 120:60-67 (July 1965); J. Howard Laeri, "The Audit Gap," a speech before the Credit Policy Committee of the American Bankers Association, February 1, 1966, reprinted in *Journal of Accountancy* 121:57-59 (March 1966). In the same issue, see also the *Journal's* editorial and the remarks of George W. Mitchell of the Board of Governors of the Federal Reserve System, pp. 31 and 60, respectively.

accounting profession. The whole profession is expanding, utilizing outside areas rather than the profession expanding from within, from its present base of knowledge." The idea is for the CPA to be a generalist, to officiate over the field of experts in information services. Several respondents of the sample suggested that management services be kept separate from public accounting and that CPAs just "preside" over the formal area, treating it as a "support group" for general practice. In this case, some businessmen's image of the CPA as a "superprofessional," a professional's professional who advises on the use of experts, would be the ideal. As previously discussed (see chapter 8, "The Large-Firm Accountant as Advisor"), this is already evident to a great extent in smaller public accounting firms. Advising on the use of experts is done much less frequently by the Big Eight, only 2 percent of the sample reporting time devoted to that type of consulting (see table 13).* This is undoubtedly due to the ability of the larger clients' managements to make their own choices in these matters. However, this will change if the large-firm accountant does become the generalist in information services, because this coordinated complex of widely varying services will require an executive assistant to suggest or choose the experts.[6]

This superprofessional or "entrepreneurial counselor," as some have called him, is now materializing, and he may become an area of serious strife between professions in such matters as advising on acquisitions, mergers, and consolidations; recruitment of executive personnel; economic analysis and forecasting; and analysis, coordination, and control of EDP systems. Most important would be the contest to decide who would advise top management on how and who should handle these matters. Because of his financial background, his wide experience, and the specialization offered in auditing, taxes, and management services by his firm, the large-firm CPA feels that he is a "natural" to fill this position.

There is a feeling among accountants that top advisory positions will constitute the only real information services profession in the future, that most of the work of professions serving organizational leadership today will be rationalized and routinized. The comment of a CPA in one Big Eight firm, a management services specialist, is a strong testimony for suggesting this trend: "We could audit IBM [ninth largest corporation in America] in almost one day with very

---

*The percentage would probably be higher if all those who did not check through the management services question (all those not engaged in any management services—57 percent, according to table 11) were to do so. Auditing partners are likely to be asked the same advice as those partners engaged in auditing *and* management services.

6. John L. Carey, *The CPA Plans for the Future* (New York: AICPA, 1965), pp. 50-51. Lyman Bryson, "Note on a Theory of Advice," in *Reader in Bureaucracy*, ed. Robert K. Merton et al. (New York: The Free Press, 1952), p. 205, describes today's predecessor position of this future advisory assistant.

little risk because their internal systems of control are so tight." As Crozier has said:

> The expert's success is constantly self-defeating. The rationalization process gives him power, but the end results of rationalization curtail this power. As soon as a field is well covered, as soon as the first intuitions and innovations can be translated into rules and programs, the expert's power disappears.
>
> ... witness the successive rise to managerial control by financial experts, production specialists, or budget analysts, according to the most important kind of difficulties organizations have had to solve to survive. As soon as the progress of scientific management or of economic stabilization has made one kind of difficulty liable, at least to a certain degree, to rational prediction, the power of the group whose role it is to cope with this kind of difficulty, and of the people who represent it, will tend to decrease.[7]

And so it happens for some specialties in auditing and management services. They are no longer useful for professionalizing, and it is realized that new knowledge must be developed. To CPAs, the knowledge required of the advisory role to management seems to be the most logical and the most powerful.

PUBLIC ACCOUNTANTS AS STRATEGIC ELITES

There are several views as to what constitutes an elite. One view sees the elite as the minority groups that rule the community.[8] Another view is more general, picturing the elite as "functional, mainly occupational, groups which have high status (for whatever reason) in a society."[9] Keller, whose definitions are utilized here, defines an elite more specifically as "a minority of individuals designated to serve a collectivity in a socially valued way," that is, effectively and responsibly. Strategic elites are "those whose judgments, decisions, and actions have important and determinable consequences for many members of society." They are "important for society as a whole"; they are "leadership groups" that have a "general and sustained social impact."[10] They are in some way responsible for the four functional processes required of a social system to maintain itself: goal attainment, the political task of defining the major goals; adaptation, the

7. Michel Crozier, *The Bureaucratic Phenomenon* (Chicago: University of Chicago Press, 1964), pp. 164-165.

8. For example, Raymond Aron, "Social Structure and the Ruling Class" (Parts I and II), *British Journal of Sociology* 1:1-16, 126-143 (March and June 1950).

9. T. B. Bottomore, *Elites and Society* (New York: Basic Books, 1964), p. 8.

10. Suzanne Keller, *Beyond the Ruling Class: Strategic Elites in Modern Society* (New York: Random House, 1963), pp. 4, 20.

economic task of producing the means and facilities to attain the goals; integration, in order to maintain order and coherence among subsystems in the light of moral and ethical traditions; pattern maintenance and tension management, in order to promote solidarity and emotional well-being.[11]

On the whole, the work of the large-firm accountant places him as a strategic elite, for his advice and decisions have profound economic and social consequences on society. However, Keller's survey of the American scene nowhere mentions public accountants as a strategic elite. She does note that the "legal elite" is an elite of achievement and apparently of ascription, but not of social function, that is, of any of the functional processes of society. Rather, theirs is a professional function, an "auxiliary of the strategic elite it serves."[12] But the large-firm accountants' independence is more than an auxiliary function, because it is the basis for an important periodic economic attest of a client for that client and for third parties. The CPA's responsibility goes beyond the client to the investors, stockholders, and creditors, to the extent of their professional knowledge and the information available to them in arriving at their attest decisions. This liability of CPAs has been upheld in the courts, and stricter, more exacting legislation may result from cases now being tried in the courts. This extension of responsibility beyond the client to third parties has partially eliminated the professional "information barrier" surrounding the CPA's performance. It is felt that this barrier is "wasteful" of clients but that "the professional is inclined to see that waste as part of a margin of error necessary to sustain his willingness to undertake what he claims is complex, uncertain, and risky work, a consequence of protecting him from others' possibly overhasty and arbitrary judgments of his difficult-to-assess work."[13] This margin of error also appears to protect the professional's area of uncertainty from invasion by the forces of rationality—it constitutes the mystique of the profession. The margin of error of public accountants has been reduced by their liability to third parties. The CPA is ultimately responsible for his decisions in the attest function. It confers upon him an authority that he imposes regularly. In one of the most important instances, the U.S. Steel case of 1948, the AICPA ruled against a depreciation practice that was supported by several major corporations, accounting groups and economists.[14]

In this role, large accounting firms, through the representation of the AICPA, constitute an integrative function in society—they adjust the deviant behavior of system units to coincide with the common objectives of the society. This is the

11. Ibid., pp. 96-98.

12. Ibid., p. 326.

13. Eliot Freidson and Buford Rhea, "Knowledge and Judgment in Professional Evaluations," *Administrative Science Quarterly* 10:123-124 (June 1965).

14. Richard Leo Smith, "A Case Analysis of External Accounting Influence over Managerial Decisions" (Ph.D. diss., Graduate School of Business Administration, Harvard University, 1955).

important function of the attest by audit; the CPA has long been known by titles like "society's policeman" and the businessman's conscience. Cases like the U.S. Steel example are repeated countlessly every year on a smaller scale. One reported case is that of a client who wanted to treat research costs as assets instead of as expenses to be deducted from profits. Presented with the auditor's negative opinion, a company officer replied to him: "'Well, we didn't think you'd let us get away with it but we thought we'd give it a try.'"[15] Another example is the comment of K. A. Randall, chairman of the Federal Deposit Insurance Corporation, before the House Subcommittee on Domestic Finance Hearings, on August 4, 1965: "The mere fact that [a bank's] management is sophisticated and able enough to use audits may by its very essence preclude it from being on the [FDIC] problem list." The searches of the auditor may uncover "inconvenient facts" that disagree with accepted procedure, which he is duty-bound to reveal if they are "material" considerations, even though he is serving a client for a fee.

Large-firm accountants are an elite of adaptation in the services that they perform in that area, but it is one of professional function (advising experts) rather than of social function. They are very influential, but it is the influence of power, not of authority.

But the power of their professional function may, with the strengthening of their role as generalists in advising on the total information system (as incorporated in the operations audit), begin to cross the line of responsibility that leads to ultimate authority. Public accountants may be held accountable for much of the advising and for some of the ultimate decisions of their clients. Their role as professionals would be jeopardized if they had too much influence. Large firms are already expressing concern about this problem in their literature dealing with the advising process of CPAs. They raise the question of how much power one can attain before he has to accept the institutional aspect of it (authority), thus destroying the concept of being a member of a profession. A great source of influence in the decision-making process of their clients would undoubtedly place large-firm accountants in the position of being strategic elites in the adaptation function. They will have successfully competed for the authority of their clients,[16] and in the process they will have lost their professional identity.

15. *Wall Street Journal,* January 21, 1964, p. 14.

16. For comments on the partial transfer of authority from manager to expert, see Reinhard Bendix, "Industrialization, Ideologies, and Social Structure," *American Sociological Review* 24:614 (October 1959). An example of transfer to large-firm lawyers is given by Erwin O. Smigel, *The Wall Street Lawyer: Professional Organization Man?* (New York: The Free Press, 1964), especially p. 161.

The CPA's continuing interest in performing societal functions has led him to a paradoxical situation; the functions can become "mutually conflictful."[17] There is a growing concern that their traditional integrative function of attest is becoming an "annual nuisance," possibly to be relegated to the technician because it is becoming so clearly defined in its operations. At the same time, there has been a move into management services—the adaptive function—but here too much influence would destroy the CPA's independence, his most important professional attribute. Others have suggested that the CPA start to lead his own cart, utilizing the deductive method in setting his basic goals, apart from any overpowering external influence.[18] One example (the investment credit issue), which was a goal-attainment function, was not supported by several of the Big Eight firms. One of the reasons surely was because many CPAs feared the possible results of limitations on alternative approaches in their work: by the action of the profession the body of knowledge will become rationalized and the power of uncertainty will be lost.

It would seem that "nothing in excess" would be the path that CPAs will have to follow—a delicate balance or posture between power and authority, uncertainty and rationality, which it must maintain in order to continue receiving the special benefits of professional standing.

THE DIALECTICS OF OCCUPATIONAL CHANGE

Large public accounting firms have gone through two major periods with regard to leadership style: the first was that of the founders, the second was the period of rapid expansion. The leaders of the third period, who are now handling affairs, are operating in an era of rapid social and technological change. Change produces uncertainty,[19] and there have been many examples of this process in the public accounting profession in the past decade. The new technology of electronic data processing, as well as the new and expanded forms of social organization both of the public accountant's clients and of those in the profession, have generated conflicts over these areas of uncertainty, areas that are the sources of new power in organizations. But because of bureaucratic tendencies in

17. Talcott Parsons and Neil J. Smelser, *Economy and Society* (New York: The Free Press, 1956), p. 18.

18. A strong argument against this position is presented by Herman W. Bevis, *Corporate Financial Accounting in a Competitive Economy* (New York: Macmillan, 1965), p. 190, in which he points out that in the legal profession the separation of lawmaking from law interpretation is much wider than it is in public accounting. The AICPA would become accountable to the courts if it (the institute) engaged in setting the "direction and pace" of accounting thought and practice.

19. Peter M. Blau and W. Richard Scott, *Formal Organizations* (San Francisco: Chandler, 1962), p. 240.

the profession, members find themselves in a dilemma. There must be detailed requirements for the reports and opinions of the CPA in order to engender the confidence of his clients and the public, yet the CPA should be free of most encumbrances such as these in order to exercise his professional judgment properly.[20] "In other words," says Crozier, "the elimination of the 'bureaucratic systems of organization' in the dysfunctional sense [routine, rigidity, inefficiency] is the condition for the growth of 'bureaucratization' in the Weberian sense [rationality stifling individualism]."[21] The latter type of bureaucracy diminishes uncertainty and the challenge that is found in uncertainty; consequently, there is an escape from reality. However, for large bureaucratic organizations of a specific type—such as large accounting firms—there is strong evidence of a dialectical trend. As routine decreases in the firms by letting the professional associations handle it, rationality increases. But this rationality itself and norms that sponsor an atmosphere of innovation are factors that produce new sources of uncertainty. Computerization has opened up a Pandora's box for public accountants; but it is unquestionably a generator of large areas of uncertainty, as, for example, the concept of total information services and operations auditing.

The sociologist Richard H. Hall has analyzed several types of professional organizations; he has concluded by hypothesizing that "the more developed the normative system of the occupation in an organization, the less need for a highly bureaucratized organizational system." Likewise, an equilibrium exists between the levels of professionalization and bureaucratization unless there is too little bureaucratization, in which case the lack of operational standards makes social control difficult.[22] James E. Sorensen, an accountant, has suggested that "perhaps the bureaucratic orientation can be increased by a rather modest decrease in professional orientation."[23]

What both these authors fail to consider is a third variable of the historical development of knowledge, as explained by the principle of uncertainty. This makes the process dialectical. The problem of rationality occurs, and an attempt is made to overcome it by acquiring new knowledge. But at the same time, the mechanism by which the problem was solved produces new ones, that is, internal problems of routine.[24]

20. The gist of this dilemma is given by Carey, *The CPA Plans,* pp. 191-192.

21. Crozier, *The Bureaucratic Phenomenon,* p. 299.

22. Richard H. Hall, "Professionalization and Bureaucratization," *American Sociological Review* 33:101, 104 (February 1968).

23. James E. Sorensen, "Professional and Bureaucratic Organization in the Public Accounting Firm," *Accounting Review* 42:565 (July 1967).

24. Blau and Scott, *Formal Organizations,* pp. 250-253, discuss the dialetical process of change in organizations.

A constantly changing profession presents serious problems, solution of which must be actively pursued by each generation of its leaders. One of the problems now faced by public accounting is the confused image and role produced by its multiplicity of tasks in three major areas—financial attestor, consultant, and tax specialist. Increasingly, scientific knowledge is entering into the judgments of the "art of accounting," especially with the application of operations or "total" auditing. The process of integrating the work and the product of CPA specialties, a task required of the highest levels, which is now extending to the lower levels of the firm, will tend to obliterate the clearly defined specialties. If all three of the major areas of public accounting are to be pursued, rather than one being concentrated upon, the education of the CPA will have to be reconsidered in terms of an orientation toward management decision-making in co-existence with the active practice of independence. The search for objective standards with which to complete a management or government agency attest will be important in this respect and might require change in many accounting concepts that are currently being used to arrive at final judgments.

There are other, more general questions to ask that bear directly on the sociology of the professions. The Big Eight are the world's largest professional organizations. It is important to examine them as going concerns, because of the trend toward bigness in nearly all types of social organization and because the professions have increased in importance in modern societies. Will other professions ultimately take the same form of social organization that these giant accounting firms now have? Those that are presently in a position to do so are management consulting and architecture. Law firms, as has been shown throughout the study, are similar in a great many respects, being smaller and less evolved in most aspects of formal organization. Even outside the professions and in the scientific occupations, would this prove to be the most successful form of organization? Would it be the most efficient form for the emerging and planned group practices of physicians and of psychiatrists teamed with psychoanalysts in mental-health work? Would it be feasible to combine into a private organization sociologists, social psychologists, physiological psychologists, and the multitude of specialists in anthropology and human biology, in order to carry out the present and expected long-term research industry on space travel and space colonization? Would the present career pattern and up-or-out system of the Big Eight firms and large law firms promote the healthiest conflict and competition within these autonomous professional and scientist groups? In its favor is the fact that "it works." But are there other alternative forms of organization that would operate more efficiently and effectively in these firms that have suddenly grown large? It is a question that is not unasked in Big Eight circles.

Studies of professionals on hospital staffs have shown a much looser formal organization of subcoalitions or factions than is the case for the large public accounting firms. Professional organization in hospitals is a "fluid" integration

184

maintained in a continual political process with established legislative forms and parliamentary procedures. These organizations seem to function very efficiently and to allow for maximum autonomy, because of the relative fluidity of alliances on specific issues. As a result, the authors of these studies feel that bureaucratic or professional theories are inadequate and that the political process of the professional-organization relationship is more accurate.25 This may be true for the hospital situation; but in the professional group that is more formally organized and is geographically and physically larger, what happens is perhaps necessarily more bureaucratic. In public accounting the nature of the work itself—organizing information—requires a minimum degree of centralization. Yet a constantly developing body of knowledge manages to generate a healthy conflict both within large accounting firms and between them and other professional organizations. *The professional-bureaucratic tension exists because of this conflict.* Whether it would be profitable for the firms to attempt to restructure for a more conflictful existence is highly questionable, especially if they begin to approach the ideal of maintaining personal freedoms while remaining strong enough to survive.

And all is not conflict. Many professions are becoming more aware of the extent of their influence on the societal level, and some of their practitioners desire to collaborate more closely. In a speech before a joint meeting of CPAs and lawyers, John W. Queenan, the senior partner of Haskins & Sells, described the "affinity" between law and accounting, foreseeing the possibility of these two professions joining together in a single associational interest group to examine their common problems, initiate policies, and defend their common position.26

The profession, and especially the Big Eight, faces many serious problems. The firms are still expanding, and their turnover rate is extremely high during a person's first few years of work. The body of knowledge is growing, yet there is the threat to independence because of that knowledge. The academicians want to build on reason plus experience; the practitioners want to build on what is "generally accepted" experience alone. For their own, it is not enough for public accountants to say that they are at a crucial stage in their development as a profession. This may have been a valid statement in a slower-changing past, but the rate of change today makes for a series of constant crucial stages. Juxtaposed, the 1931 statement of the Veblenian influenced accountant DR Scott that "the accounting profession will continue to hold a position of importance but it is hardly destined to be an Atlas and carry an economic world upon its

25. See the summary article by Rue Bucher and Joan Stelling, "Characteristics of Professional Organizations," *Journal of Health and Social Behavior* 10:3-14 (March 1969).

26. John W. Queenan, "Law and Accounting: Co-operation for Better Public Service," *American Bar Association Journal* 2:755 (August 1963).

shoulders'' may still be valid.[27] But the professing for the fully integrated information systems of the future will be accomplished by one group of generalists. Being a practical man, a "man of affairs" in the highly competive and at times ruthless world of profit motives, but at the same time being charged with the responsibility for judging the accountability of this world to his public, today's large-firm public accountant would appear to possess the qualities and resources that are necessary for survival in a nondictatorial system, in an aristocracy of intellect and energy, and perhaps he also possesses the ascription to fill this position.

27. DR Scott, *The Cultural Significance of Accounts* (New York: Henry Holt & Co., 1931), p. 240.

APPENDIX A

The Methodology and Problems of
The Collection and Analysis of Data

METHOD AND SAMPLE

The decision to make the organizational theory in this book as explicit as it is was based on the judgment that enough evidence was in from preceding studies to accept several of their findings as givens, and the choice was made to build on them. The alternatives, then, are basically between empirical exactness and the freedom of exploratory research, or, more simply, whether one knows what he wants or whether he wants to know.[1] My choice emphasized the latter.

Before much of the library research and structuring of theory was accomplished, inquiry was made with the AICPA Public Relations Division in order to obtain contacts with members of a few of the largest public accounting firms. Supplied with these names, I visited the first firm and was fortunate to meet with a person whose duties included those of "communications" and who held a master's degree in sociology. Sympathetic to my cause, he made further contacts in the firm, one of which proved to be the source for contacts with the remaining seven of the Big Eight firms.

Following the initial interviews with the first firm, I drew up a proposed outline for the study, which included a sample questionnaire, and I sent a copy to the contact at each firm for critical review. At that time I intended to have each firm mail the questionnaire to a stratified random sample of its own firm; the respondent would then anonymously return the questionnaire directly to me. A minimum amount of interviewing was planned, mostly to fill in where open-ended questions on the questionnaire proved impractical. Interviews were then held with the contacts in each firm. This resulted in a good deal of criticism of the questionnaire, especially with regard to the meaning of the questions to the prospective respondents. I was indoctrinated with regard to the peculiar language, work situations, biases, and so on, of the large-firm public accountant, and I was told directly that many of the questions were not sophisticated enough for the accountants. There also were many questions and criticisms on the structure and form of the questionaire. It was too long; certain questions might be misinterpreted; there wasn't enough space allowed to answer one

---

1. Aaron Cicourel, *Method and Measurement in Sociology* (New York: The Free Press, 1965), p. 10; Clyde Coombs, "Theory and Methods of Social Measurement," in *Research Methods in the Behavioral Sciences,* ed. Leon Festinger and D. Katz (New York: Dryden, 1953), p. 487.

question, and too much for another; one question was too general; and so on.

It became apparent that these people had much experience with questionnaires, much of it stemming from their questionnaire surveys of the internal systems of control of their clients. Much of it comes from their contact with outside researchers. My contact at one firm estimated that if they were to fill the requests of every researcher knocking at the door, the cost to the firm would run into several hundred thousand dollars a year in time and money. During several of the eight interviews the comment was made that they were besieged with requests from accountant researchers to send questionaires to firm members. It also became apparent that several firms were dissatisfied with my proposed outline of research. The contact at one firm stated quite frankly that he believed his firm would not be interested at all in the study in its then present state.

The critiques received from these eight rather arduous interviews were of inestimable value in putting the proposal into its final state. The first changes made were to fit the language and meaning of the questions to the "common-sense" world of the large-firm public accountant,[2] for this was the key to more effective communication on both the questionnaire and in the interview. The other major changes were to transfer several questions from the questionnaire to a structured interview, to delete several questions, to add several new ones, and to give equal emphasis to the interview along with the questionnaire as a major data-collecting instrument in the study.

As these changes were being made, I decided that the total universe to be sampled would be the New York City office of each of the eight largest public accounting firms in the United States (average number of personnel about 1,500), plus several "medium-sized firms" (average number about 200). The Big Eight were to be approached first; and then the medium-sized firms, upon completion of work with the Big Eight. On the basis of information received from the initial eight interviews, a suggested stratified random sample of a firm was drawn up for use with the questionnaire. This was deemed necessary, due to the structure of the hierarchy of the firm—relatively few people in the top positions, and a great number in the lower positions. Five percent of the New York City office of each participating firm were sampled.

As for the interview, research would be limited to the number of persons that I could arrange to see within a six-month period and, more especially, by the extremely tight schedules of the respondents. Therefore, I decided to attempt to meet with one representative of each major type of work on each formal level of the firm. This amounted to approximately eight interviews for each firm. For

2. Alfred Schutz, "Common-Sense and Scientific Interpretation of Human Action," *Philosophy and Phenomenological Research* 14:1-38 (1953). Cicourel, *Method and Measurement in Sociology*, p. 79, notes Schutz's view: "The well-conceived interview, complex as it may be, must have its roots in the categories of common-sense thinking, for without a knowledge of such roots the interviewer could not establish the necessary community for conducting his research."

the interviews, representativeness was limited by the nature of the public accountant's work—he is rarely at the firm's offices, and when he is, he usually has a loose and changing schedule. Perhaps the people who were too busy to be interviewed held different attitudes towards my questions. Another limitation was the method that the firm used in assigning interviewees. I stressed the necessity for obtaining a cross-section of personnel, but there were infrequent times when the enthusiasm of assigning interviews overshadowed objectivity. If a "representative" person was busy, someone else had to be substituted. In a few cases the substitute was "somebody who would be interested in talking with you." Most important, I had to depend on one man's idea of a sample of eight people that would be representative of the entire firm. The possible biases entering from these points have to be considered in the interpretation of evidence.

The research proposal—which consisted of the purpose of the study and some background information, a sample questionaire and an interview guide, and the suggested methods of sampling the firm—was then sent to three of the Big Eight firms. I felt that three was the maximum number that I could work with at one time. One firm accepted both the questionnaire and the interview for use; the other two accepted only the interview.

The first move upon acceptance was to conduct a pretest of the interview at one firm,[3] and then, after the questionnaire had been mailed, to interview a cross section of that sample. No changes were to be made on the questionnaire at this point, unless absolutely necessary, because proposals had already been sent to three more firms. The upcoming busy season for the profession was drawing near, and the plan of research had to move on. Fortunately, results were satisfactory. Only minor changes were made on the interview guide, and none were made on the questionnaire. After the data had been collected from the Big Eight, the research proposal was sent to eight medium-sized firms, and interviews were requested. By this time the accountants were well into the busy season, so questionnaires were foregone in favor of interviews. This allowed for probing in order to uncover possible differences from the large firms, and it allowed me to experience the everyday world of firms of this size.

Participation, by firms and by number of personnel, is given in table A-1.

The third method of data-gathering that is available to the sociologist—observation—was also utilized in this study. A Big Eight firm permitted me to accompany a partner on an audit of one of its larger clients and, at another time, to sit in on job interviews conducted at the firm. I was fortunate also to have

---

3. A pretest is a limited program of preliminary interviewing, whereas a pilot study is a broader, more open, more comprehensive review by interview of a proposed study. In the present study, the eight initial interviews at the eight firms were a pilot study. See Kingsley Davis, "The Sociology of Demographic Behavior," in *Sociology Today: Problems and Prospects*, ed. Robert K. Merton, Leonard Broom, and Leonard S. Cottrell, Jr. (New York: Basic Books, 1959), p. 324.

TABLE A-1

The Sample, by Number of Firms and Personnel (N=162)

Type of firm	No. of Firms	Method of Collecting Data	
		Interview	Questionnaire
Big Eight Firms	2	15	69
	1		42
	3	21	
Medium-Sized Firms	4	15	
Totals	10	51[a]	111 = 162

[a]Thirty-five interviews were included in the data-measurement and -interpretation process. The other sixteen are "background and information" interviews, conducted during the data-collection period. For explanation, see "Problems of Collecting Data" in this Appendix.

had some part-time work experience in a medium-sized public accounting firm, which was invaluable for obtaining a genuine feel for the work situation of the beginner in public accounting. In this position I was unaffected by a need to observe (which also has its disadvantages), and there was no "effect" of an observer on the interaction taking place.

PROBLEMS OF COLLECTING DATA

Examination of table A-1 indicates that the ideal data-collection goal was not reached. In the major sample (the Big Eight firms), complete participation in all phases of research was attained in two firms, and four firms accepted one data-gathering instrument for use. At one firm, a high-ranking partner agreed to a long and very informative interview, but further participation was not accorded. One firm participated only in the initial interview in the pilot study.

The major reason that complete participation was not achieved was the problem of time on the part of the accountants. The earnings of a firm are derived almost entirely from billings to its clients, and these billings in turn are based almost entirely on the time spent on client matters. Therefore, any time not spent with the client is considered time wasted. This attitude prompted more than one respondent to comment during the interviewing that "time is what we sell."

190

This concern over time required much adapting to unusual situations in the interviewing. One pilot-study interview was conducted entirely by phone. There were so many problems connected with scheduling interviews a day or two in advance that in order to solve the dilemma I spent one or more days at a firm, set myself up in a vacant office, waiting for customers. And all this before the busy season began.

But the problem was not entirely one of time. Members of firms do find extra time during the course of a week for such activities as giving a talk to a local club luncheon, drafting a technical paper for eventual publication, or doing research for an AICPA committee. In such activity there is a direct public-relations value to the firm (which is not to say that large-firm public accountants do not feel a responsibility to engage in professional association and civic affairs). This is not so evident in the case of academic research, where the value of the activity may accrue only after several years, if at all. The world of the accounting practitioner is in many areas far removed from that of the accounting theoretician. Even though the large-firm accountant is well acquainted with the value and practicality of much theory, I sometimes sensed the skepticism of the practitioner toward "half-baked ideas" and "idealism."

Still another problem that is not connected to the problem of time is the generally conservative nature of the firms. Much of this is probably due to the highly competitive nature of nearly all aspects of the firm's operations, from competition for recruits on the college campuses to competition for clients. This promotes an atmosphere of secrecy. Thus, it might be feared that an "unknown," traveling from one firm to another, even though he promised anonymity, would make too many unintentional slips to be worth the trouble of contributing to a study. This was not a serious problem. In most cases the firm members were very informative in their discussions. However, there is some information that is not divulged, or is only let out in bits, or can only be pieced together roughly because certain rules of the profession look with disfavor on such actions. Opinion Number 9 of the Committee on Professional Ethics of the AICPA states that "Information [given by an AICPA member to a reporter or writer] regarding the size of the firm, types of services which it renders, clients being served, location of offices, etc., serves no purpose other than to glorify the firm in the eyes of the reader."

Because of this, for example, accurate figures on the size of firms could not be obtained in all cases. Where they were obtained, I was obligated to restrict use of them to generalizations so that exact numbers would not be shown. The intense competition in recruitment between the eight firms has blacklisted any attempt to compare size of firms by number of partners and other personnel. Even the reputable *Fortune* magazine was admonished by the firms for the latest attempt to do this. The attraction of size, in terms of the number of members in a firm, the number of its clients, or the size of its clients, can be used as a strong selling point on college recruiting forays. Each firm is "biggest" in one or more

191

specific areas (see chapter 2), and each naturally emphasizes these positive features. Any listing of size by one arbitrary feature, such as the number of partners or offices, is considered unfair and distasteful by most firms. At three firms, one of the conditions for obtaining permission to conduct the study was to promise to withhold these figures on size.

For these reasons I have refrained from using exact figures, excepting those from previously published material. This helps to give a picture of extent of size and to serve as a basis for depicting growth and the present size of an average firm.

One other reaction was encountered on a few occasions when I phoned for interview appointments. During the months of interviewing, my time schedule was mostly open to the times requested by the respondents. All free time was devoted to library research. But to the accountant who had a calendar overloaded with appointments and several client deadlines to meet, mine was the "life of Riley," a job of ease. The question was there, although left unsaid: "Don't you feel a little guilty?"[4]

To compensate for these problems, adjustments were made where possible. In nine instances the respondent's lack of time was responsible for partial interviews. Only very broad questions could be asked, and so these interviews could not be included in the tabulation of data. In seven other cases the knowledge and position of the respondent were of such significance to the research that the interview guide was replaced by specific questions directed to his specialty. This allowed much data to be gathered on such topics as the physical structure of the firm, the effects of size on social organization, promotional advances in specialties, and so forth.

These "limiting factors" of time, a skeptical attitude towards theoreticians, and conservatism should not, however, be taken as typical of the situation faced in the course of the interviewing. Actually, in the participating firms the reception was warm, and respondents were free in giving information. For all interviews, the privacy of an office or a conference room was supplied. Perhaps one of the reasons that the firms were so receptive to this study was the straightforward manner in which the pilot study and proposal were presented. Whenever a question came up about whether a purpose should be disguised or an idea not voiced for the sake of expediency, the warnings of the experiences of other researchers were heeded.[5] Care was taken to avoid compromises with

4. A similar experience is reported by Hyman Rodman and Ralph K. Kolodny, "Organizational Strains in the Researcher-Practitioner Relationship," in *Applied Sociology*, ed. Alvin W. Gouldner and S. M. Miller (New York: The Free Press, 1965), p. 98.

5. Peter M. Blau, *The Dynamics of Bureaucracy* (2d ed.; Chicago: University of Chicago Press, 1963), pt. 4, "Methodological Epilogue," especially p. 285; Delbert C. Miller, "The Impact of Organization and Research Value Structures on Research Behavior," in *Applied Sociology*, ed. Gouldner and Miller, pp. 39-52.

regard to full disclosure of intent. This attitude directly caused one firm to switch from almost certain nonparticipation to full participation.

The temptation to follow the expedient route can disguise itself; it even affects those who are involved as subjects of the research. When I was preparing to observe the recruitment interviews at one firm, a tentative decision was made with the personnel department. They were to explain to the interviewee that I was a member of the personnel department, learning the procedures of interviews. Only after some discussion did the possible consequences of such a misrepresentation come to mind, in case any interviewee should start to ask me questions. Needless to say, the decision was changed: the true purpose of the observer during the recruitment interviews was to be disclosed.

In all, the general availability of the respondents during the eighteen months of contact with them allowed for a constant interplay of theory and research in order to strengthen the structure of the entire study.

CONSIDERATIONS IN MEASURING AND INTERPRETING THE DATA

On the basis of the three methods that were used in collecting data and on the basis of the extent of coverage of the universe from which the sample was chosen, a fair representation was attained. Although the interviews averaged five per firm instead of eight, as originally planned, substitution for missing levels of representation was made at other firms on later interviews. In this way, all levels of specialization and hierarchical position were covered in nearly equal amounts. Also, analysis of the questionnaires disclosed that there was accurate representation of the estimated ratio of each level to the total number of personnel. No exact figures could be compiled in order to determine the percentage of return for the questionnaires. However, on the basis of the approximate figures of personnel given to me at the New York offices, I estimated that there was nearly a 90 percent return from two firms, and a 65 percent return for the third.[6]

Some of the most important information in the study came from observations made during the interview period. Relations between colleagues at the same level and at different levels, with non-professional staff, and with clients could be noted in the actual work situation. There was hardly an interview during which there was not a telephone call from a client who was requesting information. Calls were continually being made by phone and in person by partners to nonpartners and vice versa. Frequently, I was invited to lunch, given tours of the firms' offices and introduced to members of the firms. Observations,

6. Request for follow-up was necessary at only one firm. With regard to the reliability of partial returns on mailed questionnaires, see Edward C. McDonagh and A. Leon Rosenblum, "A Comparison of Mailed Questionnaires and Subsequent Structured Interviews," *Public Opinion Quarterly* 29:131–136 (Spring 1965). They found that partial returns do reveal representative responses, as tested by follow-up interviews of nonrespondents *and* respondents.

such as what happened when a partner walked into a staff room or the tone of voice that he used in talking to a client, transmitted important information that would otherwise have been missed.

Before the data were collected, I decided to transfer most of the questionnaire items and some of the interview items onto IBM cards. This necessitated setting up preselected categories for the respondent to choose from. Most of the problems of too narrow, too wide, or inaccurate categories were eliminated in the pilot study and pretest. But analyzed results sometimes contained discrepancies, such as more than one category checked, and write-ins in a multiple-choice question. However, all of these proved inconsequential in number. In coding the answers to the broad, open-ended questions both on the questionnaire and in the interview, specific types were listed under the general categories, so that the reader might interpret for himself the general content of the category. An attempt was made to keep "exploitation" of similarities in data to a minimum where a new concept was being explored or a new hypothesis was being tested.[7] For the more standardized concepts, previously tested categories were accepted. But even here, open categories were maintained for possible oversights (see Questionnaire, appendix B, questions 1 and 6). The problem was also to not underexploit the data. However, the practical limitations of such a broad study prevented fuller use of devices. In a sense, this is the price one pays for opting for freedom of exploratory research.

The type of accountant examined in this work is not the "average" accountant, who is an employee of a business or who is an individual practitioner serving other individuals or small enterprises. The large-firm public accountant is the product of many years of highly specialized technical training. He is carefully selected and carefully trained by his firm to operate in the arena of big business. As such, these men are themselves practiced in the art of interviewing.[8] Their days are filled with discussions with the client on matters of production and internal controls, fact-finding investigations, or advising on mergers, acquisitions, stock issues, purchase of new equipment, tax reporting, methods of depreciation, and the like. During most interviews, I had to keep on guard not to slip into the role of interviewee, as the accountant would by habit begin to question me on my study, the size of the sample, what I had found thus far, how I was controlling for bias. On the latter point, several respondents questioned the validity of what people said as opposed to what they did, a skepticism voiced by

7. "Statistics is largely devoted to exploiting similarities in the judgments of certain classes of people and in seeking devices, notably relevant observation, that tend to minimize their differences." Leonard J. Savage, *The Foundations of Statistics* (New York: Wiley, 1954), p. 156.

8. This same situation was found with large-firm lawyers. See Erwin O. Smigel, *The Wall Street Lawyer: Professional Organization Man?* (New York: The Free Press, 1964), "Interviewing the Interviewers," pp. 24-25.

some sociologists as well.[9] There are two good reasons for disputing this idea. The first is that the combination of individual data into group properties reduces "perspectivistic distortion,"—that is, "no observer can see as much of a group or reflect its behavior as adequately as a large sample of its own members. And even the occasional facetious answer has virtually no effect on these aggregative variables."[10] Second, actions many times simply do not represent thought and may only be a "front," a cover for the more discreet intentions of the individual or group. A person who observed a potlatch, with its custom of destroying personal property, if he did not know the intent of the actors, would certainly be led to false conclusions, unless his observations took place over a very long period of time. Indeed, the underlying reasons might never be uncovered.

In measuring and interpreting the data, one special problem was anonymity. In some cases it was necessary to disguise names or to generalize or to eliminate information. (The previous example of anonymity with regard to the exact figures on the size of firms is a case in point.) But these were the exceptions rather than the rule. Because most of the respondents were aware of these problems, they gave the information and let me worry about anonymity.

A final note: the study would not have been nearly so complete without the interviews. Not only did they allow me to fit in the more prosaic bits and pieces, but, more important, the CPA was approached in person. For the first time, someone had come to him to talk about his firm instead of just sending out a questionnaire. Here he was face-to-face with someone who wanted an answer and who might start asking "why?" to that answer. It was here that I gained their respect and, ultimately, their full cooperation.

9. Pitirim A. Sorokin, *Fads and Foibles in Modern Sociology and Related Sciences* (Chicago: Regnery, 1956), p. 97, states: "The general assumption that one practices what he preaches is largely untenable: there are few, if any, individuals whose actions are identical with their vocal or written answers to the questionnaires and interviews." See also pp. 219, 297-300.

10. Hanan C. Selvin and Warren O. Hagstrom, "The Empirical Classification of Formal Groups," *American Sociological Review* 28:409 (June 1963).

APPENDIX B

1. From among the following attributes of a profession designate what you feel to be their importance in distinguishing certified public accounting from nonprofessions.

    Use the following scale and please assign a number of "x" to every attribute:

    1 = very important
    2 = important
    3 = not very important
    4 = unimportant
    x = can't tell

    _____ A *set of values*. There is an idea of a career, a "calling" in the service of the public, which through authority in its sphere of knowledge, monopoly in all matters related to its service, and objectivity in its theory and technique will advance social progress.

    _____ A *body of knowledge* which is formulated in a systematic theory or set of theories; a developed intellectual technique.

    _____ An established and formalized *educational process* to impart a body of knowledge which the professional group decides is necessary.

    _____ A standardized *formal testing* on a body of knowledge for admission to the professional group.

    _____ *Formal recognition* of the status of the profession by the society through means of state and federal licensing, thus limiting entrance into the professional group.

    _____ A *code of ethics* governing relations with colleagues, clients, and other external organizations. Included are such areas as client confidence, service motive (professional independence) over personal gain, fees, advertising.

    _____*Symbols*. Such meaning-laden items as insignias, emblems, history, folklore, and argot, the heroes and villains, the stereotypes of the client, layman and fellow professionals.

    _____ A *professional association* to facilitate colleague relations and communications and to act in concert in aiding the development, maintaining, or changing of the above seven attributes.

_____ *Personal qualities* beyond the technical competence, such as commitment to the profession through work in its associations, good judgment and poise in social relations at work and in civic activities.

_____*Unwritten rules* of behavior in social situations. Over and above the written rules and codes, these are the accepted, appropriate, proper ways of doing things all the way from the "correct" way of seeking employment to securing promotion to grooming a protégé to challenging outmoded theory.

_____Other? (please specify) _____

2. In a sentence or two, state what you think is the main reason your firm functions effectively, that is, effectively enough to remain in competition with other firms.

3. The full importance of the AICPA Code of Professional Ethics is usually realized by the CPA in—

_____pre-college training

_____college

_____graduate school

_____the first few years of work in accounting

_____both in college and in the first years of accounting

_____after many years in the field

_____is never fully realized

4. Are there any unwritten "rules" that you follow because you are a member of a large public accounting firm? If so, please list.

5. Are these unwritten rules unique to your firm?

_____yes, all of them are

_____some of them are (please mark those which are with a "U")

_____no, none of them are

_____can't tell

6. Could you estimate roughly the time you spend (in percent) in the following areas—

_____Auditing

_____Taxes

_____Administration

_____Management Services

_____Other

<u>100%</u>

Please fill out the approximate percent of time you spend in each management services area.

FINANCE AND ACCOUNTING

_____Advice on inventory valuation policies, depreciation procedures, expensing of repairs and maintenance, business organization and reorganization, credit policies, cash management

SYSTEMS AND PROCEDURES *DIRECTLY*
RELATED TO FINANCE AND ACCOUNTING

_____Development of cost systems, design of internal financial statements, advice on machine bookkeeping

SYSTEMS AND PROCEDURES
RELATED TO FINANCE AND ACCOUNTING

(a) *General Management and Administration*

_____Investigations on purchase or sale of business

_____Advice on use of special counsel or specialists

_____Other? (please specify) _____

(b) *Other*

_____Management Sciences (EDP, linear programming, statistical sampling)

_____Personnel (advice on labor contracts, wage agreements, fringe benefits, psychological testing)

_____Transportation (traffic management surveys, etc.)

_____Production (development of production standards, survey of methods, time and motion studies, factory layout)

_____Sales (market research, shipping methods and costs, public opinion polls)

_____Purchasing

_____Research and Development

_____Other? (please specify) _____

<u>100%</u>   TOTAL MANAGEMENT SERVICES

7.   (a)   Do you feel management services to be important at the present time as an aid to the growth of the public accounting profession as a "higher" profession—

_____extremely important, they are essential

_____very important

_____important

_____not very important

199

_____unimportant

_____can't tell

(b) Why?

(c) Do you think this might change in the future?—

_____yes, they will become extremely important

_____yes, they will become very important

_____yes, they will become important

_____yes, they will become not very important

_____yes, they will become unimportant

_____no, there will be no change

_____can't tell

(d) Why?

8. General
[please check where applicable]

Age: _____ 20-26 _____ 27-33 _____ 34-40 _____ 41-47 _____ 48-55

       _____ 55-61 _____ 62+

CPA: _____ yes _____ no

Job Title: _____ partner _____ principal _____ senior _____ junior

           _____ auditing _____ taxes _____ management services

           _____ administrative

[please answer if applicable]

Undergraduate major _____ Degree _____

Graduate school major _____ Degree _____

Other _____ Degree _____

1. In a sentence or two, state what you think is the main reason your firm functions effectively, that is effectively enough to maintain its position competitively.

2. Do you feel that public accounting is being molded into one of the higher professions?

    _____yes _____ no _____ already a higher profession

    What factors are helping ("preventing" in the case of no) this trend?

3. Offhand, can you think of any factors which distinguish the accounting profession (CPAs) from other professions, e.g., in principles, values, or approaches involved in their work? These factors may be distinguished as unique to public accounting or as different in degree from other professions.

4. In what area of his work do you feel the CPA utilizes the most judgment?

    (Explain to respondent if it appears necessary:)

    > Judgment is a decision(s) made in a situation of uncertainty due to the lack of facts or to the complexity of facts, or both.

    > As a consequence, the probabilities of making the correct decision are lower than usual. It is the area of "opinion" or "estimate," where foresight and good sense enter into the making of the decision. The "grey" area of the law.

5. Where does the primary responsibility of the CPA as auditor lie, that is, to which group? His client, his firm, stockholders, the public, government, the profession? Others?

    Does he ever find conflicts as to which group he owes his allegiance?

6. Would you consider any of the rules in the AICPA Code of Professional Ethics as being more important than others?

    _____yes _____ no

    If yes, which Rules come to mind?

    Generally, how well are the rules of the Code adhered to in the profession?

    In the Big Eight?

7. Are there any unwritten rules that you follow because you are a member of a large public accounting firm?

    Are any of these unwritten rules unique to your firm?

8. To conclude this discussion on rules, in your opinion what are the most important types of rules governing the profession of public accounting, the rules *external* to the firm or *internal* to the firm? (Then formal and informal)

Profession Firm

_____   _____ formal internal   (written firm rules on reports)

_____   _____ informal internal (unwritten firm rules on dress and decorum, relations with colleagues)

_____   _____ formal external   (written rules of ethics, auditing standards, state and federal regulations)

_____   _____ informal external (unwritten rules of commitment to and responsibility to profession, generally accepted accounting principles and postulates)

In your opinion, what are the most important types of rules governing your firm?

9. (a) Do you feel management services to be important at the present time as an aid to the growth of public accounting as a higher profession?

_____ extremely important, they are essential

_____ very important

_____ important

_____ not very important

_____ unimportant

_____ can't tell

(b) Why?

(c) Do you think this might change in the future?

_____ yes, they will become extremely important

_____ yes, they will become very important

_____ yes, they will become important

_____ yes, they will become not very important

_____ yes, they will become unimportant

_____ no, there will be no change

_____ can't tell

(d) Why?

10. Do clients request that you make decisions for them over and above the advice you give?

_____all the time

_____frequently

_____sometimes

_____rarely

_____never

If yes, could you give a few general areas in which such decisions are made?

Do you feel this should be part of the function of the CPA?

11. It has been hypothesized that because accounting and auditing procedures are becoming more computerized and because their principles and procedures are becoming more formally spelled out that the judgment function of CPAs will be considerably weakened. Therefore, CPAs will utilize other areas of greater judgment potential—that of management services and its related forms—to carry on, professionally strong. Does this sound plausible to you? Why, or why not?

12. General information:

CPA: _____ yes _____ no

Position in firm: _____

Major area of work: _____ auditing _____ taxes _____ administrative

_____ management services _____ other

Type of higher education: (degree and major)

Age group: _____ 20-26 _____ 27-33 _____ 34-40 _____ 41-47 _____ 48-54

_____ 55-61 _____ 62+

APPENDIX C

Tables Listing Auditors of the Largest Companies in the United States

The tables in this appendix are based on lists of largest corporations given in *The Fortune Directory* (1965), compared with the mention of auditors in *Moody's Industrial Manual, Moody's Public Utility Manual,* and *Moody's Transportation Manual* (New York: Robert H. Messner, 1965—for each manual), and *Poor's Register of Corporations, Directors and Executives* (New York: Standard & Poor's Corporation, 1965), and telephone calls to unlisted organizations. The results were found to be almost exactly the same as those of one Big Eight firm that graciously allowed this double-check after I presented my charts to them.

Research on the tables was completed in September 1966. By chance, two accountants completed the same research at the same time, because a few months later, information was published that presented the same analysis of data on auditors listed in *The Fortune Directory* for 1965. There are only a few minor differences when the charts are compared. See Stephen A. Zeff and Robert L. Fossum, "An Analysis of Large Audit Clients," *Accounting Review* 42:298-320 (April 1967).

TABLE C-1

Auditors of the 500 Largest Industrial Corporations in the United States, by Number of Corporations Audited and Their Net Sales (1964)

Firm	Net Sales of Corps. Audited, (000) Omitted	Percentage of Total Net Sales	No. of Corps.	Percentage of Total Corps.
Price Waterhouse	$70,194,534	26.7	110	24
Haskins & Sells	46,249,452	17.2	61	12
Lybrand	29,663,659	11.1	52	10
Arthur Young	27,097,445	10.2	44	9
Peat Marwick	24,165,585	9.1	61	12
Arthur Andersen	22,924,842	8.6	47	9
Ernst & Ernst	21,249,834	8.0	63	13
Touche Ross	13,040,994	4.9	26	5

205

TABLE C-1 (continued)

Firm	Net Sales of Corps. Audited, (000) Omitted	Percentage of Total Net Sales	No. of Corps.	Percentage of Total Corps.
All other firms[a]	$ 11,718,806	4.4	34	7
Totals	$266,305,101[b]	100.4[c]	498[b]	101[c]

[a]Includes: Main, Lafrentz & Co., auditing 4 companies totaling $3 billion plus; Hurdman & Cranstoun, auditing 5 companies totaling $3 billion plus; S. D. Leidesdorf, auditing 8 companies totaling $2 billion plus; Alexander Grant & Co., auditing 2 companies totaling $200 million plus; and 15 firms, each auditing 1 company, ranging from a low of $108 million to a high of $337 million, for a total of $2 billion plus.

[b]Two corporations are not audited by public accountants. They amount to only .0013 percent of total net sales for the top 500, so are omitted from the calculations.

[c]Overage due to rounding.

TABLE C-2

Auditors of the 50 Largest Merchandising Firms in the United States, by Number of Firms Audited and Their Net Sales (1964)

Firm	Net Sales of Firms Audited, (000) Omitted	Percentage of Total Net Sales	No. of Firms	Percentage of Total Firms
Touche Ross	$10,144,169	22.5	7	14
Peat Marwick	9,756,953	21.6	11	22
Haskins & Sells	6,046,410	13.4	3	6
Arthur Andersen	4,875,807	10.8	7	14
Lybrand	4,423,554	9.8	6	12
Price Waterhouse	3,352,117	7.4	5	10
Ernst & Ernst	1,970,594	4.4	3	6
S.D. Leidesdorf	1,554,396	3.4	3	6
Frazer & Torbet	786,861	1.7	2	4
Other (1 client each)	2,228,567	4.9	3	6
Totals:	$45,139,428	99.9[a]	50	100

[a]Due to rounding.

TABLE C-3

Auditors of the 50 Largest Transportation Companies in the United States, by Number of Companies Audited and Their Operating Revenues (1964)

Firm	Operating Revenues of Companies Audited, (000) Omitted	Percentage of Total Operating Revenues	No. of Companies	Percentage of Total Companies
Haskins & Sells	$ 3,830,689	26.5	13	26
Peat Marwick	3,560,767	24.6	12	24
Price Waterhouse	2,466,884	17.1	9	18
Arthur Andersen	1,331,157	9.2	5	10
Arthur Young	789,016	5.5	3	6
Lybrand	604,672	4.2	1	2
Touche Ross	460,092	3.2	1	2
Ernst & Ernst	430,297	3.0	3	6
Schutte & Williams	134,617	1.0	1	2
(No information)	825,586	5.7	2	4
Totals:	$14,433,777	100.0	50	100

TABLE C-4

Auditors of the 50 Largest Utility Companies in the United States, by Number of Companies Audited and Their Total Assets (1964)

Firm	Total Assets of Companies Audited, (000) Omitted	Percentage of Total Assets	No. of Companies	Percentage of Total Companies
Lybrand	$36,082,288	45.5	7	14
Arthur Andersen	16,067,934	19.1	13	26
Haskins & Sells	11,512,524	13.5	12	24
Price Waterhouse	11,223,506	13.2	12	24
Niles & Niles	3,446,627	3.6	2	4

TABLE C-4 (continued)

Firm	Total Assets of Companies Audited, (000) Omitted	Percentage of Total Assets	No. of Companies	Percentage of Total Companies
Peat Marwick	$ 1,697,805	2.5	2	4
Main, Lafrentz	1,474,227	2.0	1	2
Arthur Young	528,669	.6	1	2
Totals:	$82,033,580	100.0	50	100

NAME INDEX

Abel, Theodore, 140
Abelson, Robert P., 121
Adams, Bert N., 10
Adams, Donald L., 154
Adams, Sexton, 141
Akers, Ronald L., 89
Alexis, Marcus, 124
Anderson, O. J., 77
Ankers, Raymond G., 68
Anthony, Robert N., 131
Aoyagi, Bunji, 139
Arkin, Herbert, 165
Armstrong, Marshall S., 138
Aron, Raymond, 125, 179
Ashworth, John, 143
Axelson, Kenneth S., 150
Ayer, A. J., 123

Baladouni, Vahe, 137
Barber, Bernard, 59, 61-62
Barcena, John Henry, 79
Barnard, Chester, 119, 125
Barnes, James A., 48
Bedford, Norton M., 125, 168, 170
Bendix, Reinhard, 181
Bennis, Warren G., 170
Bentz, William F., 163
Beyer, Robert, 40, 156, 166, 169
Berghe, Pierre L. van den, 10, 159
Berger, Morroe, 140
Bevis, Herman W., 24, 26, 65, 125, 136,
    141, 151, 182
Biegler, John C., 103
Bierman, Harold, Jr., 83
Bierstedt, Robert, 85, 119
Bird, Caroline, 33, 79, 81
Black, John M., x
Black, William, 111
Blau, Peter M., 10-12, 85, 88, 99-100, 117,
    120, 182-183, 192
Bogoluboff, Nicholas A., 48
Bottomore, T. B., 179
Boulding, Elise, 117-118
Boulding, Kenneth E., 160

Boutell, Wayne S., 165
Bowman, Mary Jane, 126
Boyle, Edwin T., 154
Brayfield, Arthur H., 121
Brent, Philip D., 77
Briloff, Abraham J., 73
Broom, Leonard, 104, 189
Brown, Derrick M., 48
Bruns, William J., Jr., 168
Bryan, Lyman, 39, 81
Bryson, Lyman, 178
Bucher, Rue, 10-11, 159-160, 185
Buckley, John W., 137
Burke, Edward J., 95, 137
Burton, John C., 9, 51

Campfield, William L., 45, 164, 166
Caplow, Theodore, 50
Carrey, John L., 5-6, 24, 27, 29, 31, 33,
    39, 64, 70-71, 73, 77, 80-81, 83,
    88-89, 112, 120, 141, 147, 151,
    160-162, 164-165, 167, 178, 183
Carmichael, Douglas R., xi, xiii, 73, 74, 94
Carr-Saunders, Alexander, 59
Carter, C. F., 122
Casler, Darwin J., 71, 95
Chambers, R. J., 30, 133, 139
Chase, David B., 79
Chomsky, Noam, 170
Churchill, Neil C., 156, 165
Churchman, C. West, 119, 141
Cicourel, Aaron V., 94, 187-188
Clelland, Donald A., 11
Cogan, Morris L., 65
Cohen, Harry, 10
Cohen, John, 121
Cohen, Percy S., 173
Comte, August, 13
Coombs, Clyde, 187
Corwin, Ronald G., 11
Cottrell, Leonard S., 104, 189
Crozier, Michel, 12-13, 117-118, 142,
    156-157, 179, 183
Cyert, Richard M., 165

209

210

SUBJECT INDEX

accountability, 120, 125, 149
accountant, certified public (*see* certified
  public accountant)
accountant, public, 26, 70
  education of, 67
accountants
  earnings, 55
  number of, 6
  role of, 5
accounting
  deduction in, 66–67, 129, 136–139
  defined, 23–24, 137, 149, 163
  degrees in, 43
  history of, 4–6
  induction in, 66, 67, 129, 136–139
  postulates, 24–26
  principles, 27, 132
  uniformity, 131–132, 136, 139
accounting art, 136–139
Accounting Principles Board, 138
accounting, public
  independence in, 71–73, 76
Accounting Research Bulletins, 131, 138
Accounting Research Studies, 132–133
accounting science, 136–139
actuaries, 166–167
American Accounting Association, 6, 36
American Bankers Association, 38, 64
American Group of CPA Firms, 111
American Institute of Certified Public
  Accountants, 6, 36, 70, 80, 84, 139,
  160
American Management Association, 36
American Library Association, 38
American Medical Association, 38, 62
Anchin, Block & Anchin, x
Arthur Andersen & Co., 3, 15, 18, 31, 43,
  82, 131, 139
Arthur Young & Co., x, 3, 15, 22, 32, 39,
  150
Atlas Plywood, 132
audit, 26
audit opinion, 26, 55, 72, 74
audit team, 46

auditing, 28–30
  defined, 26
  standards, 27–28
authority, 119, 120
  and responsibility, 181
autonomy, 108, 111

Bank of America, 36
Big Eight
  administrative functions, 19, 34, 56, 99,
    104
  alumni, 50–51
  client changes, 9, 51
  client rates, 35
  client relations, 94
  clients, 8–9
  climate of firm, 42–43
  competition between, 191
  conflict with smaller firms, 160
  formal organization, 114
  and large law firms, 112, 115
  management services in, 145–149
  New York City offices, 20
  office layout, 22–23
  organization chart, 21
  personnel department, 34, 193
  prestige of, 9, 22
  professionalism of, (*see* professionalism)
  size, advantages of, 104–105, 108
  size of, 15–20, 191–192
  size, problems of, 101–104
  specialization, 102–103, 105, 108–109
  technical functions, 19
  training programs, 43, 46, 50, 52
  turnover, 115
  work of, 7–8
Booz, Allen & Hamilton, 177
bureaucracy, 10
  conflict with professionalism, 102
  elements of, 12
  internal, 12
  and power, 117–118, 125
  and professionalization, 100, 116, 183
  (*see also* professional bureaucracy)

214

217